Batsford Chess Library

Beating the Anti-Sicilians

Joe Gallagher

An Owl Book
Henry Holt and Company
New York

Henry Holt and Company, Inc.
Publishers since 1866
115 West 18th Street
New York, New York 10011

Henry Holt® is a registered
trademark of Henry Holt and Company, Inc.

First published in the United States in 1994 by
Henry Holt and Company, Inc.
Originally published in Great Britain in 1994 by
B. T. Batsford Ltd.

Library of Congress Catalog Card Number: 94-76059

ISBN 0-8050-3575-3 (An Owl Book: pbk.)

First American Edition—1994

Printed in the United Kingdom
All first editions are printed on acid-free paper.∞

10 9 8 7 6 5 4 3 2 1

Adviser: R. D. Keene, GM, OBE
Technical Editor: Graham Burgess

Contents

Symbols

+	Check
++	Double check
#	Checkmate
!	Good move
?	Bad move
!!	Excellent move
??	Blunder
Ch	Championship
Wch	World Championship
Z	Zonal
IZ	Interzonal
Ct	Candidates
OL	Olympiad
Corr	Postal game
(D)	Diagram follows

Introduction

No opening in chess has attracted anything like as many followers or as much interest as the Sicilian Defence. Its variations have become legendary in their own right – just think of the Najdorf and then of all its famous subvariations such as the Poisoned Pawn or the Polugaevsky, and each of them with all their fanatical followers. Virtually every single variation in the Sicilian has had a full-length book devoted to it. Is it any wonder that White players are frightened of the Open Sicilian? The amount of knowledge required to play 3 d4 confidently is colossal. Anyone who is not a full-time chess player will have great difficulty in mastering the Open Sicilian.

By selecting one of the variations in this book, White, at a single stroke, rids himself of the need for studying masses of theory, whilst he at the same time forces Black to play on territory probably more familiar to his opponent. And what's more, many of these variations are not so bad and can be considered as in no way inferior to 3 d4. For example the 3 ♗b5 of Chapter 6 is very popular at

grandmaster level and has recently been used by two world champions, Kasparov and Fischer. Not surprisingly, there are many publications advocating the use of these 'Anti-Sicilian' systems, but in my view these are not of much use to our Sicilian hero. Firstly, it is unlikely that he will want to purchase a whole book on the c3 Sicilian, for example, if he is only interested in one defence for Black, and secondly, even if he does buy such a book, he is unlikely to find what he is looking for as the book will probably be aimed, understandably so, at the player of the white pieces.

This book, I hope, will go a long way towards redressing the balance. In it you will find a complete repertoire for Black against all variations of the Sicilian where White doesn't play 3 d4. Repertoire books are a recent, but necessary concept. With the explosion of chess theory in this age of the database, it would be impossible to cover this topic fully in less than a thousand pages. Therefore I've had to be selective in my choice of defences for Black, but the lines that are chosen are covered quite thoroughly and I have very rarely restricted Black to just one narrow path. In line with the word *Beating*, which appears in the title of this book, I have selected active defences which should offer the second player reasonable chances to play for a win. For example in Chapter 7, I have recommended the slightly risky, but still sound, 3...♘d7 against 3 ♗b5+, rather than the more solid 3...♗d7 which promises Black an equal game but very few winning chances. The repertoire I have chosen is a sound one and on the whole is based on tried and tested lines for Black. Occasionally, though, I have suggested lines not so highly thought of by theory (Game 21, for example) but in these cases I have always backed up my choice with some new material (be it a recent game or my own analysis).

This book can be divided into two halves: the first where White plays something other than 2 ♘f3 should be useful to everyone who plays the Sicilian. The second part of the book, where White plays 2 ♘f3, can be divided into three further parts depending on Black's reply. I have

assumed that Black plays either 2...♘c6, 2...d6 or 2...e6. These sections may not be immediately apparent from the layout of the material, since I have preferred, for example, to include all games with an early b3 in the same chapter, rather than have them in different parts of the book depending on whether White played 2 ♘f3 or not, and whether Black played 2...e6, 2...d6 or 2...♘c6. However, use of the index will enable you to find the games specific to your repertoire. There are many transpositional possibilities which have not made my task any easier but I hope they have all been taken into account. The final chapter of the book is a discussion of move order tricks and it should help you to avoid being conned into an unfamiliar variation by a devious opponent.

My main hope is that reading this book will enable you to feel less depressed whenever an unsporting opponent sidesteps your favourite Dragon, Najdorf, Sveshnikov or even Pin Variation.

Joe Gallagher
June 1994

1 The Closed Sicilian

The variation known under this name is characterized by the moves 1 e4 c5 2 ♘c3 ♘c6 3 g3 g6 4 ♗g2 ♗g7 5 d3 d6 *(D)*.

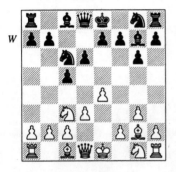

The Closed Sicilian was popularized by Boris Spassky, who employed it with considerable success in the 1960s (especially in his Candidates match with Geller). However, Black soon learnt how to defend himself against White's kingside attack and the system became a rare visitor to grandmaster practice until the late 1980s, when there was a renaissance period due to the discovery of 10 e5 (Game 3). But now that Black appears to have found the antidote to this, the Closed Sicilian is beginning to slip again in the popularity ratings.

The variation has always been popular at club level as it is very easy to learn how to play for White. I recall in my early years as a chessplayer winning game after game with this line, each one with a crushing kingside attack. As the years went by and my opponents became stronger, my attacks became less and less successful. Well, to be honest the attack never really materialized. Black would play ...f5 at some point and my pieces would be left huddled in a cumbersome manner on the kingside, whilst my opponent's queenside initiative developed freely. It was high time to learn the Open Sicilian.

The Closed Sicilian has an extremely near relative in the English Opening. After the moves 1 c4 e5 2 ♘c3 ♘c6 3 g3 g6 4 ♗g2 ♗g7, for example, we have a Closed Sicilian in reverse. One would imagine that the extra tempo would ensure White the better game, but in practice it hasn't really worked out like this. In my opinion this is mainly for psychological reasons. When White plays this system he is usually intent on a queenside attack and often fails to take the necessary defensive measures to protect his king. The extra tempo is often quite insignificant. It's not extremely relevant whether the pawn gets to a5 or a6 when mate is delivered.

Before moving on to the games I would just like to say a quick word about the move order. Black can equally play 2...d6 if White intends to play a Closed Sicilian, but the problem with this (at least in my eyes) is 3 f4, with a good version of the Grand Prix Attack (Chapter 2). I understand that 2...♘c6 may present a problem for some of you if White plays 3 ♘ge2 or 3 ♘f3, but for more about this see the discussion of move order in Chapter 10.

From the diagram White has two main continuations, 6 f4 (games 1-4) and 6 ♗e3 (games 5-6). Game 7 deals with the less frequent continuations 6 ♘ge2 and 6 ♘h3.

Game 1
Marjanović – Lputian
Erevan 1989

1	e4	c5
2	♘c3	d6
3	g3	♘c6
4	♗g2	g6
5	d3	♗g7
6	f4	e6!

Black plans never to let White advance f4-f5. With pawns on e6 and g6, a knight on e7 and a bishop on c8 this won't be possible without the supportive g3-g4. Black should then be ready to answer with ...f7-f5! (this means being careful not to leave anything loose on the long diagonal which might be *en prise* to the fianchettoed bishop after exf5). Once this kingside blockade is achieved White's attack will never get off the starting blocks. Indeed, in the long run Black has as many attacking chances as White, since he has better pawn cover around his king.

7	♘f3	♘ge7
8	0-0	0-0 *(D)*

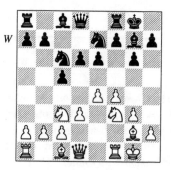

9 ♗d2

The more common 9 ♗e3 will be the subject of subsequent games. Less common alternatives are:

a) 9 ♖b1 ♖b8 and now 10 ♗d2 b5 11 a3 transposes to Marjanović-Lputian, whilst 10 ♗e3 transposes to Game 2.

b) 9 ♘e2 b6 (*ECO* gives 9...d5 10 e5 f6 11 exf6 ♗xf6 12 ♔h1 ♕d6 Mascariñas-Yurtaev, Frunze 1979, as unclear) 10 c3 f5 11 exf5 gxf5 12 d4 ♗b7 13 ♘g5 ♕d7 14 dxc5 bxc5 (Gabriel-Wirthensohn, Altensteig 1990) and Black controls all the central squares, although White will not be without his chances too.

c) 9 g4 f5 10 gxf5 gxf5 (10...exf5 11 ♗e3 ♔h8 12 ♕d2 b6 13 ♖ae1 ♗b7 with an equal game; Hennigan-Gallagher, Jersey 1985) 11 ♔h1 fxe4 12 dxe4 d5 13 e5 ♘f5 and a draw was agreed in Abou-Knežević, Bahrain 1990, although Black looks better to me.

d) 9 ♘h4 ♖b8 10 ♕e1 ♘d4 11 ♕f2 b5 12 ♘d1 b4 13 g4?! (the solid 13 ♘e3 is better) 13...f5! 14 h3?! g5! and Black is already near to winning, Schmid-Gallagher, Neuchâtel 1994.

9 ... b5

Black can employ this tricky move order (normal is 9...♖b8 10 ♖b1 b5 11 a3, transposing to the text) as 10 ♘xb5 ♖b8 wins back the pawn. An alternative approach is 9...b6.

10 a3 ♖b8
11 ♖b1 c4!

This is an important improvement over 11...a5 12 a4! which gives White an edge.

12 h3?

Novelties often have an unsettling effect, and Marjanović's response is certainly rather strange. There is clearly not going to be time to pawn-storm with the centre about to open. Lputian considers 12 ♗e3 to be best, giving the following variation: 12...d5 13 dxc4 bxc4 14 ♘d4 ♘xd4 15 ♗xd4 dxe4 16 ♗xg7 ♕xd1 17 ♖fxd1 ♔xg7 18 ♘xe4 ♗b7, which he assesses as unclear.

12 ... b4
13 axb4 cxd3
14 cxd3 ♕b6+
15 ♔h2 ♘xb4

Black already possesses a sizeable initiative.

16 ♗e1

16 ♘e1 ♗a6 17 ♖f3 d5! 18 e5 ♘f5 is awful for White.

16 ... ♗a6
17 ♗f2 ♕c7
18 ♘e1 ♖fc8

18...e5 19 ♗e3 d5 is a sharper alternative (Lputian). The next few moves see Black slowly building up his position on the queenside.

19 ♖c1 ♕d7
20 ♕d2 ♘ec6
21 ♖a1 ♘d4
22 ♖a3 ♖c7
23 ♗e3 ♘b5
24 ♖b3 ♘c6
25 ♘xb5 ♗xb5
26 ♘f3?

White should have rushed his knight to the defence of the queenside, although even after 26 ♘c2 ♖cb7 27 ♘a3 ♘d4 Black holds a clear advantage.

26 ... ♖cb7
27 ♖a1 a5

28	♖a2	♕c7
29	e5 *(D)*	

White can stand the suffering no longer and seizes his chance to grab some material.

29	...	dxe5
30	♘xe5	♘xe5
31	fxe5	♗xe5
32	♗xb7	♗xg3+
33	♔g1	♕xb7
34	♖xa5	

We can assess this position as winning for Black. For a minimal amount of material White's king has been laid bare.

34	...	♕d5
35	♖c3	♕d8?!

This move can be explained by time pressure. 35...♗d6 was pretty crushing with threats of ♕f3 and ♗b4.

36	♗a7	♖b7
37	♕g2?	

White goes down without a fight.

37	...	♕xa5!
38	♕xb7	♕a1+

39	♔g2	♕xb2+
40	♔xg3	♕xc3

The neat point behind Black's play is 41 ♕xb5 ♕c7+!.

The game concluded 41 ♕b8+ ♔g7 42 ♗e3 ♗xd3 43 ♕d6 e5 44 ♗c5 ♗c4+ 45 ♔f2 ♕c2+ 46 ♔g1 ♕c1+ 47 ♔h2 ♕f4+ 48 ♔g2 h5 0-1

Game 2
Spassky – Portisch
Toluca IZ 1982

1	e4	c5
2	♘c3	♘c6
3	g3	g6
4	♗g2	♗g7
5	d3	d6
6	f4	e6
7	♘f3	♘ge7
8	0-0	0-0
9	♗e3	♘d4 *(D)*

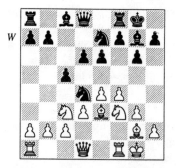

Black prevents d3-d4 and White now has to organize a way either to expel or exchange this irritating knight.

9...b6 is the subject of Game 4.

10 ♖b1

White protects his b-pawn in order to play ♘e2 and c3. There are a number of alternatives:

a) 10 ♗f2 (recently this has become Spassky's favourite, maybe because of his experience in this game against Portisch. The main idea is to be able to play ♘xd4 without losing a piece) 10...♘xf3+ (10...b6 would allow White to carry out his plan, although even here things are not so clear, e.g. 11 ♘xd4 cxd4 12 ♘e2 e5 13 c3 dxc3 14 ♘xc3 ♗e6! 15 d4 {15 f5 gxf5 16 exf5 ♗xf5 17 ♗xa8 ♕xa8 is too high a price to pay for an exchange} 15...exf4 16 gxf4 ♕d7 17 ♗h4 f6 18 d5 ♗h3 with an unclear game according to Stohl) 11 ♗xf3 ♘c6 12 ♗g2 (White preempts the move ...♘d4) 12...b6!. Black has already achieved full equality. 13 e5 ♗b7 is nothing to worry about and 13 g4 ♗b7 14 f5 ♘e5 looks like a premature attack to me, although if Black is worried about this he can always follow the example of Anatoly Karpov and play 12...♖b8. After 13 ♖b1 b6 14 ♕d2 ♗b7 15 a3 ♖c8 16 ♘e2 ♘d4 17 c3 ♘xe2+ 18 ♕xe2 a draw was agreed in Spassky-Karpov, Linares 1983. It has become apparent over the last few years that Spassky often considers the Closed Sicilian as a warm-up for the tennis that follows. I should just mention that

12...♘d4 13 e5! transposes to lines considered in the next game.

b) 10 ♕d2 (this time White plans to rid himself of the troublesome knight with ♘d1 and then c3) 10...♖b8 (Black would quite like to play 10...b6 but this runs into some trouble on the long diagonal after 11 ♗xd4 cxd4 12 ♘b5 ♘c6 {12...e5 13 ♕b4! – note that the reason 10...b6 is playable against 10 ♖b1 is that White doesn't have this possibility} 13 e5 dxe5 14 ♘xe5) and now:

b1) 11 g4 would of course be met by 11...f5, one example being Medina-Smyslov, Siegen 1970, which continued 12 gxf5 exf5 13 ♖ae1 ♔h8 14 ♔h1 ♘xf3 15 ♗xf3 b6! 16 ♗f2 ♗b7 with a good game for Black.

b2) 11 ♖ae1 b5 (11...b6) 12 e5!? (it's too late for 12 ♘d1 and c3 since 12...b4 would ensure that the b-file would be in Black's hands) 12...♘ef5 13 ♗f2 ♕c7 14 ♘g5 ♗b7 15 ♘ce4 h6 16 ♘h3 dxe5 17 c3 exf4 18 cxd4 fxg3 19 hxg3 cxd4, Bücker-Bönsch, German Ch 1991. It's difficult to know what to make of all this, but now Black definitely has good play for the piece.

b3) 11 ♘d1 b6 (the text has one big advantage over the seemingly more natural ...b5; the c-pawn is solidly defended. This ensures that the sting is taken out of any future e5, whilst also giving Black the useful option of playing d5. 11...b5 is, nevertheless, a reasonable alternative, e.g. 12 ♘h4 f5 13 c3 ♘dc6 14 ♘f3 b4 15 c4 ♘d4 with a roughly level game in Campora-Greenberg, Buenos Aires 1978) 12 ♘h4 (White hopes to gain time by forcing Black's knight to retreat, but in order to achieve this small victory he has had to behave in a rather strange manner with his own cavalry) 12...f5 (as 13 f5 might have been a threat, Black follows the golden rule) 13 c3 ♘dc6 14 ♘f3 ♗b7 and Black has achieved a more harmonious development.

c) 10 e5 is the subject of the next game.

10	...	♖b8

10...b6 immediately is probably the most accurate as White has no way to take advantage of the temporary instability on the long diagonal. Caspar-Kosten, Jurmala 1987 continued 11 ♘e2 ♘xf3+ 12 ♗xf3 ♗b7 13 ♗g2 ♕d7 14 c3 f5 15 ♖e1 ♖ad8 16 ♕c2 ♔h8 17 ♖bd1 ♕c8 18 c4 ♕a8 with a very comfortable game for Black.

11	♘e2	♘xf3+
12	♗xf3	b6
13	g4?! *(D)*	

There is no real justification for this move.

13 c3 would have been more prudent, although after 13...♗b7 14 d4 f5 Black can still look forward to the future with some confidence.

13	...	f5!

14	♘g3	♗b7
15	gxf5	exf5

This is generally the correct way to recapture in this kind of position. Black keeps his king well protected and may also be able to utilize the half-open e-file.

16 c4

White was worried about ...d5, but now Black has a nice square for his knight on d4.

16	...	♕d7
17	♕d2	♖be8
18	♖be1	♘c6
19	♗g2	♘d4
20	♔h1	fxe4
21	dxe4	h5!

Excellent play from Portisch. The h-pawn is going to cause enormous disruption in White's camp.

22 ♕d3

The e-pawn is in need of bolstering.

22	...	h4
23	♗xd4	

Forced, as White must secure f3 for his bishop.

23	...	cxd4
24	♘e2	h3
25	♗f3	

25 ♗xh3 ♖xe4!? (25...♗xe4+ 26 ♕xe4 ♕xh3 is simple and strong) 26 ♗xd7 (after 26 ♗g2 ♖e3 27 ♕xg6 ♖fe8 followed by ...d3 Black wins a piece) 26...♖xe2+ 27 ♔g1 ♖g2+ 28 ♔h1 ♖d2+ gives Black the better ending.

25	...	♕e7
26	♕d2 *(D)*	

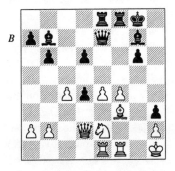

26 ... g5!
26...♗xe4 27 ♘xd4 ♕b7 28 ♖xe4 leads to complications in which Portisch, understandably, did not want to get involved. The text assures him of a large positional advantage.

27 ♔g1
27 fxg5? ♖xf3 28 ♖xf3 ♕xe4 wins for Black.

27	...	gxf4
28	♘xd4	♕f6

White is now in trouble on both long diagonals.

29	♘b5	♖d8

30 ♘xa7
White's best chance lies in some sort of simplification, although now Black's rook gains access to the seventh rank.

30	...	♖a8
31	♘b5	♖xa2
32	♕xd6	♖xb2
33	♕xf6	♖xf6
34	e5	♖g6+
35	♔h1	♗xf3+
36	♖xf3	♗xe5!
37	♖xh3	f3!

Even with such reduced material Black has a very strong attack. White is suffering terribly from the fact that his knight is totally dominated by the bishop.

38 ♖f1
38 ♖g1 allows Black to win in study-like fashion with 38...♖bg2! 39 ♖xg2 fxg2+ 40 ♔g1 ♖g5 (White has to cover ...♗xh2+, so he can only move his rook up and down the h-file; Black plans to run him out of squares) 41 ♖h4 ♔f7 42 ♖h6 (42 ♘d4 ♗d6! wins for Black) 42...♔g7 43 ♖h3 ♖g4 44 ♖h5 ♗f4 45 ♖h3 ♔g6 46 ♘d4 ♗d6 47 ♘b3 ♗e5! and White is in zugzwang.

38	...	♖bg2
39	♖d1	♗f4!

39...f2 would also win after 40 ♖g3 ♖xh2+ 41 ♔xh2 ♖xg3 42 ♔h1 ♗f4! (threat ...♗e3 and ...♖g1+) 43 ♘d4 ♖d3! (or 43...♖g1+).

40	♘d4	f2
41	♘f3	

Now 41 ♖g3 loses to 41...♖xh2+ 42 ♔xh2 ♖xg3 43 ♔h1 ♖g1+ 44 ♖xg1+ fxg1♕+ 45 ♔xg1 ♗e3+.

41	...	♗e3
42	♖d8+	♔g7
43	♖d7+	♔f6

0-1

Game 3
Langner – Stohl
Czechoslovakia 1992

1	e4	c5
2	♘c3	d6
3	f4	♘c6
4	♘f3	g6
5	g3	♗g7
6	♗g2	e6
7	0-0	♘ge7
8	d3	0-0
9	♗e3	♘d4
10	e5 *(D)*	

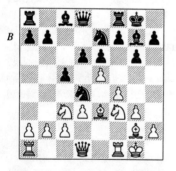

Since its introduction in 1987, this move has been the subject of a fierce theoretical debate with 10...♕b6 and 10...♘ef5 the main responses.

10	...	dxe5

But for some reason this obvious capture has been totally ignored. Let's have a look at the older lines, which will show why Black was in need of a novelty.

a) 10...♕b6 11 ♖b1! ♘ef5 12 ♗f2 ♘xf3+ 13 ♕xf3 dxe5 14 fxe5 ♗xe5 15 ♘e4 ♘d4 (15...♗d7? 16 ♗xc5 ♗d4+ 17 ♔h1! won for White in Balashov-Kiselev, Moscow 1989) 16 ♕d1 f5 17 ♘d2 (White appears to be going backwards, but he has in fact seen extremely deeply into the position) 17...♕c7 18 c3 ♘b5 19 ♕e2 a6 (otherwise d4 was very strong) 20 a4 ♘a7 21 ♘c4 ♗f6 22 b4! (Black's position begins to creak) 22...cxb4 23 ♘b6 ♖b8 24 ♘xc8 ♘xc8 25 ♕xe6+ ♔g7 26 cxb4 (White has regained the pawn and holds a clear positional advantage) 26...♕d6 27 ♕xd6 ♘xd6 28 ♖bc1 ♖f7 29 ♖c5 ♗g5 30 h4 ♗d2 31 ♗d4+ ♔h6 32 ♖d5 ♖d7 33 ♗f3 ♖bd8 34 ♗b6 ♖e8 35 ♗c5 ♖ed8 36 g4 fxg4 37 ♗xg4 ♘f5 38 ♖xd7 1-0 Balashov-Pigusov, USSR 1990. A very powerful game from White.

b) 10...♘ef5 11 ♗f2 ♘xf3+ 12 ♕xf3 ♘d4 13 ♕d1 dxe5 14 fxe5 ♗xe5 15 ♘e4 f5 16 ♘xc5 ♕d6 17 b4 ♖b8? (17...♘c6 offers better chances) 18 c3 ♘b5 19 d4 (White's pieces coordinate very well – at least compared with Black's) 19...♗f6 20 ♕b3 b6 21 ♘d3 ♗b7 22 ♗xb7 ♖xb7 23 a4 ♘c7 24 ♖fe1 ♘d5 25 c4 ♘e7

26 ♘f4! ♘c6 27 ♖xe6 ♕xb4 28 ♕d3 ♘e7 29 ♗e1 ♕b2 30 ♗c3 ♕b3 31 ♖xf6! ♖xf6 32 d5 ♔f7 33 ♘e6 ♖xe6 34 dxe6+ ♔xe6 35 ♖e1+ ♔f7 36 ♕d4 ♕xa4 37 ♕g7+ ♔e8 38 ♗f6 ♔d8 39 ♕f8+ ♔e8 40 ♖d1+ ♖d7 41 ♗xe7+ ♔c7 42 ♕xe8 1-0 Spassky-Gufeld, Wellington 1988.

c) 10...♗d7!?. This relatively unexplored move seems to offer Black fair chances. White has:

c1) 11 ♘xd4 cxd4 12 ♗xd4 dxe5! *(D)* (Stohl only considers 12...♗c6 in *Informator*)

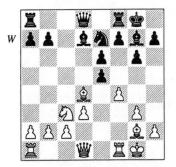

13 ♗xe5? (13 fxe5 is better, but after 13...♗c6 14 ♗c5 ♗xe5 Black has a good game) 13...♕b6+! and White resigned on account of 14...f6, winning a piece, in L.Kristensen-Feher, Århus 1992.

c2) 11 exd6?! ♘ef5 12 ♗f2 ♗c6 13 ♘e4 b6 14 c3 ♘xf3+ 15 ♗xf3 ♖c8 and Black will win back the d6 pawn with a good position.

c3) 11 ♘e4 ♘ef5 12 ♗f2 ♘xf3+ 13 ♕xf3 (13 ♗xf3 dxe5 14 ♗xc5

exf4 15 ♗xf8 ♕xf8 and Black had more than enough for the exchange in Relange-Chevalier, Paris 1991) 13...♗c6 14 c3 ♖c8 15 exd6 ♘xd6 16 ♕e2 b6 17 ♖fd1 ♕d7 18 h4 ♖fe8 19 d4 ♘xe4 20 ♗xe4 ♗xe4 21 ♕xe4 ♕b5 22 ♖d2 cxd4 23 ♗xd4 ♖ed8 24 ♕b7 ♗xd4+ 25 cxd4 ♕a5 26 ♕g2 ♖c4 27 ♕f2 ♖dc8 28 a3 ♕a4 29 ♔h2 ♖d8 30 ♖ad1 ♖d5 31 ♕e3 a5 32 f5 ♖xf5 33 b3 ♕xa3 34 d5 ♕c5 35 ♕e2 ♖c1 36 d6 ♖f2+ 0-1 Lane-Sadler, Lloyds Bank 1992. Let's not forget that Gary Lane is the author of *Winning with the Closed Sicilian*. In this game he paid the price for not considering 10...♗d7 in his book.

11 ♘xe5

11 fxe5 also deserves consideration, e.g. 11... ♘ef5 12 ♗f2 ♖b8!? 13 ♘e4 b6 14 ♘f6+ ♗xf6 15 exf6 ♕xf6 16 ♘xd4 cxd4 17 g4 ♘d6 18 ♗g3 ♕e7 19 ♗e5 f6! 20 ♗xd4 e5 21 ♗c3 ♗b7 = (21...♘b5!?) (Stohl).

11 ...   ♖b8!

This is a key move. Black removes his rook from the sensitive long diagonal and is now ready to play ...b6, which both supports c5 and prepares the fianchetto of his queen's bishop.

12 ♘e4   b6
13 c3   ♘df5

Black had taken care not to rush with ...♘ef5 as then the knight on d4 would not have had such a good retreat.

14 ♗f2 *(D)*

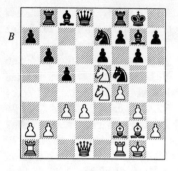

14 ...   ♗b7?!

Better was 14...♕c7 as after 15 g4 Black has a promising piece sacrifice: 15...♘d5! 16 gxf5 exf5 17 ♘g3 ♘xf4 with ...♘xg2 and strong pressure on the long diagonal to follow. If White avoids 15 g4 (15 ♘c4, for example) then play will be very similar to the actual game.

15   ♘c4?!

White misses his chance to complicate the game with 15 ♕a4. Stohl provides reams of analysis to show that 15...f6 and 15...♕c7 are good for White, but considers that 15...♔h8 and 15...♘d5 lead to unclear play.

15 ...   ♘d5
16   ♕e1   ♕c7
17   ♖d1

17 g4 ♘xf4! is killing.

17 ...   ♖bd8
18   ♔h1   ♖fe8

This type of position can quite often be reached in the Closed Sicilian and is favourable for Black for a number of reasons:

1) White's kingside is potentially rather draughty, especially if the light-squared bishops are exchanged.

2) The pawn on d3 might prove weak at some stage.

3) Since the advance ...b5 is much less committal than g4, it is easier for Black to start active play.

19   ♗g1   h6
20   ♕f2?

White slackens his grip on the e3 square, allowing Black to start a decisive attack.

20 ...   b5!
21   g4

The main point is 21 ♕xc5 bxc4 22 dxc4 ♕xc5 23 ♘xc5 ♘de3! and wins. 21 ♘xc5 ♗a8 doesn't help either.

21 ...   bxc4
22   gxf5   exf5
23   ♘xc5

23 dxc4 ♘xf4!.

23 ...   ♗a8!
24   ♘a6

This looks horrible, but Stohl shows that other moves don't help: 24 ♕g3 ♖e2!, 24 dxc4 ♘e3 or 24 ♕d2 ♗f8! 25 d4 ♗xc5 26 dxc5 ♘xf4 winning.

24 ...   ♕c6!

Black lines up.

25   ♕xa7 *(D)*

25 ♘b4 ♘xb4 26 cxb4 ♖xd3!.

25 ...   ♘xc3!
26   ♕xa8

Forced.

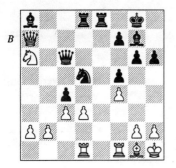

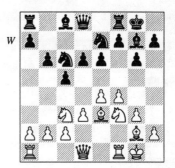

26	...	♕xa8
27	♗xa8	♘xd1
28	♘c7	

28 ♖xd1 loses to 28...♖xd3 29 ♖xd3 cxd3 30 ♗f3 ♖e1! 31 ♔g2 ♗xb2 32 ♘b4 d2 33 ♘d3 d1♕ 34 ♗xd1 ♖xd1 35 ♘xb2 ♖d2+ (Stohl).

28	...	♘xb2
29	♘xe8	♖xe8
30	♗c6	♖c8

0-1

Game 4
Abramović – Razuvaev
Paris 1989

1	e4	c5
2	♘c3	♘c6
3	g3	g6
4	♗g2	♗g7
5	d3	d6
6	f4	e6
7	♘f3	♘ge7
8	0-0	0-0
9	♗e3	b6 *(D)*

It has always been taken for granted that d3-d4 was a strong

threat, hence the habitual 9...♘d4. Recently a number of players have begun to doubt conventional wisdom and have started to experiment with the text (or maybe they were just worried about 10 e5).

10 d4

White is not forced to take up the challenge, but I would just like to quote Gary Lane, author of *Winning with the Closed Sicilian* – 'The whole system is geared towards playing d4, so it would be rather doubtful not to take advantage of the situation'.

| 10 | ... | d5!? |

10...♗a6 is also interesting, but Razuvaev's idea of countering in the centre looks impressive.

11 exd5

11 dxc5? d4 wins and 11 e5 ♘f5 12 ♗f2 ♗a6 13 ♖e1 cxd4 14 ♘xd4 ♘cxd4 15 ♗xd4 ♘xd4 16 ♕xd4 ♕c7 is good for Black.

11	...	♘f5!
12	♗f2	♘cxd4
13	♘e5	

13 dxe6 ♘xe6 will probably transpose to the game.

13 ♘xd4 cxd4 14 dxe6 ♗xe6 15 ♗xa8 dxc3 is obviously out of the question.

   13   ...   **♗a6**

   14   ♖e1

14 dxe6 ♘xe6 15 ♗xa8 ♕xa8 16 ♖e1 ♖d8 17 ♕c1 ♘ed4 looks too dangerous for White.

   14   ...   **♖c8**

   15   dxe6   **♘xe6**

   16   ♘d5

White's knights look very dominating in the middle of the board, but Black has a solid position with no real weaknesses. If the knights can be driven back or exchanged, then other factors will come into play, the most important being Black's better protected king.

   16   ...   **♗b7**

   17   c3 *(D)*

After 17 ♘f6+ ♕xf6 18 ♗xb7 ♖cd8 White has gained the two bishops, but finds his queen slightly embarrassed.

   17   ...   **♗a8!**

18 ♘f6+ was now a genuine threat.

   18   ♘d7?

White miscombines, overlooking Black's 19th move. The error was probably brought on by White's need to find something against ...♘ed4, which would seriously upset his co-ordination.

   18   ...   **♖e8**

   19   ♕a4   **♔h8!**

Black sidesteps White's tricky little threat of 20 ♘7f6+ ♗xf6 21 ♕xe8+!, and creates one of his own, 20...♗c6.

   20   ♘e5

Obviously not White's original idea, but he had little choice other than to retrace his steps as 20 ♕xa7 ♗xd5 21 ♗xd5 ♖c7 wins a piece.

   20   ...   **♗xe5**

   21   ♖xe5   **f6**

   22   ♖ee1   **♗xd5**

   23   ♖ed1

White's last hopes are based on this pin, but Black has a neat way to break it.

   23   ...   **b5!**

   24   ♕xb5   **♘d6**

   25   ♕a6   **♖c6**

   26   ♕xa7   **♗xg2**

   27   ♔xg2

Black has managed to retain his extra piece.

The game finished: **27...♕c8 28 ♕a4 ♖a6 29 ♕b3 c4 30 ♕b4 ♕c6+ 31 ♔g1 ♘e4 32 ♗d4 ♖a4 0-1**

Game 5
Yudasin – Kiselev
Podolsk 1991

1	e4	c5
2	♘c3	♘c6
3	g3	g6
4	♗g2	♗g7
5	d3	d6
6	♗e3 (D)	

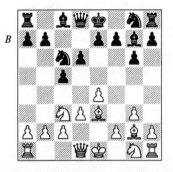

This continuation is met slightly less frequently than 6 f4, although it can be quite dangerous against the unprepared. White plans ♕d2 and ♗e3-h6 if given the chance. However, Black can upset White's scheme by delaying the development of his king's knight until ♗h6 is either no longer possible (after f4 for example) or no longer dangerous (when White is not in a position to follow up with a kingside attack).

6 ... ♖b8!?

This move highlights the main disadvantage of 6 ♗e3. White has weakened his queenside (the b2

square) so by rushing his b-pawn up the board Black hopes to exploit this. The immediate 6... b5 is dubious on account of 7 e5. 6...e6 is considered in the next game.

7 ♕d2 b5
8 f4

White has several alternatives:

a) 8 ♘f3 b4 9 ♘d1 ♗g4!? 10 h3 ♗xf3 11 ♗xf3 ♘f6 12 ♗g2 0-0 13 0-0 ♖e8 14 ♗h6 ♗h8 15 ♘e3 ♘d7 16 ♖ab1 ♖b6 17 ♘c4 ♖a6 18 a3 ♘b6 with an unclear game; Smyslov-Fischer, Zagreb 1970 (*ECO*).

b) 8 ♘ge2 and now Black may either push his b-pawn immediately, or consider delaying this:

b1) 8...♘d4 9 0-0 ♕a5!? 10 a3 e6 11 ♖ab1 ♘e7 12 ♔h1 0-0 13 ♘d5 ♕d8 14 ♘xe7+ ♕xe7 15 c3 ♘b3 16 ♕c2 c4 17 ♘c1 ♘a5 18 d4 ♗b7 19 ♘e2 f5 20 ♖fe1 ♕f7 21 h3? fxe4 22 ♗xe4 (D)

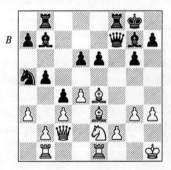

22...♕f5! and Black won in Radu-Arakhamia, Novi Sad OL 1990. White really set herself up for this classic combination. 21 ♔g1 would have been better although Black still has pressure on the long diagonal.

b2) 8...b4 9 ♘d1 ♘d4 10 0-0 e6 11 ♘c1. This is a familiar motif in the Closed Sicilian. White intends c3, but doesn't want to allow Black simply to exchange the knight off. The drawback, though, is that his own knight is not wonderfully placed. Brooks-Benjamin, Las Vegas 1992 now continued 11...♘e7?! 12 c3 bxc3 13 bxc3 ♘dc6 14 ♗h6 with unclear play. Black's 11th move broke our rule of not developing this knight while there is something else to do. Instead Benjamin recommends 11...♕a5! with the idea of 12 c3 bxc3 13 bxc3 ♘c6 with a slight advantage for Black.

c) 8 h4 h5 9 ♘h3 ♕a5 10 0-0 ♘d4 11 ♔h2 b4 12 ♘d1 ♘f6 13 f3 ♕a4! 14 b3 ♕a3 15 ♕f2 0-0 16 ♗c1 ♕a6 17 a3? ♘xf3+! 18 ♗xf3 ♗xh3 19 ♔xh3 ♘g4 and Black gained material in Hraček-Schlosser, Kecskemet 1992. If you compare this game with Radu-Arakhamia (in 'b1') it is clear that White's downfall in both games was due to the unfortunate position of the king. This might seem purely coincidental, but the truth of the matter is that there is no completely safe square for the white monarch. On h1 it can run into trouble on the long diagonal (remember that this often opens up after ...f5 by Black). On h2 something

might happen on the b8-h2 diagonal as well as on the g4 square, whilst leaving the king on g1 is usually unsatisfactory if White has played f4. This might all seem a bit abstract but I can vouch for it from personal experience.

8   ...   b4
9   ♘d1 *(D)*

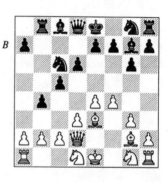

9   ...   ♕b6!?
The purpose behind this eccentric-looking queen move is to defend the knight in order to play ...f5. Black also has a couple of sensible alternatives:

a) 9...e5!? 10 ♘h3 h5 11 f5 gxf5 12 exf5 ♘ce7 13 0-0 ♗xf5 14 ♘g5 ♕d7 15 a3 b3 16 c4 f6 17 ♘f3 ♘g6 with a mess; Kupreichik-Rashkhovsky, USSR 1979.

b) 9...e6 looks the most natural move now that White has pushed his f-pawn. Ljubojević-Gelfand, Linares 1992 continued 10 ♘f3 ♘d4 11 ♘h4 ♘e7 12 0-0 f5 13 c3 bxc3 14 bxc3 ♘dc6 15 exf5 exf5 16 g4

(White is reluctant to bring his knight back into play with 16 ♘f3) 16...0-0 17 gxf5 ♗xf5 18 ♘xf5 ♖xf5 and although Black lacks his light-squared bishop he has a fine outpost for a knight on f5 and White's pawns will be more vulnerable to attack.

10 ♘f3   f5!

11 a3

11 0-0 is the obvious move, but after 11...♘f6 White is forced to enter into murky waters with 12 e5 since 12 ♘f2 ♘g4! exploits Black's control of the long diagonal. Kiselev also considers 11...♘h6 as a way to avoid the complications of 12 e5.

11 ...   a5

12 axb4   axb4

13 ♖b1?

White protects b2 in order to play ♘f2. Whilst this is a strategically sound concept, there is an enormous tactical hole in it. White should prefer 13 ♘h4 ♘f6 14 h3 or 13 0-0 ♘h6 although Black is fine in both cases.

13 ...   ♘f6

14 ♘f2   ♘g4!

15 ♘xg4

If White had an inkling of what was in store for him he would have cut his losses with 15 0-0.

15 ...   fxg4

16 ♘h4 (D)

16 ...   ♗c3!

Ouch! Suddenly White is completely lost.

17 bxc3   bxc3

18 ♕xc3   ♕xb1+

B

19	♔d2	♕b2
20	e5	♕xc3+
21	♔xc3	♔d7
22	h3	gxh3
23	♗xh3+	♔c7
24	exd6+	exd6
25	♗xc8	♖bxc8
26	f5	♘e7
27	g4	gxf5
28	gxf5	♖cf8
29	♗h6	♖f7
30	♖a1	♖b8
31	♖f1	♖g8
32	♗d2	♖g4
33	♗e1	♖g5

0-1

Game 6

Lobron – Tukmakov

Thessaloniki OL 1984

1	e4	c5
2	♘c3	♘c6
3	g3	g6
4	♗g2	♗g7
5	d3	d6
6	♗e3	e6

7 ♕d2   ♛a5!? (D)

This is not a bad square for the queen. From a5 it is well placed to support an advance of the b-pawn as well as keeping the knight on c3 semi-pinned. However, the main reason behind this move is to delay developing the king's knight. 7...♖b8 might be more natural, but this would lead to a slightly inferior version of the previous game.

Is 7...♘ge7 really so bad? Well, maybe not, but its main drawback is that it allows White to carry out his plan. In chess, success usually comes to those who manage to frustrate their opponents' ambitions. Let us take a look at the game Ljubojević-Quinteros, Mar del Plata 1981 which continued 8 ♗h6 ♗xh6 (or 8...0-0 9 h4!) 9 ♕xh6 ♘d4 10 0-0-0 (10 ♖c1 is a quieter alternative but White's king is quite safe on the queenside, unlike Lobron's in the main game) 10...♘ec6 (10...b5 11 ♘ce2) 11 ♘ge2 ♗d7 12 ♕g7!? (12

♘xd4 also led to an advantage for White in Hort-Hodgson, Wijk aan Zee 1986 after 12...cxd4 13 ♘e2 ♛a5 14 ♔b1 ♛a4 15 c3 dxc3 16 ♘xc3 ♛b4 17 d4) 12...♖f8 13 ♔b1 ♛e7 (as Lane points out, Black should have saved his h-pawn with 13...h5) 14 ♕xh7 ♕f6 15 ♕h6 ♕xf2 (otherwise White is just a pawn up) 16 ♖df1 ♕xg2 17 ♖hg1 ♕xe2 18 ♘xe2 ♘xe2 (Black has nothing to complain about material-wise, but with his only active minor piece about to be chased around the board and his king far from safety, White is clearly on top. The coming combination has an air of inevitability about it) 19 ♖g2 ♘ed4 20 c3 ♘b5 21 a4 ♘c7 22 ♖gf2 ♘e5 23 d4 cxd4 24 cxd4 ♘c6 (24...♘g4 meets a similar fate) 25 ♕xf8+! ♔xf8 26 ♖xf7+ ♔g8 27 ♖xd7 (White's rooks are totally dominant) 27...♘e8 28 ♖df7 ♘g7 29 ♖xb7 a5 30 ♖f6 ♔h7 31 d5 exd5 32 ♖xd6 1-0.

8 ♘h3

Alternatives are:

a) 8 ♘f3 ♘d4 9 0-0 ♗d7 and now the game Augustin-Byrne, Lugano 1968 continued 10 a3 ♖c8 11 ♖ab1 b6 12 ♘h4 ♘e7 13 f4 0-0 14 ♕f2 f5 with an equal game. Gary Lane recommends, in *Winning with the Closed Sicilian*, 10 ♗f4, instead of 10 a3, quoting the game Ljubojević-Am.Rodriguez, Biel 1985 which gave White an edge after 10...♕b6 11 ♖ab1 ♖c8 12 ♖fe1 ♘e7 13 e5

&c6 14 ♘e4 &xe4 15 ♖xe4 ♘xf3+ 16 &xf3 dxe5 17 &xe5 &xe5 18 ♖xe5. The natural 10...e5 is dismissed with 11 ♘xd4! cxd4 12 ♘d5 ♕xd2 13 &xd2 ♖c8 14 &b4 with advantage to White. I would replace the exclamation mark for 11 ♘xd4 with a question mark as instead of 12...♕xd2?, 12...♕d8! *(D)* leaves White's bishop trapped.

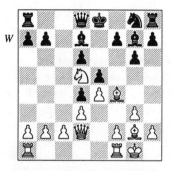

It's useful to know of errors in books such as the aforementioned, as many practitioners of the Closed Sicilian will be using this book as their main reference source. Of course you should never take anything I say on trust either. Checking lines given in books for errors is a sure way to increase your understanding of the opening and of chess in general.

b) 8 ♘ge2 ♘d4 9 0-0 ♘e7 10 ♔h1 ♘ec6 11 a3 ♘xe2 12 ♕xe2 ♘d4 13 ♕d2 0-0 14 ♖ab1 ♖b8 with an unclear game *(ECO)*.

8 ... h5

Black chooses his moment well.

White's standard response to the advance of the h-pawn in the Closed Sicilian is to play h3 (or occasionally h4) in order to meet ...h4 with g4. With the knight on h3, White has temporarily lost control of the situation.

9 f4 ♘d4
10 ♘f2 h4
11 0-0-0?

White lacks the necessary confidence to go short, but this strikes me as a move bordering on sheer lunacy.

11 ... ♘e7
12 ♔b1 ♘ec6
13 ♖c1 b5 *(D)*

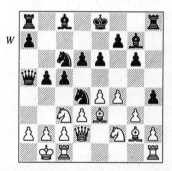

It's not often that Black has such a strong attack after a mere thirteen moves without having had to invest a considerable chunk of material.

14 e5 d5
15 ♕e1

I find it hard to offer any advice for White in this position, so I shall refrain from criticising any of his moves.

15	...	b4
16	♗xd4	cxd4
17	♘e2	♖b8
18	♖d1	♕c5

The road is now clear for the a-pawn to advance and fatally weaken the c3 square.

19	♘g4	a5
20	♘c1	a4
21	♘f6+	♔d8

Of course Black's king is not in the slightest danger with the centre so blocked.

22	g4	♘a7!
23	♖d2	♘b5
24	♖f2	a3
25	♘b3	

Or 25 bxa3 ♘c3+ 26 ♔a1 ♕a7 followed by ...♕xa3, ...♖a8 and ...♕xa2 with mate.

25	...	♕a7
26	♕xb4	♗f8!
27	♕e1	axb2

0-1

Lobron has had better days.

Game 7
Spassky – Fischer
Belgrade (22) 1992

1	e4	c5
2	♘c3	♘c6
3	g3	g6
4	♗g2	♗g7
5	d3	d6
6	♘ge2 (D)	

With this move White keeps open his options of playing with ♗e3 and

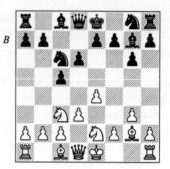

♕d2 or, alternatively, with an early f4. With the knight on c3 protected he may also start queenside proceedings with b4 (supported by a3 or ♖b1). On the other hand he has committed his knight to e2, where it can turn out to be passively placed. 6 ♘h3 (D) is another less than usual development of the knight. Black has one solid and one aggressive way to meet this:

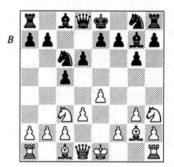

a) 6...♘f6 7 0-0 ♗g4 8 f3 ♗xh3 9 ♗xh3 0-0 10 ♗e3 ♘e8 (Black rarely leaves his knight on f6 for long in the Closed Sicilian, usually redirecting it to c7, where it doesn't block the long diagonal or the f-pawn, can support a queenside offensive, cover d5 or hop into d4 via e6. Why doesn't White resign at once?) 11 ♕d2 ♘c7 12 ♖ae1 b6 13 ♘d1 d5 14 ♕e2 e6 15 f4 f5 with an equal game; Spassky-Petrosian, Moscow Wch 1966.

b) 6...h5!? 7 f4 ♗g4 8 ♕d2 ♘d4 9 ♘g1! and now instead of 9...♕d7 10 h3 ♗e6 11 ♘ce2 h4 12 g4 which gave White the advantage in Smyslov-Romanishin, USSR 1977, Black can try 9...♕a5 or 9...e5 with an unclear game (*ECO*).

6 ...   ♘f6

As Black feels less concerned about the prospect of a kingside attack after the slightly passive ♘ge2, he has the confidence to develop his knight to f6. 6...♖b8 is a sensible alternative and play is very likely to transpose to lines considered in Game 5, as an early f4 by White seems inappropriate.

7 0-0

I should just mention that the actual move order of this game was 1 e4 c5 2 ♘e2 ♘f6 3 ♘bc3 d6 4 g3 ♘c6 5 ♗g2 g6 6 0-0 ♗g7 7 d3 (for more about these peculiarities see Chapter 10).

7 ...   0-0

8 h3

This is an integral part of White's strategy. He plans to launch a kingside pawn-storm (a standard reaction

to ...♘f6), whilst also giving himself the option of playing ♗e3 without having to worry about ...♘g4.

8 ...   ♖b8

ECO considers 8...♘d4 to be the main line, but Fischer understands that d3-d4 is not a serious threat when Black has not weakened the d6 square by playing ...e6.

9 f4

9 ♗e3 is an alternative. After the further moves 9...b5 10 ♕d2 b4 11 ♘d1 ♘e8, a double-edged position with chances for both sides has arisen.

9 ...   ♗d7

Not 9...b5?? 10 e5.

10 ♗e3   b5

11 a3   ♘e8 (D)

11...a5 is dubious on account of 12 a4!. Black should always keep an eye out for this positional trick in the Closed Sicilian. After the text Fischer is ready to meet moves like 12 ♖b1 with 12...♘c7 followed by ...a5 and ...b4. 12...♘d4 would also be worth considering.

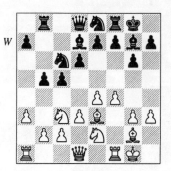

12   d4!?

This dramatically changes the nature of the game but Black has nothing to fear.

12   ...   cxd4
13   ♘xd4   b4!

Fischer is certainly not interested in the ending that arises after 13...♘xd4 14 ♗xd4 ♗xd4+ 15 ♕xd4 ♕b6.

14   ♘xc6

After prolonged thought Spassky heads for a draw. He has been criticized by several commentators for not keeping more tension in the position with 14 axb4 ♖xb4 15 ♘b3 a5 16 ♖a2 but I can't reproach him for not wishing to play in this fashion.

14   ...   ♗xc6
15   axb4   ♖xb4
16   ♖xa7   ♖xb2
17   e5!

The sole route to equality. 17 ♘d5 ♗xd5 18 exd5 ♘f6 is better for Black.

17   ...   ♗xg2
18   ♔xg2 *(D)*

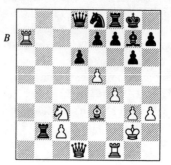

18   ...   ♘c7

18...♕c8 would have been more ambitious, but would also lead to an equal game after 19 ♘d5 ♕xc2+ 20 ♕xc2 ♖xc2+ 21 ♖f2 ♖xf2+ 22 ♗xf2 dxe5 23 ♘xe7+ ♔h8 24 ♗c5 exf4 25 ♘xg6+ hxg6 26 ♗xf8 ♗xf8 27 ♖a8 fxg3 28 ♖xe8 ♔g7 29 ♔xg3 (Balashov).

19	exd6	exd6
20	♘a4	♖a2
21	♗b6	♕e8
22	♖xc7	♕xa4
23	♕xd6	♖xc2+
24	♖xc2	♕xc2+
25	♗f2	♕e4+
26	♔g1	½-½

2 The Grand Prix Attack

An early f4 against the Sicilian was popularized by a number of young English players (Hebden, Hodgson, Watson) in the early 1980s, long before any of them became grandmasters and developed inhibitions. Another leading exponent was David Rumens, and as he and Mark Hebden both managed to win the Grand Prix (an annual prize for the best player on the British tournament circuit) using 2 f4 as their exclusive weapon against the Sicilian, the variation had found a name.

The danger inherent in this system should certainly not be underestimated. Witness the following scalpings:

Game 8
Hodgson – Nunn
Aaronson Open 1978

1	e4	c5
2	f4	g6
3	♘f3	♗g7
4	♘c3	♘c6
5	♗c4	d6

For 5...e6!, see Game 12.

6	0-0	♘f6
7	d3	0-0
8	f5	gxf5
9	♕e1	fxe4
10	dxe4	♗g4
11	♕h4	♗xf3

Hodgson gives 11...♗h5 followed by ...♗g6 as Black's best defensive chance.

12	♖xf3	♘e5
13	♖h3	♘g6
14	♕g3	♕d7
15	♘d5!	♘xd5
16	♗xd5	e6
17	♗b3	d5
18	♕f3!	c4 *(D)*

19	♗a4!	♕xa4
20	♕h5	♖fd8
21	♕xh7+	♔f8

22	&h6	&xh6
23	&xh6	&d7?
24	&f1	&e8
25	&g8+	&f8
26	&xe6+	&d8
27	&xf8+	&c7
28	&c5+	&d8
29	&h6	1-0

Whilst it is quite probable that White's attack could not survive a serious analytical examination (indeed, John Nunn, who obviously didn't enjoy typesetting this particular game, has let it be known that 23...c3! would have given Black a slight advantage), it is a nerve-racking experience defending such positions. One small slip and a young boy has checkmated a grandmaster!

Game 9
Hebden – Large
British Ch 1982

1	e4	c5
2	f4	&c6
3	&f3	g6
4	&b5	

This move is much more effective when White hasn't played &c3 as ...&d4 (see Game 13) is not really an option for Black here (it would soon be kicked away by c3).

4	...	&g7
5	&xc6	dxc6
6	d3	&f6
7	&c3	0-0
8	0-0	b6 *(D)*

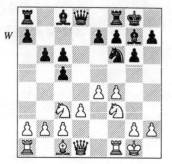

Hebden now starts the type of attack that was proving so dangerous:
9 &e1! &e8 10 &h4 &d6 11 f5! gxf5 12 e5 &e8 13 &h6 f6 14 &h1! &xh6 15 &xh6 &g7 16 &ae1 &e6 17 &e2! c4 18 &f4 cxd3 19 cxd3 &xa2 20 e6 &c8 21 &e3 &xe6 22 &xe6 &xe6 23 &xe6 &f7 24 &fe1 1-0

Terror was struck into the hearts of all Sicilian aficionados and chess purists the length and breadth of the country were appalled by the crudeness of White's play. There was an audible sigh of relief around Britain's tournament halls when the antidote was discovered. It's not clear whether 2...d5 and 3...&f6 is 100% sound, but the main point is that Black has a strong initiative right from the start of the game, and those who play the f4 Sicilian are not going to like this. For a while White dabbled with 2 &c3 and 3 f4 but they soon realized that this is not as effective a way of playing the f4 Sicilian.

The real strength of 2...d5! can be seen from the fact that Hodgson and Hebden now play 1 d4 and that Rumens gave up tournament chess!

Game 10
Hodgson – Yrjölä
Tallinn 1987

1 e4	c5
2 f4	d5!
3 exd5 *(D)*	

3 ♘c3 is the subject of Game 11.

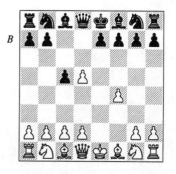

3 ... ♘f6

3...♕xd5 is playable but it doesn't fight for the initiative in the same manner as the text. By playing 3...♘f6 Black hopes to create a position where f4 will appear totally out of place and he is quite willing to donate a small amount of material in order to achieve this.

4 ♗b5+

White has to try to hang on to the pawn with c4 (obviously if he allows ...♘xd5 his opening has been an abject failure) so the only question is whether he gives this check first or not. The vast majority of players seem to reason along the lines that c4 will make this a bad bishop, so better exchange it off. It's interesting to note, though, that Hodgson considers 4 c4 to be White's best, as the light-squared bishop is a good defensive piece. He wrote (in 1985) that practical experience has been very limited with 4 c4. This is still the case today and even Hodgson has appeared unwilling to back up his prose with practical outings (this game against Yrjölä took place two years after he recommended 4 c4 and I've been unable to trace any intermediate games). According to Hodgson the critical position is reached after the moves 4...e6 5 dxe6 ♗xe6 6 ♘f3 ♘c6 7 ♘c3 (7 d4? ♘xd4! 8 ♘xd4 ♕xd4 9 ♕xd4 cxd4 10 ♗d3 ♘d7! soon led to a lost position for White in Hodgson-Salov, Leningrad 1983) 7...♗e7 8 d3 0-0 9 ♗e2 ♕c7 10 0-0. Black undoubtedly has compensation for the pawn, but who has the better chances is difficult to judge. What is clear, though, is that White is in no rush to investigate this line further. One of the few recent examples saw 9...♕d7 instead of 9...♕c7. Play continued 10 0-0 ♖ad8 11 ♔h1 ♖fe8 12 ♗e3 ♗f5 13 ♕d2 ♗xd3 14 ♗xd3 ♕xd3 15 ♕xd3 ♖xd3 16 ♗g1 b6 17 ♖ad1 ♖xd1 ½-½ Perez-Cacho, Spain 1992.

Black could also check out the alternative 7...♗d6, which is more active than 7...♗e7, but does have the disadvantage of blocking the d-file.

4   ...   ♘bd7!?

4...♗d7 is more frequently seen. After 5 ♗xd7+ ♕xd7 6 c4 e6! *(D)* White has several tries:

a) 7 dxe6 ♕xe6+ 8 ♕e2 ♗d6 9 ♕xe6+ fxe6 10 ♘e2 ♘c6 11 0-0 0-0-0 12 ♘bc3 ♘b4 13 b3 e5! and White's position was rather a wreck in the game Poloch-Tischbierek, Leipzig 1984. It's important to observe that White's weaknesses don't disappear after the exchange of queens.

b) 7 ♘f3 exd5 8 ♘e5 ♕c8!? 9 cxd5 ♗e7 (Black plans to get his king to safety and only then concentrate on rounding up the d-pawn. Note that the queen on c8 prevents 10 d4) 10 ♘c3 0-0 11 d3 ♘a6 12 0-0 ♘c7 13 ♕f3 ♕d8 14 d6?! ♗xd6 15 ♕xb7 ♗xe5 16 fxe5 ♕d4+ 17 ♔h1 ♘fd5! 18 ♘xd5 ♘xd5 19 ♗d2 ♖ab8

20 ♕xa7 ♖xb2 21 ♖ad1 ♕xd3! 22 ♗c1 ♖f2! 23 ♖g1 ♕c4 24 ♗d2 ♕c2! 25 ♕a5 h5 26 h3 ♔h7 (every Russian schoolboy knows that before one starts the final onslaught one should improve the position of one's king – assuming that one has time, which one certainly has here) 27 a4 ♖b8 28 ♖gf1 ♖e2 29 ♕a7 ♕g6! 30 ♖g1 ♖b2 31 ♕a5 ♖c2 32 ♔h2 ♘e3?! 0-1 Bhend-King, Bern 1987. How could Black have resisted 32...h4 33 ♔h1 ♕g3 with a pure zugzwang?

c) 7 ♕e2 ♗d6 *(D)* and now:

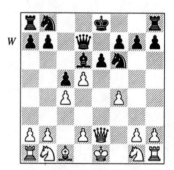

c1) 8 dxe6 ♕xe6 transposes to 'a' and 8...fxe6 will probably transpose to 'c3'.

c2) 8 f5 0-0! 9 fxe6 fxe6 10 dxe6 (even after an exchange of queens by 10 ♕xe6+, Black's massive lead in development would remain the telling factor in the position) 10...♕e8 11 ♘f3 ♕h5! (castling is now prevented on account of ...♗xh2+) 12 ♘c3 ♘c6 13 d3 ♖ae8 with a very strong attack for Black; Hebden-Davies, Nottingham 1983.

c3) 8 d3 0-0 9 dxe6 fxe6 (it is not as good for Black to exchange queens when he has already castled short) 10 ♘f3 ♘c6 11 0-0 ♖ae8 12 ♘c3 e5! 13 f5 (White has to try to keep the centre closed) 13...♘d4!? (Kasparov settled for 13...♕xf5 and after 14 ♗g5 e4 15 dxe4 ♘xe4 16 ♖ae1 ♘f6 17 ♕d1 ♖xe1 18 ♖xe1 ♘d4 19 ♗xf6 ♘xf3+ 20 ♕xf3 ♕xf3 21 gxf3 ♖xf6 the ending was about equal in Short-Kasparov, Paris Immopar rapid 1990, although Short went on to score a rare victory against the World Champion {time of writing – the day after their match in London finished}) 14 ♕d2 (14 ♘xd4 exd4 15 ♘e4 ♘xe4 16 dxe4 ♖xf5!) 14...♕xf5! 15 b3 (this is an incredibly feeble move, but 15 ♘xd4 ♕xf1+ 16 ♔xf1 exd4! gives Black a very strong attack) 15...e4 16 dxe4 ♘xe4 17 ♘xe4 ♖xe4 18 ♕g5 ♘xf3+ 19 gxf3 ♖e2 0-1 Evans-King, London 1988. White, believe it or not, is a grandmaster!

5 c4 a6
6 ♗a4?! *(D)*

This is extremely provocative. 6 ♗xd7+ is surely better. Cannings-Gallagher, Bradford 1986 continued 6...♗xd7 7 d4?! cxd4 8 ♕xd4 e6 9 ♘e2 exd5 10 cxd5 ♕a5+ 11 ♘bc3 ♗c5 12 ♕e5+ ♔f8 with a clear advantage to Black. White should have played something quieter on his

seventh move, which would have left the position unclear. 6...♕xd7 with the idea of ...e6 also deserves attention.

6 ... b5!
7 cxb5 ♘xd5

7...♘b6!? occurred in the game Watson-Razuvaev, London Lloyds Bank 1983. Play continued 8 bxa6+ ♘xa6 9 ♕xa4+ ♗d7 10 ♕c4 e6 (it's certainly not an everyday occurrence to see the normally solid Russian GM Yuri Razuvaev parting company with three pawns in the first ten moves) 11 ♘c3 and now Black could have obtained a clear advantage by 11...exd5! 12 ♘xd5 ♘xd5 13 ♕xd5 ♖xa6 14 ♘f3 ♖e6+ 15 ♔f2 ♖e2+ 16 ♔f1 ♗b5 17 ♕xd8+ ♔xd8 (Razuvaev).

8 ♘f3 g6

Black calmly completes his development. For the sake of a mere extra pawn White has a collection of weaknesses in the centre, as well as a misplaced bishop on a4.

9 ♘c3   ♘5b6
10 d4
White's best chance is to mix it up.

10 ...   ♘xa4
11 ♕xa4   ♗g7
12 ♗e3

Yrjölä awards this move a ? and considers the position to be unclear after 12 dxc5 ♘xc5 13 ♕c4 ♘d3+ 14 ♔e2 ♘xc1+ 15 ♖axc1 but I certainly like the look of Black's bishop pair, with the white king stuck in the centre as an added bonus.

12 ...   ♘b6
13 ♕a5   0-0

13...cxd4 is also awarded a question mark by Yrjölä, in view of 14 ♘xd4 ♗xd4 15 ♖d1 axb5 16 ♕b4. However, Nunn has pointed out 15...e5! 16 fxe5 ♗xc3+ 17 ♕xc3 ♕h4+ 18 g3 (18 ♔f1 ♕c4+) ♕e4, and White has nothing better than the bad ending which arises from 19 ♕c6+.

14 0-0-0

This looks quite suicidal, but White was hard pressed to meet the threat of ...cxd4 as 14 dxc5 fails to 14...♕d3.

14 ...   axb5
15 ♕xb5   ♗a6
16 ♕xc5

Possibly White had intended 16 dxc5 here, but realized too late that 16...♗xb5 17 ♖xd8 ♖fxd8 18 cxb6 ♗xc3 19 bxc3 ♖xa2 is simply winning for Black.

16 ...   ♘c4
17 ♖he1 *(D)*

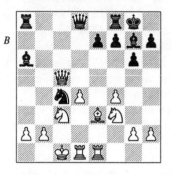

17 ...   ♕b8!

Mate is threatened and the way is cleared for the f8 rook to enter play.

18 b3

18 ♖e2 would have put up slightly more resistance, but after 18...♖c8 19 ♕g5 ♘a3 the outcome would have been the same.

18 ...   ♖c8
19 ♕xc8+

19 ♕xe7 ♗f8 followed by ...♕b4 wins for Black.

19 ...   ♗xc8
    0-1

Since after 20 bxc4, 20...♕b4 21 ♖d3 ♕xc4 wins.

Game 11
Boyd – Dorfman
Cannes 1993

1 e4   c5
2 f4   d5
3 ♘c3 *(D)*

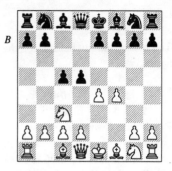

This line is commonly known on the Grand Prix circuit as 'The Toilet Variation', or more simply as 'The Toilet'. How could a variation receive such an unglamorous name? Well, a certain devotee of the f4 Sicilian was considering giving up the f4 Sicilian because of 2...d5, and then a sudden inspiration came to him in the form of 3 ♘c3. The name refers to the place where he was seated when this inspiration hit him. Unfortunately for White, the initial optimism with which his idea was greeted soon gave way to pessimism when it became clear that the most he could hope for was equality.

3 ...   dxe4

3...e6 is a solid move, transposing into other well known lines not considered part of our repertoire.

3...d4 looks a natural reaction, but strangely enough practice has been very limited. I can recall sitting next to one of the countless Hebden-Arkell encounters (I can't remember where or when) in which White had

a total disaster in the opening. Play continued (after 3...d4) 4 ♘ce2 e5 5 ♘f3 exf4 6 d3 g5! and even a King's Gambit expert such as Hebden was unable to rustle up the slightest compensation. Of course it was rather careless to have given the pawn away. Play should have gone something like this: 5 d3 ♘c6 6 ♘f3 exf4 7 ♗xf4 ♗d6 8 ♕d2 ♘ge7 with rough equality.

4 ♘b1 is probably a better way for White to play since his kingside won't become so clogged up as it does after 4 ♘e2. However, we probably won't be getting many practical examples as 3...dxe4 is doing so well for Black.

4 ♘xe4   ♘d7

4...♕c7 is also a good move so long as Black doesn't take Horn-Shabalov, Geneva 1992 as his guiding light. This game continued 5 g3 b6 6 ♗g2 ♗b7 7 ♕e2 g6?? *(D)*

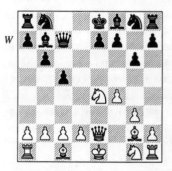

8 ♘d6+! ♔d7 9 ♗xb7 exd6 10 ♗xa8 and White was a rook up for

absolutely nothing. The fact that he managed to save a lost position after being slowly outplayed during the next thirty moves is another story; amusing, but not really relevant to this book. Shabalov was obviously confused by Horn's failure to develop his king's knight. 7...e6 would have been a sensible reply to the cheap 7 ♕e2. Now let's look at some serious stuff after 4...♕c7: 5 ♘f3 ♘f6 (the line 5...♕xf4 6 ♘xc5 shouldn't interest Black) 6 ♘xf6+ (or 6 d3 ♘bd7 7 g3 g6 8 ♗g2 ♗g7 9 0-0 with very similar play to the main game) 6...exf6 (although White has excellent chances in the king and pawn ending, he will have to negotiate a very hazardous middlegame *en route*. The pawn on f4 is very ugly and Black also has the possibility of exerting unpleasant pressure on the open central files) 7 g3 ♗e7 8 ♗g2 0-0 9 0-0 ♘c6 10 b3 ♗g4 11 h3 ♗e6 12 d3 (12 ♗b2 would have been better according to Adorjan) 12...♖fd8 13 ♗e3 ♖ac8 14 a4 b6 15 ♔h2 h6! (Black plans to play ...f5 in order to install his bishop on the long diagonal, so he rules out ♘g5) 16 ♕e2 f5 17 ♖ae1 ♗f6 18 ♕f2 ♖e8 19 ♘d2 ♗c3 and Black has a clear advantage; Ermenkov-Adorjan, Budapest 1993.

5 ♘f3

Dorfman points out that 5 ♗b5 a6 6 ♗xd7+ ♕xd7 7 ♘xc5 ♕c6 is good for Black.

| 5 | ... | ♘gf6 |
| 6 | d3 | g6 |

The bishop clearly belongs on the long diagonal.

7	g3	♗g7
8	♗g2	0-0
9	0-0	e6

Black didn't want to get involved in complications such as 9...♕c7 10 f5, and as he judged 10 ♘d6 ♕c7 11 ♘xc8 ♖axc8 to be in his favour, there is nothing wrong with the text.

| 10 | c3 | ♕c7 |

The immediate 10...b6 allows 11 ♘e5.

| 11 | ♕c2 | ♘d5! |

Dorfman was pleased with this move which hinders White's development.

| 12 | ♖e1 | b6 |
| 13 | ♗e3 | |

A rather radical solution to the question of what to do with this bishop.

13	...	♘xe3
14	♖xe3	♗b7
15	♖d1	♖ad8
16	♖ee1	♘f6
17	♘xf6+	♗xf6 (D)

Black stands better due to his superior pawn structure. There is in fact very little for White to do, and the rest of the game is an exemplary lesson in technique from the Russian/French grandmaster.

18	♘e5	♗xg2
19	♕xg2	♖d5!
20	♕e4	♗g7

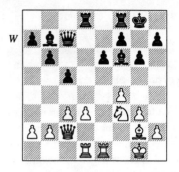

This threatens ...f5 followed by ...&xe5.

21	♘f3	♖fd8
22	♖d2	b5
23	♖ed1	a6
24	a3	h6

Dorfman's plan is eventually to open the position up with ...f5 and ...e5, but he is in no rush. Note how first he gained space on the queenside, and how now he is improving his king position. The added bonus with such a slow build-up is that one's opponent may lose his patience and self-destruct.

25	♖f1	♔h7
26	♘e1	

Dorfman criticizes this move for making it easier for Black to play ...e5.

26	...	♕b6
27	♔g2	f5
28	♕f3	e5
29	♖e2	♕c7
30	fxe5	♖xe5
31	♖xe5	♕xe5
32	♘c2	♕e6!

Once the queen gets to b3, White will be unable to hold his queenside together.

33	♖f2	♕b3
34	♘e1	♖e8
35	♖e2	♖xe2+
36	♕xe2	b4!
37	axb4	cxb4 (D)

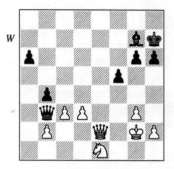

38 ♕c2

White's last chance, as after 38 cxb4 ♕xb4 the b2 pawn will also drop and then it won't take the a-pawn long to decide the issue.

38	...	♕xc2+
39	♘xc2	bxc3
40	b4	g5
41	♔f3	♗e5!

The bishop will be perfectly placed on d6.

42	d4	♗d6
43	♔e2	g4!

While the king is taking care of the c-pawn, Black will be wrapping up matters on the kingside.

44	♔d3	f4
45	gxf4	♗xf4

46 ♔xc3   ♗xh2
47 ♘e3   h5
48 ♔c4   ♔g6
49 b5   axb5+

The game concluded: **50 ♔xb5 ♗g1 51 ♘g2 ♗xd4 52 ♔c4 ♗a7 53 ♔d3 ♔g5 54 ♔e2 h4 55 ♔f1 h3 56 ♘e1 ♗b6 57 ♘d3 g3 0-1**

Games 12 & 13 feature a slightly different version of the Grand Prix Attack where White first plays 2 ♘c3, thereby avoiding the gambit line with 2...d5. However, as previously mentioned, the early development of the queen's knight is not always desirable.

Game 12
Wedberg – Kharlov
Haninge 1992

1 e4   c5
2 ♘c3   ♘c6
3 f4   g6
4 ♘f3   ♗g7
5 ♗c4 *(D)*

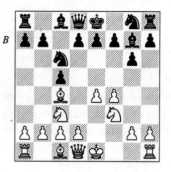

5 ♗b5 is the next game.

5 ...   e6!

This is clearly Black's best, blocking the bishop's diagonal and preparing to play ...d5.

6 f5

White's minor pieces are not ideally placed to meet ...d5, so he ensures that lines in the centre will be opened in order to give him some attacking chances. Alternatives don't promise much:

a) 6 e5 d6 (6...d5) 7 exd6 ♕xd6 (Hodgson recommends ...♘h6-f5 before recapturing the pawn) 8 ♘e4 ♕e7 9 0-0 ♘f6 and Black has an easy game. Chekhova-Zso.Polgar, Novi Sad OL 1990 continued 10 d3 0-0 11 ♕e1 ♘d4 12 ♘xd4 cxd4 13 ♗d2 ♖d8 14 ♕g3 ♕c7 15 ♘xf6+ ♗xf6 16 ♕f3 ♗d7 17 ♖ae1 b5 18 ♗b3 a5 with advantage to Black.

b) 6 0-0 ♘ge7 7 ♕e1 0-0 8 d3 d5 (8...a6 is a tricky move. Erker-Sher, Dortmund 1992 continued 9 a4 d5 10 ♗a2 b5! with a good game for Black, the point being 11 axb5 axb5 12 ♘xb5 ♘b4 13 ♘a3 ♖xa3!) 9 ♗b3 ♘a5 (with such a fluid centre it's important for Black to have the option of either taking the bishop or harassing it with ...c4) 10 ♕h4 ♘ec6! 11 ♕f2 (obviously after 11 ♕xd8 ♖xd8 12 exd5 Black can flick in 12...♘xb3) 11...b6 12 ♗d2 ♘d4 13 ♖ac1 ♘xf3+ 14 ♕xf3 c4 15 ♗a4 dxe4 16 ♘xe4 ♗b7 17 ♗xa5 bxa5 18 ♘f6+ ♗xf6 19 ♕xb7 cxd3 20 b3

♗b2! 21 ♖cd1 ♗d4+ with a winning position for Black in Carlier-Rogers, Budapest 1991.

6 ... ♘ge7!

6...exf5 7 d3 is fraught with danger and should be avoided at all costs. The untested 6...♘e5 could be worthy of investigation. Hodgson and Day give the further moves 7 ♘xe5 ♗xe5 8 0-0 ♕h4 9 g3 ♗xg3 with a draw.

7 fxe6 fxe6

7...dxe6 is equally playable. The choice of recapture is purely a matter of taste. With 7...fxe6, Black will be able to construct a big centre, but could well suffer some anxious moments due to the open spaces around his king. 7...dxe6 is safe and Black has even chances to play for the advantage as he has a good grip on the central squares, e.g. 8 d3 0-0 9 0-0 and now there are two possibilities for Black:

a) 9...♘d4 10 ♗e3 ♘ec6 11 ♕d2 (this move is awarded an ! by Hodgson and Day as they believe that if Black is allowed to play ...h6, White will have nothing constructive to undertake. Hodgson-Lawton, Ramsgate 1983 went 11 ♗b3 h6! 12 ♕d2 ♔h7 13 ♖ae1 b6 14 ♘e2 ♘xb3 15 axb3 f5 with a clear advantage to Black. In view of this it is worth considering 10...h6!?) 11...b6 12 ♗g5 ♕d7 13 ♖ae1 ♗b7 14 ♘xd4 cxd4 15 ♘e2 ♘a5 (Mokry-Plaskett, Graz 1978) and the position is given as

better for White by Hodgson and Day. I find this assessment hard to believe but Black can also play 11...♘xf3+ 12 gxf3 (12 ♖xf3 ♘e5) 12...♘d4 with a good game. (Well, at least a position I'd be happy with. I assume Messrs Hodgson and Plaskett think otherwise).

b) 9...♘a5 10 ♕e1 ♘ec6 11 ♗g5 f6 12 ♗e3 b6 13 ♘e2 ♘xc4 14 dxc4 ♗b7 15 ♖d1 ♕e7 with an edge for Black; Kosanović-Damljanović, Belgrade 1993.

8 d3

8 0-0 d5 9 ♗b5 (9 ♗b3 c4) 9...0-0 10 ♗xc6 ♘xc6 11 d3 is about equal, but rather unambitious on White's part.

8 ... d5

9 ♗b3

9 exd5 exd5 10 ♗b3 b5 transposes to the game and 9 ♗b5 is similar to the previous note.

9 ... b5!

10 exd5 exd5 (D)

11 0-0!?

11 ♘xb5 has been the normal move here, and over the years there has been a theoretical debate on the merits of 11...♕a5+ 12 ♘c3 d4 after which Black nets a piece at the cost of a dangerous attack. Black has in fact a much stronger way to win a piece, namely 12...c4!. Nobody seems to have paid any attention to Hodgson and Day who gave this as the refutation of White's attack back in 1985. The point is that Black will win the powerful bishop rather than the knight. Research for this book enabled me to chalk up an easy point in the game Sudan-Gallagher, Geneva 1993. After 12...c4 my opponent seemed shell-shocked. There quickly followed 13 dxc4 dxc4 after which he spent the next hour staring at the ceiling, apart from the occasional mournful glance at the unopened chocolate bar which he'd placed very purposefully beside the board at the start of the game. It had obviously been intended to boost his flagging powers in the final hour of the session. Finally he played 14 ♗xc4 ♗xc3+ 15 ♗d2 ♗xd2+ 16 ♕xd2 ♕xd2+ 17 ♔xd2 and although he managed to stagger on into the fourth hour, you normally require more than a chocolate bar to save an ending a piece down. I should just mention that it's not even clear that 13...dxc4 is the strongest. 13...d4 has a lot to be said for it, now that the bishop's diagonal is closed.

11 ...	**c4**

In Hodgson-Strauss, London 1979, Black made the panicky decision to part company with his dark-squared bishop. After 11...♗xc3 12 bxc3 c4 13 ♘g5 ♗f5 14 dxc4 dxc4 15 ♕e2 White had a strong attack, although Strauss went down without a fight: 15...h6?! (15...cxb3 16 axb3 ♕d5! is not so clear) 16 ♖xf5! hxg5 17 ♖xb5 cxb3 18 axb3 ♕d6 19 h3 0-0 20 ♗xg5 ♘f5 21 ♖d1 1-0.

12 dxc4	**dxc4**
13 ♕xd8+	**♘xd8!**

Kharlov, annotating in *Informator*, considered this recapture worth two exclamation marks. After the alternative 13...♔xd8 14 ♘xb5 (14 ♖d1+!?) 14...cxb3 15 axb3 White has some dangerous threats (♘g5 or ♗f4) which Black is not ideally placed to deal with.

14 ♘xb5	**cxb3**
15 ♘c7+	**♔d7**
16 ♘xa8	**bxc2!** (D)

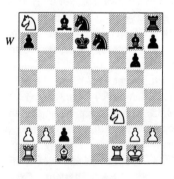

17 ♗f4?!

Kharlov considers 17 ♖f2! to be the only move. After 17...♗b7 18 ♖d2+ ♔c8 19 ♖xc2+ ♘ec6 20 ♗f4 ♗xa8 21 ♖ac1 he gives the position as unclear. However, Blatny has pointed out that 18...♘d5! leaves Black with a clear advantage.

17 ...   ♖f8!
18 ♘e5+

After this Black has the chance to exchange a pair of rooks. Normally with two minor pieces against a rook one tries to keep the rook, but here the strength of the c2 pawn multiplies as White's back rank becomes less secure. The alternative is 18 ♗g3 but Black keeps a sizeable advantage after 18...♘e6 19 ♖ac1 ♗b7 20 ♖xc2 ♖xa8 21 ♖d2+ ♔e8 22 ♖e1 ♗xf3! (Kharlov).

18 ...   ♗xe5!
19 ♗xe5   ♖xf1+
20 ♖xf1   ♘dc6
21 ♗c3   ♗a6
22 ♖c1   ♗d3
23 ♔f2   ♘d5
24 ♗d2   ♘cb4
25 a3   ♘c6

Now Black has the b3 square at his disposal. It's impressive how Black won the game without even bothering about the knight on a8: 26 ♖e1 ♗f5 27 h3 h5 28 ♔g3 ♘d4 29 ♔h4 ♘b3 30 ♗g5 ♗d3 31 ♔g3 ♘c5 32 ♔f3 ♘e6 33 ♗c1 h4 34 ♔f2 ♗f5 35 g3 ♘c5 36 ♔f3 ♘d3 37 ♖g1 ♘xc1 38 ♖xc1 hxg3 39 ♔xg3 ♘e3 0-1.

Game 13
Hodgson – Petursson
Reykjavik 1989

1 e4   c5
2 ♘c3   ♘c6
3 f4   g6
4 ♘f3   ♗g7
5 ♗b5 (D)

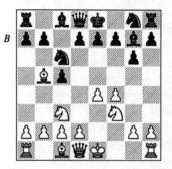

This is a more positional approach than 5 ♗c4. If he can, White will capture on c6 after which Black will have trouble finding a constructive plan. After, for example, 5...d6 6 ♗xc6+ bxc6 White's position is more favourable than in Game 27, as the pawn on f4 gives White extra space on the kingside.

5 ...   ♘d4!

Black doesn't fall in with White's plans.

6 ♘xd4

White's idea is quite simple: play c3, forcing Black to exchange, after which he can hope to create a broad centre. However, this is not so easy to carry out as White's position lacks cohesion. There are a whole host of alternatives, many of them involving ♘xd4 at some later point:

a) 6 0-0. White shows no respect for the two bishops, considering his piece on b5 to be rather peripheral to the proceedings. Black now has:

a1) 6...♘xb5 7 ♘xb5 d6 (I always assumed that it was common knowledge that 7...d5 was a simple way to equalize, e.g. 8 exd5 a6 9 ♘c3 ♘f6 or 8 d3 a6 9 ♘c3 d4. However, everybody seems to play the text) 8 a4 (this rules out any early activity by Black on the queenside) 8...a6 9 ♘c3 ♘f6 10 ♕e1 0-0 11 d3 (White should have taken the time to play a5) 11...e6 12 ♔h1. This was White's last chance to play 12 a5!. The game Hebden-Ftačnik, Hastings 1982-83, was from now on an exemplary performance by Black and a game worthy of close study. 12...b6! 13 ♗d2 ♗d7 14 ♘d1 b5 15 axb5 axb5 16 ♖xa8 ♕xa8 17 ♕h4 ♗c6 18 ♘f2 ♕d8 19 f5 exf5 20 ♗g5 (D)

20...h6! 21 ♗xh6 ♘xe4! 22 ♗g5 ♘xf2+ 23 ♕xf2 ♕d7 24 b3 ♖e8 25 h4 ♖e6 26 ♗f4 ♕e7 27 ♕g3 ♗xf3 28 gxf3 ♗f6 29 h5 ♗h4 30 ♕h3 g5 31 ♗g3 ♗xg3 32 ♕xg3 ♔g7 33 d4 cxd4 34 ♖d1 f4 35 ♕f2 ♔h6 36 ♖f1 ♖e3 37 ♕d2 ♕f6 38 ♕a5 g4 39 ♕a8 gxf3 0-1.

a2) 6...e6 7 d3 ♘e7 8 ♘xd4 cxd4 9 ♘e2 0-0 10 ♗a4 d6 11 ♗d2 ♗d7 12 ♗b3 ♖c8 13 ♕e1 ♔h8 14 ♔h1 f5 15 ♘g3 ♘c6 16 ♕f2 ♘a5 17 ♗xa5 (White needs his light-squared bishop to defend c2, but this in conjunction with his next move cannot be good) 17...♕xa5 18 exf5 exf5 19 ♘e2 ♕c5 (Moutousis-Topalov, Biel IZ 1993) and Black has a clear advantage. White will soon begin to appreciate what a big hole he has on e3.

b) 6 ♗c4 e6 7 d3 (or 7 e5 d5 8 ♘xd4 cxd4 9 ♗b5+ ♗d7 10 ♗xd7+ ♕xd7 11 ♘e2 f6 with an unclear position; Tarasov-Ilivitsky, USSR 1966) 7...♘e7 8 ♘xd4 cxd4 9 ♘e2 0-0 10 0-0 d5 11 ♗b3 dxe4 12 dxe4 ♕b6 13 ♔h1 ♗d7 14 c3 ♗c6 with advantage to Black; Nikolić-Stanojoski, Yugoslav Ch 1991.

c) 6 ♗a4?! ♕a5 7 ♗b3 b5 8 ♘xd4 cxd4 9 ♘b1 ♗b7 10 ♕e2 ♘f6 11 e5 ♘e4 12 ♘a3 a6 13 0-0 ♘c5 14 d3 0-0 15 ♕f2 d6 16 exd6 e6 with an edge for Black; Damljanović-Ribli, Reggio Emilia 1988/89.

d) 6 ♗d3 d6 7 ♘d5!? (7 ♘xd4 cxd4 8 ♘e2 ♘f6 transposes to

Hodgson-Petursson) 7...e6 8 ♘e3 ♘e7 9 c3 ♘xf3+ 10 ♕xf3 (White has gone to great extremes in trying to avoid ♘xd4. It's a shame such an imaginative approach is so poorly rewarded) 10...d5 11 exd5 ♘xd5 12 ♘xd5 ♕xd5 13 ♕xd5 exd5 14 0-0 ♗f5!? leading to a slight edge for Black; Izrailov-Donaldson, New York 1991.

e) 6 a4 a6 (Black transposes to 'b' or 'd' where the inclusion of ...a6 and a4 shouldn't be too relevant. Black should be able to keep White sufficiently occupied, so that he can't find the time to fix the queenside with a5) 7 ♗d3 d6 8 ♘xd4 cxd4 9 ♘e2 ♘f6 10 ♘xd4 ♘xe4 11 ♗xe4 ♗xd4 12 ♕f3 ♕c7 13 c3 f5!? 14 ♗d5 e6 15 ♗a2 ♗f6 with an equal game; Kindermann-Ribli, Altensteig 1992.

| 6 | ... | cxd4 |
| 7 | ♘e2 | ♘f6 |

7...♕b6 is also good, e.g. 8 ♗d3 d5! 9 e5 f6 10 c4 fxe5 and Black was already better in Romanishin-Sisniega, Taxco IZ 1985.

| 8 | ♗d3 | d6 |

8...e5!? 9 fxe5 ♘g4 10 ♘xd4 ♘xe5 11 ♘f3 ♘xd3+ 12 cxd3 d5! with good play for the pawn; Lupu-Rotshtein, Val Thorens 1991.

| 9 | 0-0 | |

9 ♘xd4 ♘xe4 is similar to 'e' in the note to White's 6th move.

| 9 | ... | 0-0 |
| 10 | c3 | dxc3 |

10...e5!?.

| 11 | bxc3 | b6! |

By immediately pressurizing e4, Black prevents White from expanding in the centre.

12	♗c2	♗b7
13	d3	♕c7
14	♔h1	♖ac8
15	f5?	*(D)*

White could have kept his disadvantage to a minimum by remaining solid and playing something like 15 ♕e1. In that case Petursson intended to play 15...♘d7, meeting 16 ♕h4 with 16...♗f6 and 16 ♗d2 with 16...b5.

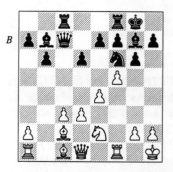

| 15 | ... | d5! |

This needed careful calculation, as Black obviously doesn't want to allow e5 without having a strong rejoinder.

| 16 | ♗f4 | ♕c6! |
| 17 | ♗a4 | |

After 17 e5 d4 18 ♖f3 ♘g4! the threat of ...♕xf3 gives Black a winning position.

17 ...	b5
18 ♘d4	♕c5!

18...♕xc3 19 ♘xb5 is not so clear. Now if White takes on b5, 19...dxe4 is strong.

19 e5	bxa4
20 exf6	♗xf6
21 fxg6	hxg6 *(D)*

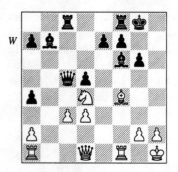

22 ♕g4

Hodgson remains true to his style and throws everything into the attack, even if this particular one is doomed from the outset.

22 ...	♕xc3
23 ♘f5!	♕xd3!

Black has not only won a couple of pawns, but has greatly increased the activity of his queen.

24 ♘h6+	♔g7
25 ♖ad1	♕a3

26 ♘f5+	♔g8
27 h4 *(D)*	

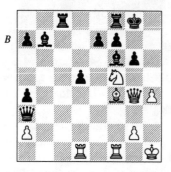

27 ♘h6+ was slightly more dangerous but Petursson has shown that with cool defence Black should win: 27...♔h7 28 ♖f3 ♖c3 29 ♕h3 ♖xf3 30 gxf3 ♗c8! 31 ♘g4+ ♔g8 and the attack has run out of steam.

27 ...	♖c4!

Black's major pieces combine attack and defence.

28 h5	g5
29 ♖f3	♕b4
30 ♖df1	♗c8!

There are a large number of pins on the board.

31 ♘h6+	♔h7
32 ♕g3	♖xf4
33 ♖xf4	gxf4

0-1

3 The c3 Sicilian

1 e4　　　　c5
2 c3 (D)

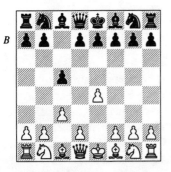

This variation is well supported right through the chess spectrum from beginner to grandmaster. With grandmasters such as Rozentalis and Sveshnikov never playing anything else against the Sicilian, 2 c3 certainly deserves some respect. The idea behind the move is very simple. White plans to play d4 and in the event of ...cxd4 to recapture with the pawn, thereby avoiding the positional disadvantages of the Open Sicilian. Black's two most active and common replies are 2...♘f6 and 2...d5, neither of which allow White to set up his ideal position with

pawns standing abreast on the central squares d4 and e4.

Games 14-20 follow my main recommendation 2...♘f6. After the standard moves 3 e5 ♘d5 4 d4 cxd4 5 ♘f3 e6 6 cxd4 I am suggesting the slightly unusual continuation 6...b6 which I believe gives Black more winning chances than the main lines. Of course the fact that it is slightly unusual is an asset in itself as White might not be as familiar with the subtleties of the position as in some of the other lines. I have to warn you that Black often has to soak up some early pressure on the kingside (as is the case with a lot of the lines in the c3 Sicilian), but if he takes care there is no real danger and as the game progresses he may well be able to take advantage of the weakened queenside that White usually possesses.

Game 21 features an alternative line with 2...d5 followed by an early ...e5 break. This line has a bad reputation but I believe that this is undeserved and that Black has as many chances here as in any of the other lines. The main advantage of this line is that there is a lot less theory to learn. Before we move on to the games, a quick word is required about the c3 Sicilian Deferred. After the moves 1 e4 c5 2 ♘f3 e6 3 c3 Black should be able to transpose to our main line with 3...♘f6 4 e5 ♘d5 5 d4 cxd4 etc. but after the moves 1 e4 c5 2 ♘f3 ♘c6 3 c3 Black, if he wishes to follow the proposed repertoire, has to play 3...d5 in order to reach Game 21. The position after 1 e4 c5 2 ♘f3 d6 3 c3 offers no transpositional possibilities to this chapter, and as play is usually of quite a different nature I feel that a separate section is warranted. This line is featured in Chapter 8.

Game 14
Braga – Gutman
Ostend 1984

1	e4	c5
2	c3	♘f6
3	e5	

Of course this is not forced, but other moves are rarely seen and can be met by using common sense. Here is an example: 3 ♗d3 ♘c6 4 ♕e2 (4 ♘f3 c4 is interesting) 4...e6 5 f4 a6 6 ♘f3 ♕c7 7 g3 (White seems to be trying to play all the variations in this book in the same game) 7...b5 8 ♗c2 ♗b7 9 d3 ♗e7 10 ♘bd2 d6 11 a3 g6 and Black's forces were more harmoniously deployed in Sarapu-Rogers, Wellington 1988.

3	...	♘d5
4	d4	cxd4
5	♗c4 *(D)*	

White offers a pawn in return for some vague attacking chances. Apart from the normal 5 cxd4, 5 ♘f3 is frequently seen, after which 5...e6 6 cxd4 or 6 ♕xd4 will transpose to subsequent games.

5 ... ♕c7!

5...♘b6 is the alternative, but the text has the advantage of forcing the bishop to the less active d3 square (as we shall see).

6 ♕e2

Other moves quickly lead to a good game for Black, e.g. 6 ♕xd4 ♘b6 7 ♗b5 ♘c6 8 ♗xc6 dxc6! 9 ♘f3 ♗f5 10 0-0 ♖d8! (Chandler) or 6 ♕b3 ♕xe5+ 7 ♘e2 d3 8 ♗xd3 e6 (*ECO*).

6 ... ♘b6

7 ♗d3

7 ♗b3?! d3! 8 ♕e4 ♕c6 9 ♕f4 d5 10 ♘f3 (10 exd6 e6) ♕g6 11 0-0 ♘c6 12 ♘a3 ♗g4 with advantage to

Black; Lukić-Rabar, Yugoslav Ch 1955.

7 ...   ♘c6
8 ♘f3 *(D)*

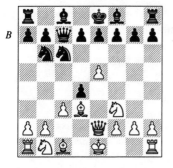

8 ...   d5!

Gutman's improvement on 8...g6 after which White has decent play for the pawn, for example 9 0-0 (9 cxd4? ♘xd4) 9...dxc3 10 ♘xc3 ♗g7 11 ♗f4! 0-0 12 ♖ac1 f6 13 ♘b5 ♕b8 14 ♗g3 fxe5 15 ♘g5! ♘d5?! 16 ♗c4 e6 17 ♗xd5 exd5 18 ♕d3 d4 19 ♕c4 with advantage to White; San Marco-Leontxo, Ales 1984. With the text move, Gutman shows that he has no qualms about returning the pawn as he expects to be left with some positional advantage, either in the form of White's isolated pawn on d4 or, if White decides to capture with a piece on d4, because of his central pawn majority.

9 exd6
Obviously not 9 cxd4 ♘xd4.

9 ...   ♕xd6
10 ♘xd4

Analysis by Gutman shows that 10 0-0 ♗g4! is good for Black. He continues 11 ♖d1 g6 12 cxd4 ♗g7 13 ♘c3 0-0 14 ♗e3 ♖ad8 15 h3 ♗xf3 16 ♕xf3 ♕b4! 17 ♗a6 ♕xb2 18 ♗xb7 ♘xd4 19 ♗xd4 ♗xd4 with a clear advantage to Black.

10 ...   g6!
10...♘xd4 11 cxd4 e6 12 ♘c3 gives White more attacking chances.

11 ♘b5
Gutman gives 11 ♘xc6 bxc6 as unclear, but Black's position looks preferable to me.

11 ...   ♕b8
12 0-0   ♗g7
13 ♗g5   ♘d5
13...0-0! is safer. Gutman gives 14 ♗xe7 ♖e8 15 ♗d6 ♖xe2 16 ♗xb8 (16 ♗xe2 ♗g4!) 16...♖xb2 17 ♗d6 ♘e5 18 ♖e1 ♗d7 with a clear advantage to Black.

14 ♗c4   h6!
15 ♗h4   ♘f4
16 ♕e3   g5
17 ♗g3   a6
18 ♘5a3   h5!

Black's extremely energetic play begins to bear fruit.

19 h4   ♗h6
20 hxg5   ♗xg5
21 ♘d2 *(D)*
21 ...   ♘h3+!

This little combination guarantees the win of a pawn.

22 gxh3   ♗xe3
23 ♗xb8   ♗xd2
24 ♗c7   ♗xh3

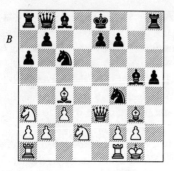

25 Rfd1   Rc8
26 &g3   &g5
27 &d5   h4
28 &h2   &g4
29 f3   &h3

29...&f5 looks more natural. From this point on, Black's play begins to deteriorate due to extreme time shortage.

30 &f2   e6
31 &e4   &e7?!

31...b5 was better.

32 &d6   &d8

Here Gutman prefers 32...Rg8.

33 ©c4   b5?

This is a blunder. ...b5 should have been played earlier to prevent the knight getting to c4. 33...Rg8 was again to be preferred.

34 Rh1?

White misses his chance. 34 &e5! would have won material, although Black certainly has compensation for the exchange after 34...bxc4 35 &xc6+ Rxc6 36 &xh8 &c7.

34 ...   bxc4
35 Rxh3   f5

36 &xc6+   Rxc6
37 &e5   Rg8
38 Rd1   Rc5!
39 &d4   Rd5
40 f4?

White blunders a second pawn, no doubt due to his anxiety over ...e5.

40 ...   Rg4
41 &f3   &c7

0-1

Game 15
Blatny – Jansa
Czechoslovakia 1986

1 e4   c5
2 c3   ©f6
3 e5   ©d5
4 d4   cxd4
5 ©f3   e6
6 cxd4   b6 *(D)*

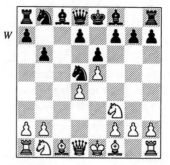

As the bishop has absolutely no future on the c8-h3 diagonal, this is a very logical move. Depending on White's reply, Black can either deploy his bishop actively on the long diagonal or alternatively choose ...♗a6 to swap off White's most dangerous attacking piece.

7 ♗d3

The most critical continuation, 7 ♘c3, will be seen in subsequent games.

7 a3 ♗e7 (this is the most flexible move as Black wants to keep open the option of ...♗a6) 8 ♗d3 (if White wants to avoid the bishop exchange he might try 8 ♘bd2 as in P.Littlewood-Nikalsson, Krinsja 1978. Play continued 8...0-0 9 ♘e4 ♗b7 10 ♗d3 f5 11 exf6 gxf6 12 h4 with a good game for White, but 11...♘xf6 is obviously better, with about equal chances) 8...♗a6 (8...♗b7 is riskier as White is allowed to keep his dangerous bishop, but Black's bishop could also prove to be a very strong piece. Sanz-Miles, Amsterdam 1978 continued 9 0-0 ♘a6 10 ♖e1 ♘ac7 11 ♘bd2 0-0 12 ♘e4 f5 13 exf6 gxf6 with unclear play. This position is less dangerous than Littlewood-Nikalsson quoted above, as White's rook cannot be introduced into the attack so quickly) 9 ♗xa6 (if White doesn't take, Black's knight will be able to develop to the better square c6, e.g. 9 0-0 0-0 10 ♖e1 ♗xd3 11 ♕xd3 ♘c6 12 ♘bd2 f5 13 ef ♘xf6 with a good game for Black; Gaprindashvili-Kushnir, Pitsunda Women's Wch 1972) 9...♘xa6 10 0-0 0-0 11 ♘bd2 f5 (this is the standard way of reducing White's kingside attacking

chances) 12 exf6 gxf6!? 13 ♘e4 ♔h8 (Black's king is quite safe in the corner and the open g-file may prove to be dangerous for White) 14 ♘e1 ♖g8 15 ♘d3 ♖c8 16 ♕a4 ♘ac7 17 ♗d2 (not 17 ♕xa7 ♖a8 18 ♕b7 ♘b5 and the queen is trapped) 17...♕e8 18 ♘g3 a5 19 ♖fe1 ♖g4 20 ♖e4 ♖xe4 21 ♘xe4 f5 22 ♘g3 d6 and Black had slightly the better of it in Wians-Kouatly, Budel 1987.

7 ... ♗b4+

Theoretically Black is swapping off his good bishop but these rules should not be adhered to too strictly as many factors have to be weighed against each other. In this case White has more space so Black decides to exchange off all the bishops; this will give him a freer game as well as reducing White's attacking potential.

8 ♗d2 ♗xd2+
9 ♕xd2

9 ♘bxd2 doesn't look correct as White loses the right to challenge the knight on d5. 9 ♘fxd2!? frees the way for White's queen, but a timely ...f5 should neutralize the attack, e.g. 9...0-0 10 ♕h5 (10 ♘c3 ♗b7 11 ♗e4 can be met by 11...d6, as 12 ♕f3 ♘c6! gives Black good play) 10...h6 11 ♕g4 ♗a6! 12 ♗xa6 ♘xa6 13 0-0 ♖c8 14 ♘e4 f5 15 ef ♘xf6 16 ♘xf6+ ♕xf6 with at least equality for Black; Nun-Koch, Dortmund 1989.

9 ... ♗a6
10 0-0

White also has:
a) 10 &e4 *(D)*.

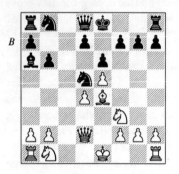

Various sources have considered this to give White an edge, quoting the following game: 10...♘c6 11 ♘c3 ♘xc3 12 bxc3 ♖c8 13 h4 ♘e7 14 ♖c1 h6 15 ♖h3 ♕c7 (Cvitan-Marjanović, Yugoslav Ch 1986) 16 ♖g3 with a slight advantage to White. I'm not sure I agree with this final assessment, but in any case Black's play was rather passive. Why not meet 13 h4 with 13...f5 (this time we're obeying the rules – countering a flank attack with play in the centre) 14 exf6 (bishop moves don't look right, e.g. 14 &d3 &xd3 15 ♕xd3 ♘a5; 14 &c2 ♘a5; 14 &xc6 dxc6 with good play for Black in each case) 14...♕xf6 with an unclear position. One thing worth noting is that Cvitan is now playing this line with Black. *ECO* suggests that after 10 &e4 White should play the following moves: &xd5, ♘c3 and 0-0-0 with a slight advantage. If we examine this a little more concretely, it is easy to see that this is incorrect: 10...♘c6 11 &xd5 exd5 12 ♘c3 ♘b4 13 0-0-0 ♖c8! 14 a3 (what else?) 14...♘a2+ 15 ♔b1 ♘xc3+ 16 bxc3 ♕e7 and Black's prospects are clearly not worse.

b) 10 ♘c3 ♘xc3 11 bxc3 0-0 12 0-0 &xd3 13 ♕xd3 ♘c6 14 ♖ad1 *(D)* (Barlov-Rajković, Kragujevac 1977) is given as slightly better for White in *ECO*.

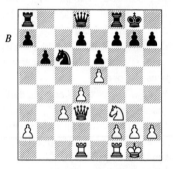

Whilst admitting that the position is not tremendously exciting, I don't believe that Black stands worse, e.g. 14...d6 15 exd6 (15 d5 leads nowhere and 15 ♖fe1 dxe5 16 ♘xe5 ♘xe5 17 ♖xe5 gives Black a favourable pawn structure) 15...♕xd6 16 ♘g5 g6 17 ♘e4 (17 ♕h3 h5 18 g4? ♕f4) 17...♕f4 18 g3 ♕f5 and Black has an easy game. These variations may be quite drawish, but if Black manages to blockade the queenside he will have some chances.

10 ... 0-0

11 ♞a3!?

Blatny wishes to retain some life in the position and sends his knight off towards the e5 or d6 squares. 11 ♞c3 is much more common and after 11...♞xc3 12 bxc3 ♝xd3 13 ♛xd3 ♞c6 14 ♖ad1 d6 we have transposed to the previous note.

11 ... ♝xd3
12 ♛xd3 ♞c6
13 ♞c4 f6!

Opening the f-file will give Black good attacking chances.

14 ♖fe1 fxe5
15 dxe5?!

This falls in with Black's plans. 15 ♞cxe5 ♞xe5 16 ♞xe5 ♖c8 17 a3 was better, with a roughly level game.

15 ... ♛e8!
16 ♖ad1 ♛h5
17 ♛d2? *(D)*

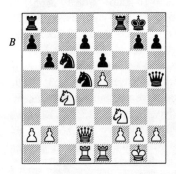

White actually seems to be provoking Black into a crushing exchange sacrifice. The best chance was 17 ♖e4 after which Black

should prepare to double on the f-file with 17...♖f7 as 18 ♖h4 ♖xf3 19 ♖xh5 ♖xd3 20 ♖xd3 ♞f4 21 ♖hh3 b5 is very good for him.

17 ... ♖xf3!
18 gxf3 ♖f8
19 ♖e4

Black's intended ...♞f4 must be prevented.

19 ... ♖xf3
20 ♖de1 ♞f4!

But it can't be!

21 ♔h1 ♞d3
22 ♖1e2 b5
23 ♞e3 ♞cxe5
24 ♞f1 ♞g4
25 ♔g1 ♞gxf2
26 ♞g3 ♖xg3+
0-1

Game 16
Sariego – Estevez
Sagua la Grande 1987

1 e4	c5
2 c3	♞f6
3 e5	♞d5
4 d4	cxd4
5 ♞f3	e6
6 cxd4	b6
7 ♞c3	♞xc3
8 bxc3	♛c7! *(D)*

This move is a very important part of Black's opening strategy. White has only one sensible way to parry the attack on c3, 9 ♝d2, after which the bishop is passively placed. Its best square is usually f4, from where

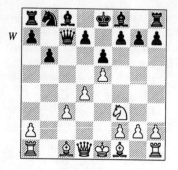

it would take a more active part in the battle for the centre which occurs when Black plays ...d6. In fact White often plays ♗f4 anyway a few moves later. It is also possible to sacrifice the pawn with 9 ♗e2, although this won't be to everybody's taste. Play becomes extremely complex after 9...♕xc3+ (Black is advised to accept the sacrifice as otherwise White will be able to develop his bishop actively to f4, e.g. 9...♗b7 10 0-0 d6 11 ♗f4 ♘d7 12 d5 exd5, Yrjölä-Jansa, Berlin 1986, and now 13 ♕a4! would have left White on top) 10 ♗d2 ♕a3 *(D)*

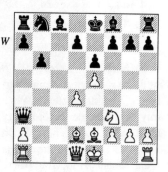

White has attempted to develop his initiative in several alternative ways:

a) 11 0-0 ♘c6 12 ♗c1?! ♕a5 13 ♘g5 ♗e7 14 ♕d3 ♗b7 15 ♖d1 ♘b4 16 ♕b1 ♖c8 17 a3 ♘d5 with a clear advantage to Black in Polasek-Lanc, Prague 1989.

b) 11 d5 ♗b4 12 0-0 0-0 13 ♘d4 ♗xd2 14 ♕xd2 ♗a6 15 ♖c1 ♗xe2 16 ♕xe2 ♘a6 17 ♘b5 ♕a4 18 ♖c3 ♘c5 and Black has a good game (Polasek-Haba, Prague 1989).

c) 11 ♖c1 ♘c6 12 ♖c3 (12 d5 is suggested by Chandler, but after 12...exd5 13 0-0 ♗c5 I cannot believe that White has two pawns worth of compensation) 12...♕e7 13 ♘g5. The game Van Mil-Krasenkov, Budapest 1989 continued 13...f5 (13...♘xd4 is unplayable due to 14 ♗h5 g6 15 ♘e4! when 15...gxh5 loses to 16 ♘d6+ ♔d8 17 ♗g5!) 14 exf6 ♕xf6 15 ♘xe6! dxe6 16 ♗b5 ♗d7 17 ♗xc6 ♗xc6 18 ♖xc6 ♗e7 19 ♕e2 ♕xd4 20 ♕xe6? ♖d8 21 ♖c2 ♕d5 with a slight advantage to Black. However by 20 ♗c3! White could have maintained a strong initiative. Instead of 13...f5, I believe Black should try 13...h6 14 ♘e4 ♕h4 with a double-edged position.

9 ♗d2 ♗b7

Black has an alternative move order in 9...d6 10 ♗d3 ♘d7 11 0-0 ♗b7 transposing back to the main line, but this does allow White the extra attacking possibility 11 ♘g5!?

as well as Smagin's latest try 10
♗b5+.

10	♗d3	d6
11	0-0	♘d7
12	♗f4	

White's other way of protecting
e5, 12 ♖e1, is featured in Game 17.

12 exd6 has been seen from time
to time, but this allows Black a very
comfortable game, e.g. 12...♗xd6
13 ♖e1 0-0 14 h3 ♖ac8 15 a4 ♗f4!
(in this type of position it is a good
idea for Black to exchange pieces as
this will emphasize the weakness of
White's queenside pawns) 16 ♗e3
♘f6 17 c4 ♖fd8 18 a5 ♗xe3 19 fxe3
♗e4 20 axb6 axb6 21 ♗f1 h6 and
Black stood better in Landenbergue-
Cvitan, Suhr 1992.

12	...	♗e7
13	♖e1	0-0
14	♖e3 (D)	

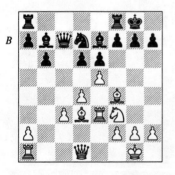

14	...	♗xf3!?

This is probably the correct idea
as Black's bishop is not taking part
in the battle for e5. Black naturally

assumes that he can weather what-
ever White might throw at him on the
kingside and that he will eventually
be able to take advantage of White's
weakened queenside.

15	♕xf3	g6!

Obviously some precautions are
necessary on the kingside.

16	♖ae1	dxe5
17	dxe5	♖fd8!
18	♗h6	

White plans ♕f4 followed by
♖f3, but the drawback to this plan is
soon revealed.

18	...	♖ac8
19	♕f4	♘xe5!
20	♗a6	

Otherwise a pawn has been lost
for nothing.

20	...	♘c4!
21	♖e4!	♘d6!?

The complications continue. This
is much stronger than 21...♘d2? 22
♖4e2! or 21...♕xf4 22 ♗xf4 ♘d6 23
♗xd6 with an edge for White.

22	♗xc8	♖xc8
23	♕e5?! (D)	

23 ♖4e3? ♘f5! is good for Black.

23 ♖4e2 ♕xc3 (Estevez considers
23...♘f5 to give Black a clear advantage) 24 ♖c1 ♕xc1+ 25 ♕xc1
♖xc1+ 26 ♗xc1 ♘c4 and Black has
slightly the better of a probable draw.

23	...	♕xc3!
24	♖c1	

24 ♕xc3 ♖xc3 is clearly better for
Black.

24	...	♕xc1+!

25 ♗xc1   ♗f6!

This pretty move is awarded a couple of exclamation marks in *Informator*, but this seems somewhat excessive to me as 25...♘xe4 also leaves Black with a considerable plus.

26	♕f4	g5!?
27	♕e3	♘xe4
28	h3	♖c4!

With rook, knight and two pawns for a queen, plus active pieces, Black has a winning position.

29	♕e1	b5
30	♗e3	a6
31	h4	h6
32	hxg5	hxg5
33	f3	♘c3
34	♕d2!	g4?!

More exact is 34...♖a4! as after 35 ♗xg5 ♖xa2 White does not possess a good square for his queen (36 ♕e3 ♗d4!).

35	♕d6!	♘d5
36	♗c5	♘e7??

An incredible blunder. After 36...♗e7! 37 ♕b8+ ♔g7 38 ♗xe7

♘xe7 39 fxg4 ♖xg4 40 ♕d6 ♘d5! 41 ♕xa6 b4! White would still have had plenty of suffering in front of him.

37	♕d8+	1-0

Game 17
Rizzitano – Miles
USA 1980

1	e4	c5
2	d4	cxd4
3	c3	♘f6
4	e5	♘d5
5	cxd4	e6
6	♘f3	b6
7	♘c3	♗b7
8	♗d3	♘xc3
9	bxc3	♕c7
10	♗d2	d6
11	0-0	♘d7
12	♖e1	(D)

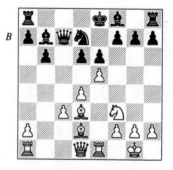

12	...	dxe5

12...♗e7 is an interesting alternative, even if it offers White more possibilities than the text:

a) 13 ♘g5!? dxe5 (White cannot
be allowed to play such a blatant attacking move free of charge – its
soundness must be tested. If 13...h6
then 14 ♕h5 0-0 {14...g6 15 ♗xg6}
15 ♘h7 ♖fe8 16 ♗xh6 gxh6 17
♕xh6 with a crushing attack) 14
♕g4 *(D)*:

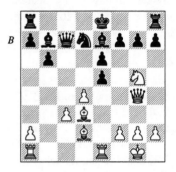

a1) 14...h5 occurred in Rausis-
Gallagher, Nîmes 1992. The game
continued 15 ♕h3 (the queen sacrifice doesn't work: 15 ♕xe6 fxe6 16
♘xe6 ♗d6!) 15...♗xg5 (the dangerous knight has to be removed) 16
♗xg5 f5 (Black has trouble finding
another plausible defence because
16...exd4 17 ♖xe6+ fxe6 18 ♕xe6+
♔f8 19 ♗e7+ is the end) 17 ♖ad1
0-0! (17...e4 18 ♗xe4! ♗xe4 19
♖xe4 with the same mate as in the
previous note if Black takes on e4)
18 dxe5 g6 with a very unclear position.
a2) After 14...♗xg5, we have:
a21) 15 ♕xg5 0-0 16 dxe5 (the
direct 16 ♖e3 can be met by 16...f5)

16...♖fd8!?. I like this move, which
places the rook on the open d-file
and doesn't commit the knight too
early. Often a knight on f8 will be
sufficient to hold the kingside whilst
Black develops an initiative on the
other wing. Note that 17 ♖e3 allows
17...♘xe5! 18 ♗xh7+ ♔xh7 19
♖xe5 ♖xd2 20 ♕h4+ ♔g8 21 ♖h5 f6
and White's attack is worth considerably less than a piece, e.g. 22 ♖h8+
♔f7 23 ♕h5+ ♔e7 24 ♖xa8 ♗xa8
25 ♕h8 ♕xc3.
a22) 15 ♗xg5. Now 15...h5 16
♕h3 transposes to Rausis-Gallagher,
whilst 15...exd4 loses to the usual 16
♖xe6+. 15...f5 is interesting, but after 16 ♕h5+ ♔f8 (16...g6 17 ♕h6 is
very strong) 17 dxe5 the natural
17...♘c5 runs into 18 ♗xf5! exf5 19
e6 g6 (the only way to stop e7-e8) 20
♕h6+ ♕g7 (20...♔e8 21 e7) 21 ♕h4
with a very strong attack.
b) 13 ♗g5. White has similar aggressive intentions to the above
lines, but figures that he will have
more chance of success if he keeps
his knight. Black now has:
b1) 13...♕d8 14 ♗f4! ♗xf3 (the
line 14...dxe5 15 ♘xe5 ♘xe5 16
♗xe5 is good for White as 16...0-0
loses to 17 ♕h5! g6 18 ♕h6 ♗f6 19
♖e3 ♗xe5 20 ♖h3 ♖e8 21 dxe5.
Maybe 14...♕c7 is best, transposing
to Sariego-Estevez with a tempo
less) 15 ♕xf3 dxe5 16 dxe5 0-0 17
♖ad1 ♕c7 18 ♗xh7+! ♔xh7 19
♕d3+ ♔g8 20 ♕xd7 with advantage

to White; Smagin-Dizdarević, Zenica 1987.

b2) 13...♗xg5 14 ♘xg5 (D):

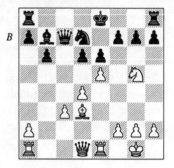

b21) 14...h6 15 ♕h5 0-0 16 ♘h7 (16 ♘xe6 is too optimistic: 16...fxe6 17 ♕g6 dxe5 18 ♕xe6+ {18 ♕h7+ ♔f7 and there is no mate} 18...♖f7 19 ♗g6 ♘f8! with advantage to Black) 16...♖fd8 17 ♘f6+ (or 17 ♖e3 dxe5! 18 dxe5 {18 ♖g3 e4! 19 ♕xh6 ♕xg3!} 18...♘xe5!) and now:

b211) 17...gxf6? is too dangerous: 18 exf6! ♘xf6 19 ♕xh6 ♕c6 (19...♕xc3 20 ♕xf6 ♕xd3 21 ♖e3 and 19...♕e7 20 ♖e3 win for White) 20 ♗f1! (20 f3 is less good as White won't be able to swing his rook across via the third rank. Black can defend himself with 20...♕xc3 21 ♕g5+ ♔f8 22 ♕xf6 ♕xd3 23 ♖xe6 ♕h7!) 20...♘h7 (20...♘e4 21 ♖e3 intending ♖h3 followed by ♗d3) 21 ♖e3 ♔h8 (21...♘f8 22 ♖g3+ ♘g6 23 ♗d3) 22 ♖h3 ♕e4 23 ♕f6+ (or 23 ♖g3!? ♖g8 24 ♗d3 ♕xg2+ 25 ♖xg2 ♖xg2+ 26 ♔f1) 23...♔g8 24

♖g3+ ♔f8 25 ♕h6+ ♔e7 26 ♗d3 and White should be winning.

b212) 17...♔f8 18 ♘xd7+ (18 ♘h7+ might be a draw. Black would have to be feeling very brave to try 18...♔e7) 18...♖xd7 and White's attack is history.

b22) 14...dxe5!. Smagin claimed that White can now gain a clear advantage by 15 ♕h5 ♘f6 16 ♘xe6 ♕c6 17 d5 ♕xd5 18 ♘c7+ ♔f8 (18...♔d8 19 ♘xd5 ♘xh5 20 ♖xe5) 19 ♕h3!. However, Nunn points out that this variation is nonsense as 17...♕xe6! wins a piece. 17 ♘xg7+ (instead of 17 d5) is also insufficient, e.g. 17...♔f8 18 d5 ♕xd5 19 ♗g5 ♖g8 20 ♖xe5 ♕d8! 21 ♕h6 ♖xg7 22 ♖g5 ♘e8 and Black is winning.

c) 13 a4 0-0 14 a5 dxe5 15 ♘xe5 ♘xe5 16 dxe5?! (White played this whole game in a very passive manner; 16 ♖xe5 is unclear) 16...♖fd8 17 ♕c2 g6 18 axb6 axb6 19 ♖xa8 ♗xa8 20 ♗f1 (20 ♗e4 ♕c4 gives Black a safe edge whilst 20...♕xe5 is interesting: 21 ♗xg6 {21 ♗xa8 ♕d6!} 21...♕d5 22 ♗xh7+ ♔g7 23 ♗e4 ♕xd2 24 ♕xd2 ♖xd2 25 ♗xa8 ♗c5 26 ♖f1 ♖c2 with some chances) 20...♗d5 21 ♕b2 h5 22 h3 ♖a8 23 ♗e3 (White gives up a pawn without a fight. The key line was 23 c4 ♗xc4! 24 ♖c1 {24 ♗xc4 ♕xc4 25 ♕xb6 ♗c5 is good for Black} 24...♗a3! 25 ♕a1 b5 {better than 25...♗xc1 26 ♕xa8+ ♔h7 27 ♗xc1

♗xf1 28 ♗h6! ♗c4 29 f4} 26 ♗b4 ♗xc1 27 ♕xa8+ ♔h7 with good winning chances for Black) 23...♕xe5 24 ♕xb6 *(D)*

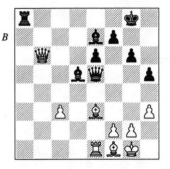

24...♗d6! (forcing a loosening of the kingside as 25 g3 ♕e4 26 f3 ♕xf3 27 ♕xd6 ♕h1+ 28 ♔f2 ♕h2+ wins for Black) 25 f4 ♕xc3 26 ♖c1 ♕a3 27 ♕d4 ♗f8 28 ♕c3 ♗g7 29 ♕xa3 ♖xa3 (Black has excellent chances to win this ending) 30 ♖c8+ ♔h7 31 ♔f2 ♗f6 32 ♖c2 ♔g7? (32...♗e4 33 ♖d2 ♗h4+ 34 ♔e2 ♗b7! would have won) 33 g3 ♗e4 34 ♖d2 ♗c3! 35 ♖d6?! (the last chance was 35 ♗c5 although after 35...♗xd2 36 ♗xa3 h4! Black should be winning the ending. His idea is to play ...hxg3 followed by ...g5! creating connected passed pawns) 35...♗d5 (a simpler move than 35...♗e1+; now White's rook is out of the game) 36 ♗e2 h4! 37 gxh4 ♗e1+ 38 ♔xe1 ♖xe3 39 ♔f2 ♖xh3 0-1 Preissmann-Gallagher, Geneva 1993.

13	♘xe5	♘xe5
14	♖xe5	♗d6 *(D)*

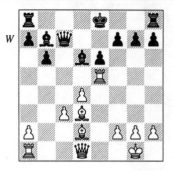

15 ♖h5

15 ♗b5+ ♗c6 16 ♕f3 can be met by 16...♖c8.

15 ... g6
16 ♗b5+

16 ♖h3 is the latest try, with White pinning his hopes on a kingside breakthrough. Black has:

a) 16...♕c6?! 17 f3 0-0 18 ♕e1 ♕d7 19 ♕h4 f5 20 ♗b5 ♕f7 21 ♖e1 h5 22 ♕g5 ♕f6 23 ♖xe6! and White wins as 23...♕xe6 24 ♗c4! is terminal; Smagin-Plachetka, Trnava 1987. There are a number of places where Black can improve on this débâcle, e.g. 18...♗e7 would have stopped ♕h4.

b) 16...0-0 *(D)* (after this White's attack doesn't seem too fearsome):

b1) 17 ♕g4 f5! (Black defends his weak h7 square along the second rank. 17...e5 would be too risky: 18 ♕h4 f5 19 ♗c4+ ♔h8 20 ♗h6 and White wins as 20...♗e7 fails to 21

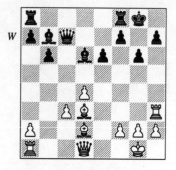

W

&g7+! &xg7 22 ♕xh7+ &f6 23 ♖g3 with mate to follow shortly) 18 ♕h4 ♖f7 (preventing any &c4 ideas) 19 ♖c1 ♕c6 20 f3 b5 21 &g5 ♖e8 22 &f6 &e7 23 &xe7 ♖fxe7 and Black's position was preferable in Dominguez-Kouatly, Manila OL 1992.

b2) 17 &h6 (this is double-edged as Black is often able to take the c-pawn) 17...♖fe8 18 ♕g4 e5 (countering in the centre) 19 ♕h4 &e7 (19...♕xc3 also deserves serious consideration, e.g. 20 ♖c1 ♕xd4 21 ♕f6 &f8 22 &c4 &d5 23 ♖d3 ♕xc4 24 ♖xc4 &xc4 25 &xf8 ♖xf8 with advantage to Black) 20 &g5 &xg5 21 ♕xg5 ♕xc3 22 ♖c1 ♕xd4 23 ♕h6 e4 24 ♕xh7+ &f8 and Black stood better in Grosar-Striković, Geneva 1991.

16 ...   &c6

16...&f8 worked out very well for Black in M.Hansen-P.Cramling, Gausdal 1987, which continued 17 ♖h3 ♖c8 18 &h6+ &g8 19 ♕d2 a6 20 &f1 (Nunn suggests 20 &a4 intending &b3) 20...f6 21 &e3 (White

was worried about ...g5 but this move is just hopeless) 21...♕xc3 22 ♕d1 ♕c2 and Black had a winning position.

17 ♕f3!   0-0-0!
18 &xc6   gxh5
19 a4 *(D)*

The little tactical skirmish has led to the win of the exchange for Black, but White has some compensation on the light squares.

B

19 ...   a6
20 &e4   &b8
21 ♕xh5   &f4
22 &e1   f5
23 &d3   &a7
24 ♕e2?

This seems wrong as Black's attack develops much quicker than White's.

24 ...   &xh2+
25 &h1   ♖dg8!
26 g3

White is not just trying to trap the bishop but also avoiding a devastating rook sacrifice, e.g. 26 &xa6

Ⅱxg2! 27 ♔xg2 Ⅱg8+ 28 ♔h3 ♕g7! followed by mate.

The game concluded: **26...h5! 27 ♔xh2 h4 28 ♔g1 hxg3 29 fxg3** (29 ♕e5 ♕xe5 30 dxe5 g2 is no better) **29...Ⅱxg3+ 30 ♗xg3 ♕xg3+ 31 ♕g2 ♕e3+ 32 ♔f1 ♕xd3+ 33 ♔f2 ♕d2+ 34 ♔f1 ♕f4+ 35 ♔e1 ♕c7** (Black cuts out White's ♕g7+, whilst ...Ⅱh2 remains a threat) **36 Ⅱc1 Ⅱh2 0-1**

Game 18
Govedarica – Plachetka
Trnava 1987

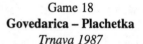

	1	e4	c5
	2	c3	♘f6
	3	e5	♘d5
	4	d4	cxd4
	5	♕xd4 *(D)*	

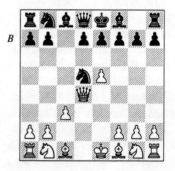

This capture (or 5 ♘f3 e6 6 ♕xd4) strikes me as being somewhat illogical having played c3, but it can, nevertheless, prove quite dangerous against an unprepared player.

5	...	e6
6	♘f3	

6 ♗c4 ♘c6 7 ♕e4 ♘de7 (the knight heads for g6, whence strong pressure can be brought to bear on the white e-pawn. White's development now looks rather silly) 8 ♘f3 ♘g6 9 0-0 (9 ♗b5 ♕c7 10 ♗xc6 ♕xc6 has also occurred in practice, but obviously Black can have no complaints about this position) 9...♕c7 10 Ⅱe1 b6!? (Black considers that there is no need to risk 10...♘cxe5 11 ♘xe5 ♘xe5 12 ♕xe5 ♕xc4 13 ♘a3 when White has a little play for the pawn) 11 ♗b3 ♗b7 12 ♕e2 f6! (taking control of the centre) 13 exf6 gxf6 14 ♘a3 ♗xa3 15 bxa3 0-0-0 with a clear advantage for Black; Timoshchenko-Zaichik, USSR 1987.

6	...	♘c6
7	♕e4	d6 *(D)*

The solid option. 7...f5 can be seen in the next game.

| 8 | ♘bd2 | |

The knight heads for c4, from where it hopes to exert a strong influence on the centre. This is the main line, but there are a number of other possibilities:

a) 8 &c4 dxe5 9 ♘xe5 &d6 (9...♕c7!?) 10 ♘xc6 bxc6 11 0-0 0-0 and Chandler considers that Black stands better after 12 ♘a3 ♕c7 or 12 ♘d2 ♕c7 13 ♘f3 e5.

b) 8 &b5 (this is White's latest try) 8...&d7 9 c4 ♘c7 (9...♘b6 – Plachetka) 10 exd6 &xd6 11 0-0 ♘xb5 12 cxb5 ♘e7 was Stein-Plachetka, Copenhagen 1990, and now 13 ♘c3 ♕c7 14 ♖d1 0-0! (14...♖d8 allows an interesting exchange sacrifice: 15 ♖xd6 ♕xd6 16 &f4) 15 ♕d3 ♘d5 16 ♘xd5 exd5 17 ♕xd5 &e6 and White can't capture on d6 because of 18...♖ad8. Black's two bishops and lead in development offer fine compensation for the half a pawn he is down.

c) 8 c4 is rare but can produce very unclear play. Short-Browne, London 1980 continued 8...f5 9 ♕e2 ♕a5+ 10 &d2 ♘db4 11 exd6 &xd6 12 &c3 &e7!? 13 ♘bd2 &f6 14 ♘b3 ♕b6 15 &xf6 gxf6 with a mess.

8   ...   &d7!?

There is nothing wrong with 8...dxe5 except that it leads to rather dull positions, e.g. 9 ♘xe5 ♘xe5 10 ♕xe5 ♕d6 11 &b5+ &d7 12 &xd7+ ♕xd7 13 0-0 ♘f6 (13...♕d6 14 ♕xd6 &xd6 15 ♘e4 might offer

White a small edge) with a roughly equal position; Rogers-Gallagher, Biel 1992.

9   exd6

9 ♘c4 can be met by 9...♘xc3!? 10 bxc3 d5 11 ♕f4 dxc4 12 &xc4 &e7 13 0-0 (13 &d3 ♕a5 14 &d2 g5! 15 ♘xg5 ♘xe5 16 &e2 Buljovčić-Browne, Novi Sad 1979 and now 16...0-0-0 17 ♘xf7 ♘xf7 18 ♕xf7 &g5 19 f4 &h4+ 20 g3 ♕d5! with advantage to Black) 13...0-0 14 &d3 ♕a5 15 ♕g3 ♖fd8! 16 ♘g5 g6 17 &f4 &e8 18 ♘e4 ♘xe5! 19 &xe5 ♖xd3 20 f3 (White plays for an attack, as he believed that after 20 ♕xd3 ♕xe5 Black had very good compensation) 20...♕d8 21 ♕f4 f5 with advantage to Black; Sveshnikov-Beliavsky, USSR 1978.

9   ...   &xd6
10   ♘c4   &c7
11   ♘ce5?! *(D)*

This natural move leads White into serious difficulties. An alternative is 11 &d3 ♕e7 12 ♘ce5 0-0-0 13 0-0 ♘xe5 14 ♘xe5 (Buljovčić-Sigurjonsson, Novi Sad 1976) which is given as unclear by Chandler. 14...♕d6 looks worthy of investigation, e.g. 15 ♖e1 f6 16 ♘f3 (16 ♘f7 ♕xh2+ 17 ♔f1 ♕h1+ 18 ♔e2 ♕h5+) 16...♘xc3! 17 bxc3 &c6 with advantage to Black.

11   ...   ♘xc3!

A superb, original sacrifice, the point being that after 12 bxc3 &xe5 13 ♘xe5 ♕a5 the double threat to e5

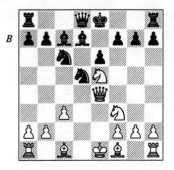

and c3 seems decisive, e.g. 14 ♘xd7 (14 ♘c4 ♛xc3+ 15 ♔d1 ♛xa1 16 ♘d6+ ♔e7 also leads nowhere for White) 14...♛xc3+ 15 ♔d1 (15 ♔e2 ♛xa1) 15...0-0-0.

12 ♛g4!

White finds a way to complicate the game.

12	...	♘xe5
13	♛xg7	♘xf3+
14	gxf3	♖f8
15	♗h6	♗d6
16	♛xc3	♖c8?!

Why give up material? The simple 16...♖g8 would have left Black clearly better.

17	♛d2	♛b6
18	♗xf8	♗xf8
19	a3	♖c5
20	♗d3	♖e5+

Stohl considers 20...♖d5! to be stronger. 21 ♛e2 loses to 21...♛a5+! 22 ♔f1 (22 b4 ♗xb4+) ♖xd3! and 21 0-0-0 ♗a4 22 ♖de1 ♛d4! is excellent for Black.

| 21 | ♔f1 | ♖d5 |
| 22 | ♖c1 | ♗g7 |

Stohl gives the following variation: 22...♛d6 23 ♔e2 (23 ♖c3 ♗g7 24 ♖b3 ♗a4) 23...♛e5+ 24 ♔f1 ♖xd3 25 ♛xd3 ♗b5 26 ♖c8+! ♔e7 27 ♖c7+ ♔f6 (27...♔e8=) 28 ♖c4 ♛d5 29 ♛c3+ followed by b3.

23 ♔g2   ♛d4?

23...♛xb2 24 ♛xb2 ♗xb2 25 ♖b1 ♖xd3 26 ♖xb2 ♗c6 is safe and good.

The game concluded: **24 ♖hd1 ♛h4 25 ♖c4 ♖g5+ 26 ♔f1! ♛h3+ 27 ♔e2 ♖d5 28 ♛f4 ♗e5 29 ♛g5 ♗c6 30 ♖h4 ♗g7 31 ♛f4 ♖e5+ 32 ♗e4 ♛f5** and Black lost on time (1-0), though he is in trouble anyway after 33 ♛e3 ♛f6 34 ♖f4.

Game 19
Vorotnikov – Sveshnikov
Lvov 1983

1	e4	c5
2	c3	♘f6
3	e5	♘d5
4	d4	cxd4
5	♛xd4	e6
6	♘f3	♘c6
7	♛e4	f5 *(D)*

This is the most dynamic of Black's possible seventh moves. White has a difficult choice (although he will have no doubt made it at home) between taking on f6 and retreating the queen to e2 (8 ♛c2 ♛c7!). In the first case he will receive some attacking chances whilst conceding the centre to Black, and in

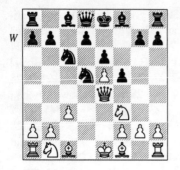

the latter he maintains the strong e5 pawn, but impedes his development.

8 exf6

Or 8 ♕e2 ♕c7 9 g3 and Black has a number of moves:

a) 9...♘de7 (intending to lay siege to the e-pawn, but the evidence suggests that White can maintain his grip in the centre) 10 ♘a3 ♘g6 11 ♘b5 ♕b8 12 ♗f4 a6 13 ♘bd4 ♘xd4 14 ♘xd4! b5 15 ♗g2 ♗b7 16 0-0 ♗e7 17 ♖fd1 0-0 18 ♖d3 and White had an edge in Rozentalis-Yakovich, USSR 1986.

b) 9...b6 10 c4 (not 10 ♗g2? running into 10...♘cb4! 11 ♕d2 ♗a6 12 cxb4 ♗xb4 13 ♘c3 ♘xc3 14 a3 ♘b1! and Black won in Baker-Basman, London 1978) 10...♗a6 11 b3 ♗b4+ 12 ♗d2 ♗xd2+ 13 ♘bxd2 ♘db4 14 ♘b1 ♘xe5 15 ♘xe5 ♘c2+ 16 ♔d2 ♘xa1 17 ♕h5+ g6 18 ♘xg6 0-0-0 19 ♘xh8 ♗b7 20 ♘c3! and White emerged from the tactics with the advantage in Vorotnikov-Georgadze, Tbilisi 1979. However, I think Black missed a chance on his fourteenth move, when instead of the dubious 14...♘xe5, he could have tried 14...g5! *(D)*.

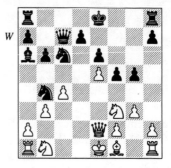

For example: 15 ♘xg5 (15 a3 g4!) 15...♘c2+! 16 ♔d1 (if 16 ♔d2 then Black can even play 16...h5 and collect the rook in his own good time) 16...♘xa1 17 ♕h5+ ♔d8 18 ♘f7+ ♔c8 (18...♔e7 allows a perpetual: 19 ♕g5+ ♔xf7 20 ♕f6+ ♔g8 21 ♕g5+) 19 ♘xh8 ♕xe5 and Black stands clearly better. One possible continuation is 20 ♕e8+ ♔c7 21 ♕xa8 ♕e4 22 ♘d2 ♕c2+ 23 ♔e1 ♗b7! and White will soon be mated. White needs an improvement in this line (maybe 10 ♘bd2).

c) 9...d6 (Black takes immediate action in the centre, hoping that his lead in development will allow him to advance his e-pawn in time) 10 exd6 ♗xd6 11 ♗g2 0-0 12 0-0 (White can also delay castling, e.g. 12 ♘bd2 ♘f6 13 ♘c4 e5 14 ♘xd6 ♕xd6 15 ♗e3 f4 Vorotnikov-Machulsky, Vilnius 1977 which is assessed as sharp by Chandler) 12...♘f6 (Black prepares ...e5 by moving his knight from the sensitive long diagonal) 13 c4 (Vorotnikov's latest try; the alternative is 13 ♘bd2 e5 14 ♘c4 e4 15 ♘g5 h6 16 ♘xd6 ♕xd6 17 ♘h3 g5 with chances for both sides in Vorotnikov-Tseitlin, Leningrad 1978) 13...e5 14 c5 ♗e7 15 ♘c3 a6 16 ♕c4+ ♚h8 17 b4 h6 18 ♘a4 with advantage for White; Vorotnikov-Gorbatov, Moscow 1992. However, Black could have tried 15...e4, as after 16 ♗f4 (16 ♘b5 ♕d7 17 ♘g5 ♘e5) 16...♕a5! (not 16...exf3?? 17 ♕c4+) 17 ♕c4+ ♚h8 18 ♘g5 ♕xc5! 19 ♘f7+ ♚g8 20 ♘h6+ ♚h8 there is no smothered mate (21 ♕g8+?? ♘xg8), so White must be content with a draw.

    8 ...   ♘xf6
    9 ♕h4 *(D)*

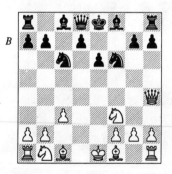

Other queen moves are rare as White normally attacks on the kingside. Nevertheless, it is necessary to be familiar with them:

    a) 9 ♕c2 e5!? (9...♕c7 10 ♗g5 ♘e5! 11 ♘bd2 b6 12 ♗e2 ♗b7 Hort-Hartston, Hastings 1975/76, is quite playable, but it looks tempting to construct a broad centre immediately) 10 ♗g5 d5 11 ♗b5 e4 12 ♘d4 ♗d7 13 ♘d2?? (White blunders, but Black's position was already quite good) 13...♘xd4 14 ♗xd7+ ♘xd7! and Black wins a piece; Konovalov-Koblents, Moscow 1959.

    b) 9 ♕a4 ♗e7 10 ♗d3 b6!? 11 ♘bd2 ♕c7 12 0-0 ♗b7 with a pleasant position for Black.

    9 ...   d5

This seems the most natural, but Miles' move 9...e5!? deserves special attention. Hort-Miles, BBC Master Game 1979 continued 10 ♗g5 d5 11 ♗b5 ♗d6 12 c4 0-0 13 0-0 e4 14 cxd5 exf3 15 dxc6 fxg2 16 ♚xg2 (16 ♖e1 ♕c7 17 ♗xf6 gxf6 18 ♘c3 bxc6 19 ♗c4+ ♚h8 20 ♖e3 ♗e5 was good for Black in Wockenfuss-Hartston, Berlin 1980) 16...bxc6 17 ♗c4+ ♚h8 18 ♘c3 ♕c7 with an edge for Black, although he still has to take care as the game continuation proved: 19 ♖ad1 ♗b7 20 ♗d3 ♖ad8 21 ♗f5 ♗e5? 22 ♗xh7!.

    10 ♗d3   ♗d6
    11 ♗g5 *(D)*

Checking on g6 will prove very time consuming for White, e.g. 11 ♗g6+ ♚e7 12 ♗c2 h6 13 ♗g6 (White must stop ...g5) 13...♗d7 14 ♗f4?! e5 15 ♗g3 ♗e8 16 ♗xe8 ♖xe8 with a clear advantage for

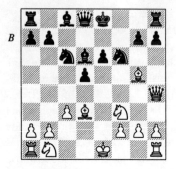

Black in Novopashin-Sveshnikov, USSR 1981.

11 ...   &f7!

This shows excellent under-standing of the position. Black saw that 11...e5 12 &g6+ &e7 13 &c2 h6 14 &xf6+ gxf6 was not so clear, so instead he prepares to play ...h6 on his next move.

12 ♘d4

Sveshnikov considers that 12 0-0 h6 13 &xf6 ♛xf6 would be only slightly better for Black.

12	**...**	**h6**
13	**&e3**	**♘e5**
14	**&c2**	**g5**
15	**♛h3**	**♘g6**
16	**g3**	**e5!**
17	**♘f5**	**♘e7**
18	**f3**	

18 ♘xd6+ ♛xd6 19 ♛g2 d4 is terrible for White.

18	**...**	**d4!**
19	**&f2**	

19 cxd4 exd4 20 &xd4 &xf5! 21 &xf5 ♛a5+ wins a piece.

19	**...**	**♘xf5**

20 &xf5   ♛b6!

And White's queenside caves in. The remaining moves were: **21 ♘d2 ♛xb2 22 ♖d1 ♛xc3 23 0-0 &xf5 24 ♛xf5 ♛c8 25 ♛b1 ♛c6 26 ♖c1 ♛d5 27 ♘e4 ♖ad8 28 g4 ♘xe4 29 fxe4 ♛e6 30 ♛xb7+ &g6 31 &g3 ♖h7 32 ♛a6 ♛xg4 33 ♖c6 ♖hd7 34 ♛c4 ♖e7 35 ♛a6 ♛d7 36 ♖c2 d3 37 ♖d2 ♛e6 38 &g2 &b4 39 ♛xe6+ ♖xe6 40 ♖dd1 d2 41 ♖f5 ♖c8 42 &f3 ♖c1 0-1.**

Game 20
Short – Kasparov
London (rapid) 1993

1	**e4**	**c5**
2	**c3**	**♘f6**
3	**e5**	**♘d5**
4	**g3!? (D)**	

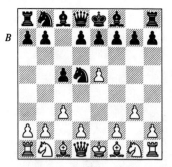

Up until this game, 4 g3 had been virtually the exclusive property of Lithuanian grandmaster Eduard Rozentalis, who has employed it with reasonable success over the last couple of years. It is strange that the idea of fianchettoing in this position had not occurred to anyone before.

4 ... d6

This is the most natural move, immediately exchanging the pawn on e5 before it can do any harm. Another idea is to attack the advanced pawn, e.g. 4...♘c6 5 ♗g2 ♕c7! 6 f4 (6 ♗xd5 ♕xe5+ is obviously not possible, but 6 ♕e2 is also bad: 6...♕xe5! 7 ♕xe5 ♘xe5 8 ♗xd5 ♘d3+ 9 ♔d1 e6 10 ♗g2 ♘xf2+ with advantage to Black – Shirov) 6...e6 7 ♕e2 ♗e7 (or 7...a6 8 d3 b5 9 ♘f3 d6 Rozentalis-Shirov, Manila OL 1992, and now Shirov considers that 10 c4! bxc4 11 dxc4 ♘b6 12 exd6 ♗xd6 13 0-0 would give White a slight advantage) 8 ♘f3 a6 9 0-0 (9 d3) 9...b5 10 a4 bxa4!? 11 ♖xa4 ♘b6 12 ♖a1 c4 13 d3 cxd3 14 ♕xd3 a5 with an unclear position in Rozentalis-Kotronias, Manila OL 1992.

5 exd6 e6

Black can also recapture at once with the queen, e.g. 5...♕xd6 6 ♗g2 ♘c6 7 ♘e2 (7 ♘f3 ♗g4 is annoying) 7...♗f5 8 d4 cxd4 9 ♘xd4 ♘xd4 10 ♕xd4 ♕e6+ 11 ♗e3 (11 ♔f1 ♖d8 is very dangerous for White) 11...♘xe3 12 fxe3 ♕a6 13 ♕d5 (Rozentalis-Gelfand, Tilburg 1992) and now 13...♗g4 14 ♗f1 ♕d6 15 ♗b5+ ♔d8 16 ♗c4 would be equal according to Blatny.

6 ♗g2 ♗xd6
7 ♘f3 0-0

The most recent game in this line is Rozentalis-Shirov, Tilburg 1993, and here Black played 7...♘c6 at once, which provoked Rozentalis into a more aggressive response: 8 d4 cxd4 9 ♘xd4 ♗d7 10 0-0 0-0 11 c4 ♘de7 12 ♘b5 ♗e5 13 ♘1c3 a6 14 ♘d6 ♕c7 15 c5 ♖ad8 16 ♖e1 ♗c8 17 ♕h5 ♗xd6 18 cxd6 ♕xd6 19 ♘e4 ♕b4 (Black is a healthy pawn up, so White invests another one for cheapo chances) 20 ♗e3 ♕xb2 21 ♗c5 e5 22 ♘d6 ♖d7 23 ♗h3 g6 24 ♕h4 f5 25 ♕c4+ ♔g7 26 ♖ad1 b5 27 ♕e6 ♖c7 28 ♘xc8 ♖f6 29 ♕b3 ♕xb3 30 axb3 ♘xc8 and Black finally won 50 or so moves later.

8 0-0 ♘c6
9 d3

White is in fact playing a King's Indian Attack but with a tempo less than normal. For example, take the moves 1 e4 c5 2 ♘f3 e6 3 d3 ♘c6 4 g3 d5 5 ♘bd2 ♗d6 (I recommend 5...g6 in Game 43) 6 ♗g2 ♘ge7 7 0-0 0-0 8 exd5 ♘xd5 9 c3 and you will notice that we have the same position as in Short-Kasparov, apart from the fact that White has an extra ♘bd2 – and this is Short's next move! How did White lose this tempo? Well, in the main game he played e4, e5 and exd6 – three moves – whilst in the King's Indian Attack he played e4 and exd5, arriving in the same structure using only two moves. If this is the best White can do, I don't predict a very bright future for the Rozentalis variation.

9	...		b6
10	♘bd2		♗b7
11	♕e2		♗c7
12	♘c4		♖e8
13	a4		h6
14	♗d2		♕d7
15	♖ad1		♖ad8
16	♗c1		e5 *(D)*

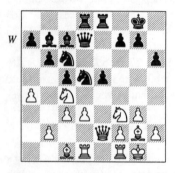

Both sides have now completed their development and Kasparov feels that with White threatening d3-d4 it is time for ...e5. I don't wish to comment too much on these moves as each player had only twenty minutes for the whole game. In my experience quickplay games can have some exceptional moments but are very rarely of a high quality for any length of time.

17	♖fe1		f5
18	♘h4		

This looks like the start of a dubious plan. White should probably have played 17 ♘h4 a move earlier.

18	...		♕f7
19	♗f3		♖f8
20	♗h5		♕d7
21	♘g6		♖fe8
22	♕f1		♘f6!

White's little flurry of activity is over and now it's time to retrace his steps.

23	♗f3		♔h7
24	♘h4		g5

Now it's Black's turn.

25	♘g2		f4
26	♕e2		♔g7
27	♕c2		♕h3
28	♘d2 *(D)*		

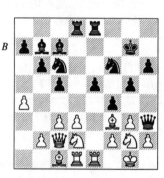

White's bishop was in need of protection. A quick comparison between the last two diagrams reveals a rather tragic picture for White. Black is now ready for the decisive breakthrough.

28	...		e4!
29	♖xe4		

29 dxe4 or 29 ♘xe4 are met by 29...♘e5!.

29	...		♘xe4

30	♗xe4	♖xe4!
31	dxe4	♘e5
32	♘e1	

32...♖xd2 was threatened.

32 ...   ♗a6!

The bishop is switched to the most sensitive diagonal. ...♖xd2 is again threatened but this time there is no defence.

The game concluded **33 c4 ♖xd2! 34 ♖xd2 ♗xc4 35 ♖d3 ♗xd3 36 ♘xd3 ♘f3+ 37 ♔h1 ♕f1# (0-1)**

The players had obviously been instructed to give the crowd at the Savoy Theatre their pound of flesh.

Game 21
Howell – Gallagher
ARC Young Masters 1984

1	e4	c5
2	c3	d5
3	exd5	♕xd5
4	d4	♘c6
5	♘f3	

White has an alternative here in 5 dxc5, which won't be relevant to those of you who reached this position via the move order 1 e4 c5 2 ♘f3 ♘c6 3 c3 d5 4 exd5 ♕xd5 5 d4 (and this game is primarily included for your sake). However, for those of you who prefer this line to playing 2...♘f6 we shall take a look at an interesting piece of Soviet analysis (by Kuindzhi and Plisetsky) that Chandler dug up for his book on the c3 Sicilian: 5...♕xd1+ (5...♕xc5 is a

solid alternative offering equal chances) 6 ♔xd1 *(D)*

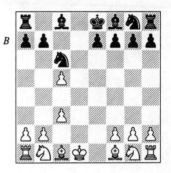

Black now has:

a) 6...e5!? 7 b4 ♘f6 8 ♗e3 (8 ♗b2 ♗f5 9 ♘d2 0-0-0 10 ♔e1 ♘d5 11 ♘e2 ♗e7 12 a3 ♗g5 13 ♘f3 ♗h6 with a good game for Black) 8...♗f5 9 ♗b5 0-0-0+ 10 ♘d2 ♘e4!; or 7 ♗e3 ♘f6 8 f3 ♗f5 9 ♘d2 ♘d5 10 ♗f2 0-0-0 11 g3 (Izvozchikov-Gudimeako, Rostov-on-Don 1977) 11...e4! 12 fxe4 (or 12 ♗d4 ♘xd4 13 cxd4 ♘e3+) 12...♘xc3+ 13 bxc3 ♗xe4 14 ♗h3+ ♔b8 and Black will win material.

b) 6...♘f6 7 b4 (or 7 ♘f3 ♗f5 8 ♗e3 0-0-0+ 9 ♔e1 ♘d5! 10 ♗b5 e5 11 ♗xc6 bxc6 12 ♘xe5 ♖e8 13 ♘c4 ♗xc5 with an edge for Black) 7...♗f5 8 ♘f3 (8 ♗b5 0-0-0+ 9 ♔e1 ♘e5!) 8...0-0-0+ 9 ♔e1 e5 10 ♗b5 ♘d5 11 ♗d2 ♗e7 12 ♗xc6 (12 ♘a3 e4 13 ♗xc6 exf3 14 ♗xd5 ♖xd5 15 gxf3 ♗h4!) 12...bxc6 13 ♘xe5 ♗f6 14 ♘xc6 ♖he8+ 15 ♔f1 ♘xc3! with an overwhelming attack.

| 5 | ... | cxd4 |
| 6 | cxd4 | e5!? *(D)* |

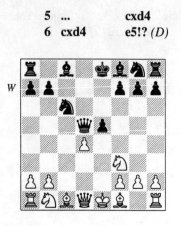

W

This line has quite a poor reputation but it seems to me to offer as good a chance of equality as some of the more recognized variations. The positions that arise are quite strange and when you add this to the fact that White will have not faced this line too often, one has achieved a perfect mix for confusing the opponent.

7   ♘c3

7 dxe5?! ♕xd1+ 8 ♔xd1 ♗g4 is good for Black. The board is much too open for White to be able to live happily with his king stuck in the centre. One example is Vollin-Conquest, Brest 1979 which continued 9 ♘bd2 0-0-0 10 ♗e2 ♗c5 11 ♘g5 ♘h6 12 ♔e1 ♘xe5 13 ♘b3 ♗b4+ 14 ♔f1 ♖he8 with advantage to Black.

7   ...   ♗b4

This pin is of course the main reason why this system is playable.

8   ♗d2

8 ♗e2 has been suggested in various places (Sir Stuart Milner-Barry is the originator, according to Chandler), White's idea being that after 8...e4 9 0-0 ♗xc3 10 bxc3 exf3 11 ♗xf3 he has a very dangerous attack for the piece. I was a bit surprised that nobody had taken the natural 8...♘xd4 into account. As far as I could see, Black wins a pawn for not too much, e.g. 9 ♘xd4 ♕xd4 10 ♗b5+ ♗d7; or 9 ♕a4+ ♕d7!. I was all set to recommend 8...♘xd4 as a strong novelty, when *Informator 48* appeared on the scene containing analysis of this very line by a chap called Finkel. His conclusion was that 9 ♗d2! leads to a better game for White. Whilst admitting to having overlooked this move, I cannot endorse the claim that White is better. The critical line appears to be 9...♗xc3 (9...♕d6?! 10 ♘xd4 ♕xd4 11 0-0 and 9...♘xf3+ 10 ♗xf3 ♕d7 11 ♕e2 {11 ♕b3} both give White compensation for the pawn) 10 ♗xc3 ♘xf3+ 11 ♗xf3 ♕xd1+ 12 ♖xd1 f6 13 ♗a5! ♗d7 14 ♗xb7 ♖b8 15 ♗d5 with advantage to White (Finkel). This is true, as capturing on b2 fails to 16 ♗b3, but 15...♗d7? is a serious error. Black can achieve a comfortable game with 13...♗e6!, e.g. 14 ♗xb7 ♖b8 15 ♗c6+ ♔f7 and although White has the bishop pair, Black has a strong centre and a lead in development (the threat to the b-pawn has to be dealt with and ...♘e7

is coming with tempo). I consider the position to be about equal. White has one other surprising try after 8...♘xd4, namely 9 ♔f1!?. Play could continue 9...♕a5 10 ♘xd4 exd4 11 ♕xd4 (not 11 ♗b5+? ♔f8 12 ♕xd4 ♗xc3 13 ♕c5+ ♘e7 14 bxc3 a6! winning) and now Black has no need to play 11...♗xc3, which looks a little better for White after 12 ♕xc3, but can play instead 11...♘f6!, as 12 ♗b5+ ♔f8 and 12 ♘b5 0-0 13 a3 ♗e7 14 ♗d2 ♕d8 are nothing to worry about.

8 ♕d2!? is an alternative, but extremely rare, way to break the pin (at least the official pin). After 8...♗xc3 9 bxc3 exd4 10 cxd4 ♘ge7 11 ♗e2 ♗e6 12 0-0 0-0 13 ♖d1 White has a passed but isolated d-pawn which Black has solidly blockaded. I am inclined to agree with Chandler's assessment of unclear rather than Rozentalis' of slightly better for White.

8 ... ♗xc3

Don't forget to play this (I've seen it happen!)

9 ♗xc3 e4
10 ♘e5 ♘xe5
11 dxe5 ♘e7 (D)

This position can be considered as the theoretical starting point for this variation. The inverted e-pawns give the position quite an original look. Strategically speaking, Black would like to exchange off the light-squared bishops, which would not only deprive White of the bishop

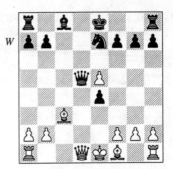

pair, but could also leave Black with the superior minor piece. It is not clear which of the e-pawns will prove weaker, but White always has to keep an eye out for the possibility of the desperado advance ...e3, whilst equally Black must watch out for e6.

12 ♕a4+

The text is just one of several queen moves White has tried in the diagram position. The alternatives are:

a) 12 ♕c2 0-0 13 ♖d1 ♕xa2 and now:

a1) 14 ♕xe4 ♗f5 15 ♕xb7 ♖ad8! 16 ♕xe7 ♖xd1+ (otherwise White will come under a strong attack) 17 ♔xd1 ♕b1+ 18 ♔e2 ♕d3+ with perpetual check. Instead of grabbing the b-pawn, White can also try 15 ♗c4. The game Nun-Witkowski, Hradec Kralove 1975/76 was rather exciting: 15...♗xe4 (15...♕xb2 could be worth investigating) 16 ♗xa2 ♗xg2 17 ♖g1 ♗c6 18 e6 f6 19 ♗b4 ♖fe8 20 ♖d7 ♘g6 21 ♖f7 ♖ad8 22

♖xg6 hxg6 23 e7 ♔h7 24 f3 ♗d5 25 ♔f2 ♗xa2 26 exd8♕ ♖xd8 27 ♖xb7 a6 28 ♗e7 ♗d5 29 ♖c7 ♖b8 30 ♗xf6 ♖b7 ½-½.

a2) 14 ♗b4 *(D)*

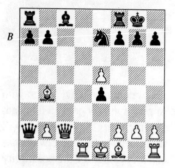

14...♗g4! (this sacrifice has re-vitalized the whole variation. Pre-viously 14...♕e6 15 ♕xe4 had been played, with White gaining the ad-vantage after 15...♖e8 16 ♗b5 ♘c6 17 0-0) 15 ♗xe7 ♖fc8 16 ♕xe4 (the line 16 ♕b1 ♕a5+ 17 ♖d2 e3! 18 fxe3 ♕xe5 19 ♗h4 ♕xe3+ 20 ♗e2 ♗xe2 21 ♗f2 ♗d3+! is one of the elegant points behind Black's idea) 16...♗xd1 17 ♗d3 g6 (Afek-Peretz, Israel 1990) 18 0-0 ♕a4! 19 ♕e3 ♗c2 20 ♗f6 ♕b4! (Afek) and Black can easily defend the dark squares.

b) 12 ♕e2!? 0-0 13 ♖d1 ♕c6 (un-fortunately after 13...♕xa2 14 ♗b4! Black is forced to play 14...♕e6, which after 15 ♕xe4 transposes to the part of 'a2' considered favour-able for White) 14 ♖d6 ♕a4 15 ♕c4 (15 b3 ♕a3 16 ♕d2 ♕c5 17 ♗c4

♗e6! was very unclear in Schmittdiel-Hodgson, Bad Wöris-hofen 1994) ♕xc4 16 ♗xc4 ♘f5 17 ♖d1 ♗e6 18 ♗xe6 fxe6 19 ♔e2. We have been following the game Ubi-lava-Zaichik, USSR 1976 where Black now rather carelessly played 19...♖ac8 allowing 20 ♖d7 ♖f7 21 ♖hd1 with a clear advantage for White. Better was 19...♖f7 20 ♖he1 h5! (now that g4 is prevented White finds it difficult to make any pro-gress but even if Black went wrong with something like 20...♘e7 21 ♔f1 ♖af8 22 ♖d2 ♘d5 23 ♖xe4 ♖c7 the win would be extremely prob-lematic as Black's knight is such a strong piece) 21 ♖d2 (21 ♔f1 e3 22 f3 ♖c8 doesn't get White anywhere) 21...♖af8!? (threat ...♘e7-d5) 22 ♗b4 ♖c8 and Black is not worse.

12 ...   ♗d7
13 ♕a3

13 ♕b4 has also been seen, after which 13...♕c6 transposes to analy-sis given below in the note to 14 ♗e2 (14 ♕b4 ♕c6 to be precise).

13 ...   ♕e6!

Black prepares to castle, removes his queen from the d-file and vacates the d5 square for his knight. A useful move!

14 ♗e2

It has been common knowledge for a long time that 14 ♖d1 0-0 15 ♖d6?! is good for Black. Marić-Ros-solimo, Novi Sad 1972 continued 15...♕f5 16 ♗e2 ♗e6 17 0-0 ♘g6 with good attacking chances. 15 ♖d2 is given by Rossolimo as about equal.

14 ♕b4 is awarded an ! by Chandler whose analysis runs as follows: 14...♗c6 15 ♗b5 ♗xb5 16 ♕xb5+ ♕c6 17 ♕e2 ± with the idea of 18 0-0 and 19 ♖fe1. Chandler points out that 17...♘d5 is met by 18 ♕xe4, but he doesn't consider 17...0-0 18 0-0 ♘d5! when 19 ♕xe4? loses to 19...♘xc3 20 ♕xc6 ♘e2+. The problem with this variation for Black is not 17 ♕e2 but 17 ♕xc6+ as after 17...♘xc6 18 0-0-0 he is very likely to lose his e-pawn. But don't despair, as there are several other opportunities to improve on this analysis, e.g. 14...♕c6!? with the possible variation:

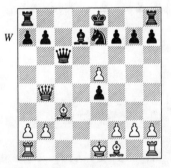

15 ♖d1 (15 ♗e2 ♘d5 16 ♕xe4 ♘xc3 17 ♕xc6 ♗xc6 18 bxc3 ♗xg2 19 ♖g1 ♗e4 with rough equality) 15...e3!? 16 fxe3 (16 f3 ♘d5 17 ♕c4 ♕xc4 18 ♗xc4 ♘xc3 19 bxc3 ♖c8!?

20 ♗xf7+ ♔e7 21 e6 ♗b5 looks fine for Black) 16...♘d5 17 ♕d4 ♘xc3 18 ♕xc3 (18 bxc3 ♗e6) 18...♕xc3+ 19 bxc3 ♗e6 and if anyone is better it's Black.

Another possible improvement is 14...♗c6 15 ♗b5 e3, e.g. 16 fxe3 ♘d5 17 ♕c5 ♘xc3 18 bxc3 ♖c8; in both these cases White's extra doubled pawn is pretty useless. Black can probably even draw quite easily after 14...♗c6 15 ♗b5 ♘d5 16 ♗xc6+ ♕xc6 17 ♕xe4 ♘xc3 18 ♕xc6+ bxc6 19 bxc3 0-0-0 when he is very active in the rook ending, e.g. 20 0-0 ♖he8 21 f4 (21 ♖fe1 ♖d3 22 ♖ac1 ♖d2) 21...♖d3 22 ♖ac1 f6. Enough! All this really goes to show is that you must never take anyone's analysis on trust (as I've already commented elsewhere in this book).

14	...	0-0
15	0-0	♘g6
16	♖fd1	♘f4
17	♗f1	♕g6!?

Howell's plan of simply completing his development was pretty timid and Black could have considered playing for more here with 17...♗c6. I'm afraid I've no idea what my thoughts were at the time (to be honest I was surprised to find that this game even existed).

18	♖xd7	♘h3+
19	♔h1	♘xf2+
20	♔g1	½-½

4   b3 Systems

An early b3 against the Sicilian has never enjoyed a great reputation and consequently you will be up against this line quite rarely. White can either play b3 immediately, which gives him the option of entering into a dubious version of the King's Gambit (which I imagine most of you regard as pretty doubtful at the best of times). This is examined in Game 22.

Alternatively White can first play 2 ♘f3 and only play b3 after 2...e6 (3 b3 makes much less sense against 2...d6 or 2...♘c6 (Game 23) as the diagonal will be firmly closed after ...e5). Black's best system is then to enter into a type of Hedgehog, but knowing the sort of players who play 2...e6 in the Sicilian, this should suit them down to the ground.

Game 22
Grosar – Kupreichik
Ljubljana 1989

1	e4	c5
2	b3	e5

This is the most principled move, hoping to block the bishop out of the game. I, personally, would prefer the move order 2...♘c6 3 ♗b2 e5, actually waiting for the bishop to get on the long diagonal before playing ...e5. 2...b6 is another possibility, with play similar to Game 24. This will suit those of you who can appreciate a good Hedgehog.

3	♗b2	♘c6
4	f4!?	*(D)*

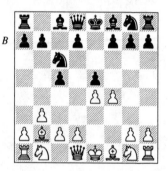

This gives rise to a strange sort of King's Gambit. I believe that the inclusion of these queenside moves favours Black. The pawn on c5 will prevent the formation of a broad centre and with his bishop posted on b2 White will have not much chance of winning his pawn back. White does have some advantages (he will be able to castle long quickly and he has some pressure on long diagonal) but these are clearly not the critical factors in the position.

The alternative, 4 ♘f3, transposes to Game 23.

4 ...   exf4
5 ♘f3

5 ♗c4 ♕h4+ (connoisseurs of the King's Gambit will understand that this check is often more trouble than it's worth. Alternatives are 5...d6!? with the idea of transposing to the note to Black's 5th move or 5...♘f6 6 e5 ♘e4 7 ♕h5! ♕e7 8 ♘e2 with an unclear game according to Lukin) 6 ♔f1 ♘f6 7 ♘f3 ♕h6 8 ♘c3 d6 9 ♘b5 ♔d8 10 e5 ♘e4 11 d4! cxd4 (taking the rook, now or later, with 11...♘g3+ 12 ♔g1 ♘xh1 13 ♔xh1 gives White excellent attacking chances) 12 ♘bxd4 ♗d7 13 ♗xf7 ♘xe5 14 ♘xe5 dxe5 15 ♘e6+ ♔c8 16 ♕d5 f3! 17 ♕xe4 fxg2+ 18 ♕xg2 ♗xe6 19 ♗xe6+ ♕xe6 20 ♕e4 ♗d6 21 ♔g2 ♔c7 22 ♖he1 ♖ae8 23 ♖ad1 ♕g6+ 24 ♕xg6 hxg6 25 ♖e4 ♖e6 ½-½ Lukin-Shirov, Klaipeda 1988.

5 ...   ♘f6 (D)

Without the mess on the queenside (I'm entitled to regard it as that as author of *Winning with the King's Gambit*) this would be known as the Schallop defence, a variation with a justifiably dubious reputation. As we shall see, though, it seems quite effective in this particular position. A

less aggressive approach is 5...d6. The game Veličković-Gallagher, London Lloyds Bank 1990 continued 6 ♗c4 ♗e6 7 ♕e2 ♗xc4 8 ♕xc4 ♘f6 9 ♘c3 ♘e5 10 ♕e2 ♗e7 11 0-0-0 ♕a5 12 ♔b1 ♖c8 13 ♖hf1 0-0 (Black delayed castling until the rook had left the h-file so that the standard g3 would be less dangerous) 14 g3 fxg3 15 ♘xe5 dxe5 16 hxg3 ♕a6!? 17 ♕h2 b5 18 ♖f5 b4 19 ♘a4 c4! 20 ♕e2 (taking on e5 allows ...♘g4) 20...♖c6! (threatening 21...cxb3 22 ♕xa6 bxc2+) 21 d3 c3 22 ♗c1 ♘d7 with a clear advantage to Black.

6 e5

6 ♘c3 ♗e7! 7 ♕e2 0-0 8 e5 (otherwise Black plays ...d5) 8...♘g4 9 ♘d5 d6 10 0-0-0 ♖e8 11 h3 ♘gxe5 12 ♘xf4 ♗f8 left White with no compensation for the pawn in Veličković-Antić, Yugoslav Ch 1991.

6 ...   ♘h5

6...♘d5 has been played more often, but I like the text which keeps the d5 square free for a pawn advance.

7	♗e2	d5
8	0-0	♗g4
9	h3?	

It's a serious mistake to allow the black knight into g3. 9 ♘e1 should be considered, but the position after 9...♗xe2 10 ♕xe2 ♕h4 11 e6 0-0-0 12 exf7 ♗d6 looks very dangerous for White.

9	...	♗e6
10	♘h2	♘g3
11	♖xf4	♕g5
12	♖f2	♘e4
13	♖f3	c4!
14	d4	cxd3
15	cxd3	♗c5+
16	d4 *(D)*	

| 16 | ... | ♕xe5!! |

How enjoyable it must have been to play this! White is now completely lost.

17	♗b5	♗b6
18	♔h1	♘g3+
19	♔g1	

There's no way out of the deadly pin.

19	...	0-0
20	♗xc6	bxc6
21	♘a3	♘e2+
22	♔h1	♗xd4
23	♗xd4	♘xd4

0-1

Game 23
de la Riva – P.Cramling
Barcelona 1991

1	e4	c5
2	♘f3	♘c6
3	b3	d6

This is a convenient move order for your writer as it also covers 2...d6 3 b3 ♘c6.

4 ♗b5

White can fianchetto first, but he normally plays ♗b5 at some stage as this bishop hasn't really got an active role to play. The game Rausch-Szalanczy, Dortmund 1992 confirms this view: 4 ♗b2 e5 5 c3 g6 6 ♗e2 ♗g7 7 d3 ♘f6 8 0-0 0-0 9 ♘a3 ♘h5 10 ♘c4 ♘f4 11 ♘e3 f5 with a healthy initiative for Black.

4 ... e5

4...♘f6!? 5 ♕e2 e5 6 c3 ♗e7 7 d4 cxd4 8 cxd4 0-0 9 ♗xc6 bxc6 10 dxe5 dxe5 11 ♗b2 led to a small advantage for White in Yudasin-Smirin, USSR Ch 1990. However, Black's play can be improved upon. For example, instead of 8...0-0, 8...exd4 9 ♘xd4 ♗d7 10 ♗b2 0-0 should give Black equal chances. White has a better pawn structure but is somewhat lagging behind in development.

5 c3

5 &b2 is again the most natural, but it's all likely to end up in the same position as White's only decent plan is to play c3 and d4. In Mordue-Rahman, British Ch 1991, he tried something else but found himself in dire straits after a mere ten moves: 5 &xc6+ bxc6 6 ♕e2 ♘e7 7 d3 ♘g6 8 c3 &e7 9 &e3 0-0 10 0-0 f5.

5	**...**	**g6**
6	**0-0**	**&g7**
7	**d4** *(D)*	

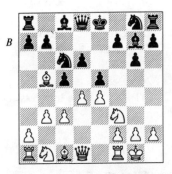

7 ... exd4!

Of course Black captures in this fashion in order to exploit the pin on the long diagonal.

8	**cxd4**	**♘ge7**
9	**&b2**	**0-0**
10	**h3**	

10 ♘bd2? cxd4 11 &xc6 ♘xc6 12 h3 ♖e8 13 ♖e1 &e6 14 ♘c4 d5

15 exd5 ♕xd5 was a total disaster for White in Manolov-Pavlović, Burgas 1991.

10	**...**	**a6**
11	**&xc6**	**♘xc6**
12	**♘a3**	**&e6**

Whilst Cramling's idea is interesting, 12...f5 is a good alternative. Both 13 exf5 (13 e5 cxd4) 13...&xf5 14 ♖e1 ♕f6! and 14 ♘c4 &e4 should favour Black.

13	**♕d2**	**d5**
14	**e5**	**f6**

14...cxd4 15 ♖fe1 ♕b8 16 &xd4 enables White to keep the centre blockaded.

15	**exf6**	**&xf6**
16	**♖fe1**	

16 dxc5 &xb2 17 ♕xb2 ♖xf3 is good for Black.

16	**...**	**♕d7**
17	**♖e3**	

White protects his knight in order to capture on c5.

17	**...**	**&f5**

17...c4 18 ♖ae1 is awkward as 18...♖ae8 19 bxc4 dxc4 20 d5! wins for White. One idea for Black is 17...cxd4 18 ♘xd4 &xd4 19 &xd4 ♖f4!. 20 &b2 is met by 20...♖af8 and 20 ♖xe6 by 20...♘xd4!; best is 20 ♘c2 with an unclear game.

18	**dxc5**	**d4**
19	**♖ee1**	**&xh3!?**

Otherwise there is not enough for the pawn.

20	**♕f4?**	

The sacrifice had to be accepted.

After 20 gxh3 ♛xh3 21 ♘h2! the
onus is on Black to prove that her
idea is correct. The critical line looks
like 21...♗e5 (21...♗h4 22 ♖f1 ♖f5
23 f4 and 21...♗g5? 22 ♛xg5 ♖xf2
23 ♛d5+! are insufficient for Black,
but 21...♘e5 and 21...♖ad8 might be
worth examining, although intuition
tells me that Black will have a maxi-
mum of a draw in these lines) 22
♖xe5 ♘xe5 23 ♛xd4 ♖f5 24 ♛d5+
♘f7 25 ♛xb7 ♖d8 *(D)*.

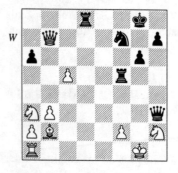

Of course Black has a strong attack but the white queen and bishop
are also extremely active and are
quite capable of rustling up a
counter-attack. White now has:

a) 26 ♘f1? ♖g5+ (26...♖d2 27
♛b8+! ♘d8 28 ♛g3) 27 ♘g3 ♖xg3+
28 fxg3 ♛xg3+ 29 ♛g2 ♛e3+ 30
♛f2 ♛g5+ 31 ♛g2 ♛xc5+ 32 ♔h1
(now 32 ♛f2 ♛xf2+ is good for
Black) 32...♖d5 33 ♛e4 ♖h5+ 34
♔g2 ♖g5+ 35 ♔h1 ♛f8!! and the
only move to avoid immediate disaster is 36 ♗g7.

b) 26 ♘c4! (as there seems to be
no immediate threat White has time
to bring his worst-placed piece into
the game, which now covers important squares such as e5 and e3)
26...♖dd5 (26...♖h5 27 ♘f1 ♖g5+
28 ♘g3 ♖xg3+ 29 fxg3 ♛xg3+ 30
♛g2 leads nowhere this time;
26...♖d7 27 ♛e4 {or 27 ♖e1} ♘g5
28 ♛e8+ ♖f8 29 ♛e5 is also good
for White) 27 ♛c8+! (27 ♘e3
♖xf2!) 27...♘d8 (27...♖d8 28 ♛c6!
♘g5 29 ♘d6) 28 ♘e3 ♖g5+ 29
♘hg4! h5 30 c6! and White wins. All
these variations show how brilliant a
knight is when defending his king.

20	...	♗g4
21	♘c4	♗xf3
22	♛xf3	♗h4
23	♘b6	♖xf3!
24	♘xd7	♗xf2+
25	♔h2	♖f7
26	♘e5	

26 ♖f1 ♖d8 is quite hopeless for
White.

26	...	♖f5

0-1

Game 24
Grosar – Sokolov
Portoroz 1987

1	e4	c5
2	♘f3	e6
3	b3	

This is more popular against
2...e6 than other moves as Black is
now unable to block the diagonal

with ...e5 (at least without looking stupid).

3   ...   b6! *(D)*

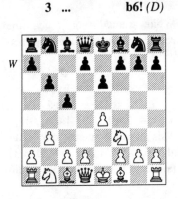

If Black is going to adopt a Hedgehog set-up, then it's important to fianchetto immediately as the attack on the e-pawn can actually be quite awkward for White to meet.

4 ♗b2

4 c4 ♗b7 5 ♘c3 is a major alternative, after which Black has two possibilities:

a) 5...♘f6 6 ♗d3 (6 e5 ♘g4 7 h3 ♘h6 looks OK for Black) 6...♘c6 7 ♗b2 ♗e7 (7...d6 reduces Black's possibilities. The game Short-Illescas, Barcelona 1989 continued 8 0-0 ♗e7 9 ♖c1 0-0 10 ♗b1 ♘d4?! 11 ♘xd4 cxd4 12 ♘e2 e5 13 ♘g3 g6 14 f4 with advantage to White) 8 0-0 0-0 9 ♖e1 ♘g4! 10 e5 (White was worried about 10...♗f6) 10...♕b8 11 ♕e2 f6 12 exf6 ♘xf6 13 ♘e4 ♕f4! (the queen is brought to the kingside where it can both attack and defend) 14 g3 ♕h6 15 ♘eg5 ♕h5 16 h4

♘b4! 17 ♗b1 h6 and Black has a clear advantage; Tseitlin-Psakhis, Berlin 1991. The game continuation 18 ♗xf6 gxf6 19 ♗e4 ♗xe4 20 ♘xe4 ♘c2 left Black the exchange up.

b) 5...a6 6 ♗b2 ♕c7 7 d4 cxd4 8 ♕xd4 ♘f6 9 e5?! ♗c5 10 ♕f4 ♗xf3 11 gxf3 ♘c6 12 ♘e4 ♘xe4 13 ♕xe4 ♗b4+ 14 ♔e2 0-0 15 f4 ♖ad8 16 ♖g1 g6 17 ♖d1 b5 18 a3 ♗e7 19 b4 bxc4 20 ♕xc4 ♕b6 21 ♔f3 f6 22 ♕e4 ♖f7 23 exf6 ♗xf6 24 ♗c1 a5 25 ♗e3 ♕b7 0-1 Dreev-Illescas, Oviedo 1992.

4   ...   ♗b7 *(D)*

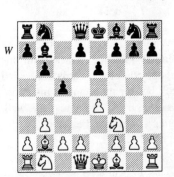

5 ♘c3

White has a number of other ways to defend his e-pawn:

a) 5 d3 d6 6 ♗e2 ♘f6 7 0-0 ♗e7 8 ♘bd2 ♘c6 9 ♖e1 0-0 10 ♗f1 ♖c8 11 a3 a6 12 ♖b1 ♖e8 13 b4?! (this doesn't fit in with White's passive set-up. 13 c3 would have been better) 13...cxb4 14 axb4 d5! with advantage to Black; Bhend-Gallagher,

Suhr 1992 (the reason I'd played 2...e6 is that I knew my opponent often played 3 b3).

b) 5 ♕e2 d6 6 d4 cxd4 7 ♘xd4 ♘f6 8 ♘d2 ♘bd7 9 g3 a6 10 ♗g2 ♕c7 11 0-0 ♗e7 12 c4 0-0 13 f4 ♖fe8 with a fairly typical hedgehog set up; Romero-Illescas. However, the fact that the white knight is on d2 rather than c3 means that Black might find it easier to free his position with d5 or b5.

| 5 | ... | ♗e7 |

5...d6 or 5...a6 are equally playable.

6	d4	cxd4
7	♘xd4	a6
8	♗d3	

White is probably hoping for an eventual kingside attack with his bishops pointing towards the castled king, but for the moment his minor pieces don't coordinate very well. Better would have been 8 g3.

| 8 | ... | d6 |
| 9 | ♘ce2 | |

This is primarily a prophylactic move against ....♗f6. If Black ever manages to exchange the dark-squared bishops White will be left with a horribly weakened queenside. That White is reduced to a move such as the text is proof that his set-up is artificial.

9	...	♘f6
10	f3	♘bd7
11	0-0	b5
12	♕d2	0-0

Black has achieved a very harmonious Sicilian set-up.

13 c4?!

White should not touch the queenside pawns. 13 ♘g3 looks better.

13	...	♕b6
14	♔h1	bxc4
15	♗xc4	♘e5
16	♖ac1	h6?! *(D)*

This allows White to complicate. With 16...♖fc8 Black would have obtained the better game without any risk.

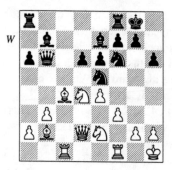

17 ♗xe6!

This is of course pretty desperate but it's usually a good idea to try to change the course of a game that's not going well.

17	...	fxe6
18	♘xe6	♖fc8
19	♗d4	♖xc1!

19...♕b5 20 ♘c7 ♕d3 21 ♕b2 is difficult for Black.

| 20 | ♖xc1 | ♕b5 |
| 21 | ♘c7 | ♕d3! |

22 ♕b4!

Now 22 ♕b2 is less good due to the weakness of White's back rank: 22...♘xf3! 23 ♘xa8 ♘xd4 24 ♘xd4 ♗xa8 and Black wins.

22 ... ♖b8 (D)

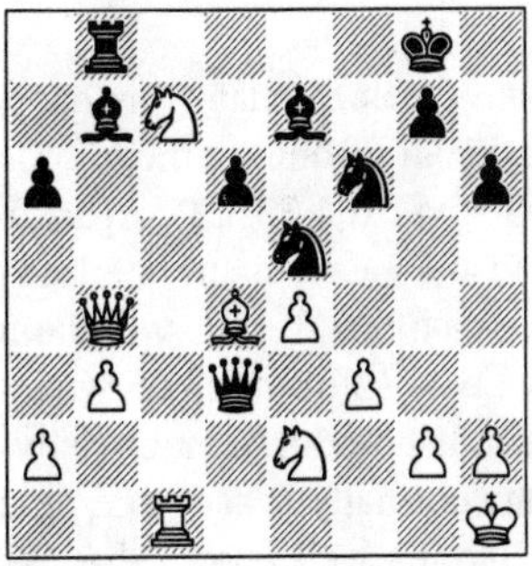

22...♕xe2?! 23 ♘xa8 ♗xa8 24 ♗xe5.

23 ♗xe5?

Losing without a fight. White could have played 23 ♘f4! a5 24 ♘xd3 axb4 25 ♘xb4 with an unclear game.

23	...	♕xe2
24	♗xf6	♗xf6
25	♘d5	♗e5
26	♘e7+	♔h7
27	♘c6	♗xc6!
28	♕xb8	♕d2
29	♖b1	♕f4
30	♔g1	♕xh2+
31	♔f2	♗d4+

0-1

5 Gambits

Ackermann – King
Bern 1992

1	e4	c5
2	d4	cxd4
3	c3	(D)

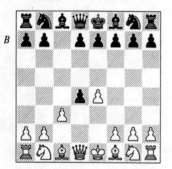

This introduces the so-called Morra Gambit. White sacrifices a pawn in order to achieve a lead in development and possibly some pressure on the open c-file. This line is much more popular (and dangerous) at club, rather than master, level where there is probably more respect for a central pawn.

Instead of 3 c3, White could also play 3 ♘f3 with the idea of getting into an Open Sicilian (this happens occasionally from the move order 1 d4 c5 2 e4 cxd4 3 ♘f3). Apart from the usual assortment of moves, Black can play 3...a6! with the idea of 4 ♘xd4 ♘f6 5 ♘c3 e5 when we have transposed into an O'Kelly Sicilian (normally 2...a6) and against this line it's well known that White shouldn't play 3 d4. Of course if White plays now 4 c3 we are back in the Morra Gambit. I should just mention that Black shouldn't try to hang on to the pawn with 3...e5?, as then 4 c3! is good for White.

	3	...	dxc3

If you wish, you can play 3...♘f6 4 e5 ♘d5, transposing to the c3 Sicilian. I recommend this approach only for those who have little time on their hands and will consequently be delighted to reduce two variations to one, or those who love playing against the c3 Sicilian. My own view is that the latter is one of the best ways to meet the Sicilian (apart from 3 d4) and that the Morra constitutes the win of a pawn for just a little suffering (but not too much).

4	♘xc3	♘c6

5 ♘f3   d6

It has not been easy to find a system to recommend against the Morra as Black seems to have four or five reasonable ways of playing. A popular alternative to the text is 5...e6. *ECO* gives 6 ♗c4 a6 7 0-0 ♘ge7 8 ♗g5 f6 9 ♗e3 b5 10 ♗b3 ♘g6 11 ♘d4 (11 ♕e2 ♘a5 12 ♗c2 ♗e7 13 ♖ad1 0-0 with advantage to Black; Ferismo-Gheorghiu, Istres 1975) 11...♘xd4 12 ♗xd4 ♗d6 13 ♕g4 0-0 14 f4 with reasonable attacking chances for White. However, 11...♗b7 looks like a clear improvement to me.

6 ♗c4   a6

Black has to pay great attention to his move order. For example, the immediate 6...♘f6 is bad on account of 7 e5! dxe5 8 ♕xd8+ ♘xd8 9 ♘b5 ♖b8 10 ♘xe5 e6 11 ♘c7+ ♔e7 12 ♗e3 with a dangerous attack for White; Kristiansson-Roberts, Harrachov 1967.

7 0-0   ♘f6

There is another decent system in which Black delays developing this knight, the idea being to avoid an annoying ♗g5, e.g. 7...e6 8 ♕e2 ♗e7 9 ♖d1 ♗d7 10 ♗f4 e5 11 ♗e3 and only now 11...♘f6 when ♗g5 involves a loss of time.

For those of you who wish to follow Danny King's idea in this game, please make sure you don't play 7...♗g4?? as 8 ♗xf7+ would be embarrassing.

8 ♕e2 *(D)*

8 h3 would prevent Black's next, but in my experience Morra players are creatures of habit and like to play their first ten or so moves before looking up to see what Black has done. Of course there will be exceptions to prove this rule, so let's take a look at 8...e6 (in reply to 8 h3). Play is quite likely to continue 9 ♕e2 ♗e7 10 ♖d1 ♗d7 (White was threatening e5) 11 ♗f4 (11 ♗g5 ♕b8!?) and now Black has a choice:

a) 11...b5 12 ♗b3 ♕b8. Black avoids the weakening ...e5, and if White now continues quietly he can follow up with 13...♘e5!. Therefore, the game Montavon-Gallagher, Neuchâtel 1994 continued 13 e5 (13 ♘d5 exd5 14 exd5 ♘a5 15 ♖e1 ♘g8 should be OK for Black) 13...dxe5 14 ♘xe5 ♘xe5 15 ♗xe5 ♕b7 (the point behind 11...b5 is revealed) 16 ♗xf6 ♗xf6 17 ♘e4 (17 ♘d5 ♗d8!; 17 ♗d5 ♗c6) 17...♗e7 18 ♗d5 ♗c6! and now instead of the totally unsound 19 ♗xe6?, White should have tried 19 ♗xc6+ ♕xc6 20 ♖ac1 ♕b6 21 ♕f3 with some drawing chances.

b) 11...e5 12 ♗g5 ♗e6! with a position quite typical of the Morra. I consider Black's chances to be slightly better, although White has good drawing chances (as long as he plays for one) as Black's extra pawn is backward and on an open file.

8 ♗g5!? is another possibility. The game Lendwai-Lutz, Graz 1993 continued 8...e6 9 ♕e2 h6! 10 ♗h4 g5 11 ♗g3 ♘h5 12 ♖ad1 ♘xg3 13 hxg3 ♕f6 with a good game for Black.

8 ...   ♗g4!

This is the big idea behind Black's strange move order. He will now be able to set up his small centre with the bishop actively deployed outside the pawn chain. His game will now be a lot less cramped and he won't have to worry much about any central breakthroughs from White, as a key attacking piece, the knight on f3, is pinned.

9 ♖d1   e6

Of course 9...♘e5 is met by 10 ♘xe5!.

10 ♗f4   ♕b8!

This is an excellent defensive square for the queen. From b8 she will be able to hold the centre whilst development is completed. 10...♕c7 would unnecessarily expose her to harassment on the c-file.

11 h3

The piece sacrifice 11 ♘d5 is insufficient: 11...exd5 12 exd5+ ♘e5 (that pin again).

A sounder alternative is 11 ♖d2, in order to gang up on the d-pawn. After 11...♗e7 12 ♖ad1 0-0 13 ♗xd6 (13 ♖xd6 e5) 13...♗xd6 14 ♖xd6 ♘e5 White has won his pawn back, but will now incur some kingside weaknesses. If White doesn't capture on move 13, then Black will be able to protect his pawn with either ...♖d8 or ...♘e5.

11 ...   ♗xf3

There's no point in messing around with 11...♗h5. After he captures on f3, there is nothing to stop Black completing his development and achieving a fairly normal Sicilian position with an extra pawn thrown in for good measure.

12 ♕xf3   ♗e7
13 ♖ac1   0-0
14 ♗b3   ♖c8
15 ♕e3   b5

Black's previous move, which protected the knight, ensured that this was possible. Invasions on b6 are not going to be permitted.

16 ♗g5   ♘a5
17 f4 (D)

White goes onto the offensive, but Black has a little combination to make him wish he'd stayed quiet.

17 ...   h6!
18 ♗h4   ♘g4!
19 hxg4   ♗xh4

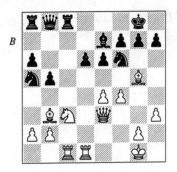

The game concluded **20 g5 hxg5
21 f5 ♘xb3 22 axb3 g4 23 fxe6 fxe6
24 ♕f4 ♗f6! 25 ♕xg4 (or 25 ♕xd6
♕xd6 26 ♖xd6 b4) 25... ♖e8 26 e5
♗xe5 27 ♘e4 ♕b6+ 28 ♔h1 ♕e3
29 ♖c7 ♕h6+ 30 ♔g1 d5 0-1**

Game 26
K.J.Lutz – De Firmian
Biel 1993

1 e4   c5
2 b4 *(D)*

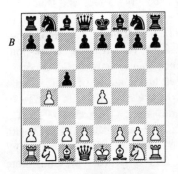

The Wing Gambit is a forgotten
relic, having hardly set foot in a
tournament hall since the days of
Frank Marshall and Rudolf Spielmann. White sacrifices a pawn for ...
well, not a lot. Maybe he hopes to
build a big centre but Black can easily counter this with ...d5. Open files
on the queenside? Yes, but it's far
from clear if he will be able to exploit these with the centre still in a
state of fluidity.

Before continuing, let's take a
brief look at the Wing Gambit Deferred (after 2 ♘f3):

a) 2 ♘f3 e6 3 b4 cxb4 4 d4 (4
a3!? bxa3 5 ♘xa3 d6 6 d4 ♘f6 and
White hasn't enough for the pawn,
but at least here he has something ap-
proaching the amount of compensation one could expect out of the
Wing Gambit's dubious comrade,
the Morra Gambit) 4...d5 5 e5 ♘c6 6
a3 bxa3 7 c3 a6 8 ♘xa3 ♗d7 9 ♗d3
b5 with a slight advantage for Black
according to Boleslavsky.

b) 2 ♘f3 d6 3 b4 cxb4 4 d4 ♘f6 5
♗d3 e6 6 0-0 ♗e7 7 ♘bd2 d5 8 e5
♘fd7 9 ♘e1 (one of the problems
with the Wing Gambit Deferred is
that ♘f3 often proves to be premature, especially if Black adopts a
French-like structure) 9...♘c6 10
♕g4 0-0 11 ♘df3 f5 12 ♕h3 ♕e8
with a clear advantage to Black; Cor-
den-Gligorić, Hastings 1969/70. The
only positive aspect of having played
b4 is that Black can't attack the centre in the traditional French manner
(...c7-c5). However this is far from

being sufficient compensation for the wreckage that answers to the name of White's queenside.

c) 2 ♘f3 ♘c6 3 b4. Yes, it's even been played here! Most people would probably take with the knight without much thought, but my one insane experience of this line is 3...cxb4 4 d4 e6 5 d5 ♛f6 *(D)*

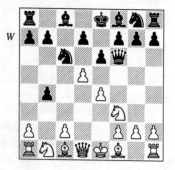

6 c3 bxc3 7 dxc6 c2 8 ♛xc2 ♛xa1 9 ♛b3 a5 10 cxb7 ♗xb7 11 ♗d3 ♗b4+ 12 ♔e2 ♛f6 13 a3 ♛e7 with a mess; Stanton-Gallagher, somewhere in London in the early eighties. After 3...♘xb4 4 c3 ♘c6 5 d4 d5 6 exd5 ♛xd5 a c3 Sicilian has arisen where White has swapped his b-pawn for a tempo.

Anyway all these lines are pretty academic. If you get one every ten years it will probably be above average.

2   ...   cxb4
3   a3

Eccentric Swedish grandmaster Jonny Hector experimented with 3

c4?! here, but after 3...e5!? 4 ♘f3 ♘c6 5 ♗b2 d6 6 d4 exd4 7 ♘xd4 ♘f6 8 ♘d2 ♗e7 9 ♗d3 0-0 10 0-0 ♘xd4 11 ♗xd4 ♘d7 he had little to show for his investment in Hector-Kudrin, Palma 1989.

3 d4 is a more conventional alternative, after which play can continue 3...d5 4 e5 (4 exd5 is considered doubtful by *ECO* which gives the following example: 4...♘f6! 5 ♗b5+ ♗d7 6 ♗c4 ♗g4 7 f3 ♗f5 8 a3 ♘xd5 9 axb4 ♘xb4 10 ♘a3 e6 11 ♘e2 ♗e7 12 0-0 0-0 13 c3 ♘d5 14 ♗b3 ♘c6 with advantage to Black; Ozsvath-Varnusz, Hungary 1973) 4...♘c6 5 a3 ♛b6 6 ♘e2 (and here *ECO* only considers 6 ♗e3 as leading to an unclear position after 6...♗f5 7 ♗d3 ♗xd3 8 ♛xd3 e6 9 ♘e2 ♘ge7 10 0-0 ♘f5 11 ♘d2 bxa3 although I would certainly rather have the position with the extra pawns, e.g. 12 c4 ♘xe3 13 fxe3 ♗e7 14 cxd5 {14 c5 ♛c7 and Black can later break with ...f6} 14...exd5 15 e6 fxe6 16 ♘f4 0-0 17 ♘xe6? ♘b4) 6...♗g4 (a previous correspondence game, Caliprano-Del Vasto, 1990 had continued 6...♗f5 7 axb4 ♘xb4 8 ♘a3 ♖c8 9 ♘f4 ♘xc2+ 10 ♘xc2 ♗xc2 11 ♘xd5 ♛b3 12 ♛f3 ♛xf3 13 ♗b5+ ♔d8 14 gxf3 with good compensation for the pawn) 7 f3 ♗f5 8 g4 (the previous note doesn't work now, if only because 12 ♛f3 is no longer possible) 8...♗g6 9 h4 h5 10 axb4 hxg4 11

fxg4 e6 12 c3 f6 13 ♘f4 ♗f7 14 exf6 ♘xf6 15 g5 ♘e4 16 g6 ♗g8 17 ♗e3 ♗e7 18 ♕g4?! (better is 18 h5 although Black still has the superior chances) 18...♘e5! with advantage to Black, Caliprano-Kalinichenko, Corr 1991.

3 ... d5!

The harsh reality of modern chess. Marshall and Spielmann, more often than not, found themselves up against 3...bxa3 which, though not a bad move in itself, suggests that Black is in a more carefree frame of mind than is good for him. One historic example is: 4 ♘xa3 d5 (4...e6) 5 exd5 ♕xd5 6 ♗b2 ♘c6 7 ♘b5 ♕d8 8 ♕f3 e5 9 ♗c4 ♘f6 10 ♕b3 with advantage to White in Spielmann-Sämisch, Baden-Baden 1925. I must admit that when I recently came face to face with the Wing Gambit for the first time in years I couldn't resist 3...bxa3 (not really a question of honour, more a case of lack of knowledge). After 4 d4 d5 5 exd5 (5 e5) 5...♕xd5 6 c4 ♕d8 7 ♘xa3 ♘f6 8 ♘b5 e6 9 c5! ♘c6 10 ♗f4 ♘d5 11 ♗d6 White had some play for the pawn in Haub-Gallagher, Biel 1992.

4 exd5

The strange 4 e5 is also possible and play is likely to transpose to the note to White's third move after 4...♘c6 5 d4 ♕b6.

4 ... ♕xd5

5 ♘f3

Of course 5 axb4 loses to 5...♕e5+.

ECO recommends 5 ♗b2, giving the following line: 5...e5 6 axb4 ♗xb4 7 ♘a3 ♘c6 8 ♘b5 ♕d8 9 ♘f3 ♘f6 10 ♗e2 0-0 11 0-0 ♖e8 12 d4 and makes the ludicrous claim that White has enough compensation for the pawn. After the plausible continuation 12...exd4 13 ♘fxd4 ♘xd4 14 ♘xd4 ♗d7 15 ♗f3 ♕c7 White obviously has nothing for the pawn.

5 ... e5

6 axb4 ♗xb4

7 c3

Lutz is something of a specialist in the Wing Gambit and this looks like his attempt at improving over the line given in *ECO*: 7 ♘a3 ♘f6 8 ♘b5 0-0 9 ♘c7 ♕c5 10 ♘xa8 e4 11 ♘g1 ♖e8 with the threat of ...e3. If 12 c3 then 12...♘g4 13 ♘h3 e3 looks strong.

7 ... ♗e7

8 ♘a3 *(D)*

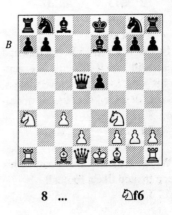

8 ... ♘f6

De Firmian is quite happy to give back the pawn (and more) in order to obtain a lead in development. However, 8...♘c6 is certainly worth considering, with the idea of 9 ♗c4 ♛e4+ (queen retreats allow 10 ♛b3) and now 10 ♗e2 ♘f6 11 ♘b5 0-0 looks fine for Black (as long as he avoids 12 d3 ♛g6?? 13 ♘h4; 12...♛f5 is the move). Maybe White should try 10 ♔f1!? after which 10...♗g4 or 10...♗e6 look playable (not 10...♘f6 11 ♗xf7+). To summarize, a complicated game will ensue, with Black having already banked an extra pawn. One of the problems with the Wing Gambit is that White doesn't even achieve a lead in development.

9   ♘b5   ♛d8
10 ♘xe5   ♘c6!

Obviously this is a position where speedy development takes precedence over pawn structure niceties.

11 ♘xc6   bxc6
12 ♛f3   ♗d7
13 ♘d4   0-0
14 ♗a6

14 ♘xc6 ♗xc6 15 ♛xc6 ♖e8 and White will find it difficult to evacuate his king to safety. Nevertheless, this line deserved serious consideration.

14 ...   ♛c7
15 h3

White wishes to avoid having his queen treated like a football.

15 ...   c5

16 ♘f5   ♛e5+
17 ♘e3   ♗d6!
18 ♗e2   ♗c7
19 ♘c4   ♛e6
20 ♛e3

After 20 0-0 Black can play 20...♖fe8 21 ♛e3 ♘e4 transposing to the game or search for a stronger 21st move.

20 ...   ♘e4
21 0-0   ♖fe8
22 ♗d3   f5
23 ♖e1

23 f3 ♘g3 is very bad for White.

23 ...   ♛d5

Black has a beautifully coordinated position, whilst White's flanks are totally disconnected.

24 ♛f3   ♗b5!
25 ♘b2   c4
26 ♗f1   ♗b6
27 ♘d1 (D)

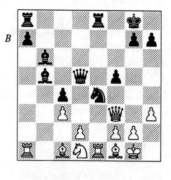

27 ...   f4!
28 ♛xf4

Otherwise White will have difficulty in finding legal moves.

28 ...	♘xf2!
29 ♘e3	

29 ♖xe8+ ♖xe8 30 ♘xf2 ♖f8 is terminal.

29 ...	♘d3
30 ♗xd3	♕xd3

This game was played on a board very near mine in Biel and I recall being rather envious of De Firmian's position around about here. His only problem was the clock, although two minutes for ten moves is hardly out of the ordinary for him.

31 ♔h1	♖e4
32 ♕g5	♗c6
33 ♗b2	

And here De Firmian was visibly shocked for about two seconds until he saw the finish.

33 ...	♕xd2
34 ♖ad1	♖xe3!
35 ♖xd2	♖xh3# (0-1)

6   1 e4 c5 2 ♘f3 ♘c6 3 ♗b5

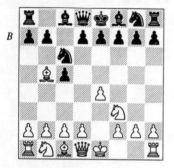

This line is often known as the 'Rossolimo Variation', after the Ukranian-born grandmaster. Of all the lines in this book, this is the one which is most often encountered at grandmaster level. Black has a number of ways to combat this system, such as 3...e6 or 3...♘f6, but in this book I'm going to recommend 3...g6, which also happens to be the main line. The long diagonal is clearly where the king's bishop belongs, and this plan of development gives Black more space than the 3...e6 line. White's most common plan is to try to create a strong centre with c3 and d4, so the fianchettoed bishop will obviously be able to take part in the struggle against this.

4 ♗xc6 is White's most simplistic approach to the position. This capture looks so naïve that *ECO* failed even to consider it. However, this move is certainly worthy of our respect as it has recently been adopted by two gentlemen who know rather more about the game of chess than the rest of us – Fischer and Kasparov. Basically, White wishes to clarify the situation so that he can select an appropriate plan. Against 4...bxc6 he will aim to open up the centre as quickly as possible to exploit his lead in development, whilst against 4...dxc6 he will play a slower manoeuvring game. Black's choice of recapture is a matter of taste, but I should point out that he tends to be more successful with 4...dxc6.

Game 27
Fischer – Spassky
Sveti Stefan (11) 1992

1	e4	c5
2	♘f3	♘c6
3	♗b5	g6
4	♗xc6	

This should come as no great

surprise considering Fischer's affection for the Exchange Variation of the Ruy Lopez.

4 ...   bxc6

4...dxc6 is the subject of the next game.

5 0-0   ♗g7

6 ♖e1 (D)

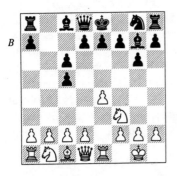

6 ...   e5

In Game 13 of the same match, Spassky produced quite a surprising novelty, 6...f6!?. Play continued 7 c3 (7 e5 fxe5 8 ♘xe5 can be met by 8...d6!) 7...♘h6 8 d4 cxd4 9 cxd4 0-0 10 ♘c3 d6 11 ♕a4 and instead of 11...♕b6 12 ♘d2! (I must admit that I'm very tempted to suggest the dogmatic rule of never playing ...♕b6 in any of the variations of the ♗b5 line. It's usually more trouble than it's worth), Black should have played 11...♗d7. His position looks rather passive, but there is a fair amount of dynamism just beneath the surface. There are a number of central pawn breaks waiting to be timed correctly,

as well as a bishop pair in case the position opens up. Playing for a win with Black is not always an easy affair, so accepting double-edged positions such as this one is often not a bad idea.

6...♘f6 has been quite frequently played, but this does seem to lead to a good game for White after 7 e5 ♘d5 8 c4 ♘c7 9 d4 cxd4 10 ♕xd4. The pawn on e5 severely cramps Black who will only be able to break out by weakening his position. Here are a couple of examples:

a) 10...0-0 11 ♕h4 d6 12 ♗h6 ♘e6 13 ♘c3 f6 14 ♗xg7 (Kasparov considers the continuation 14 exf6 ♖xf6 15 ♘g5 to be more accurate) 14...♔xg7 (14...♘xg7!) 15 exf6+ ♖xf6 16 ♘g5 ♘xg5 17 ♕xg5 with a clear advantage to White; Kasparov-Salov, Dortmund 1992.

b) 10...♘e6 11 ♕h4 h6 12 ♘c3 d6 13 ♖d1 ♗b7 14 ♗e3 c5 15 ♘d5? dxe5! 16 ♘f6+ ♗xf6 17 ♖xd8+ ♖xd8 and Black's central grip gave him a clear advantage in Kharlov-Andersson, Haninge 1992. However, 15 ♘d5 was a serious error. Kharlov considers that 15 exd6! exd6 16 ♕g3 would leave White with the better game.

c) 10...d5!? is untested.

7 b4!?

Fischer plays in Wing Gambit style, which is the most obvious way of gaining access to the holes in the centre created by Black's last move.

Nevertheless White has also scored quite well with the quieter 7 c3, for example: 7...⚘e7 8 d4 cxd4 9 cxd4 exd4 10 ⚘xd4 0-0 11 ⚘c3 ♖b8 (D)

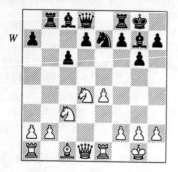

12 e5!? (12 ⚘b3 also promises White a small advantage. Black's problem is the same as after 7 b4 – weak central dark squares) 12...c5 13 ⚘b3 ⚘c6 14 ⚘xc5 ⚘xe5 15 ⚘5e4 ♗b7 16 ♗g5 f6 17 ♗e3 ♗a8 18 ♗c5 f5 19 ♗xf8 ♕xf8 20 ⚘d6 and Black had insufficient compensation for the exchange in Spassov-Ivanović, Nikšić 1991.

> **7 ...   cxb4**
> **8 a3   c5**

Black could try to return the pawn with 8...b3 but 9 ♗b2! would then keep the initiative.

> **9 axb4   cxb4**
> **10 d4   exd4**
> **11 ♗b2**

White is a pawn down but Black's position is extremely ragged.

> **11 ...   d6**
> **12 ⚘xd4   ♕d7**

Spassky considered 12...♕b6 to be an improvement, but as usual the queen is exposed on this square: 13 ⚘d2! with the following variation given by Timman in *Informator*: 13...♗xd4 14 ⚘c4 ♗xf2+ 15 ♔h1 ♕c5 16 ⚘xd6+ ♔e7 17 ♖f1 ♕xd6 18 ♕f3! with a very strong attack.

> **13 ⚘d2   ♗b7**

Timman gives 13...⚘e7 as equal although after 14 ⚘c4 I can't see anything better than 14...♗b7 (if 14...0-0 then 15 ⚘b6 whilst 14...♖b8 is met by 15 ⚘c6!) transposing to his next note, where he gives 15 ⚘b5 as slightly better for White. Even here 15 ⚘f5! looks a more forceful continuation.

> **14 ⚘c4   ⚘h6 (D)**

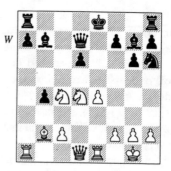

> **15 ⚘f5!?**

Fischer can't resist this adventure, but 15 ⚘b5 leaves White better.

> **15 ...   ♗xb2**

Of course 15...⚘xf5 16 exf5+ ♔f8 17 f6 is crushing.

> **16 ⚘cxd6+   ♔f8**

17	♘xh6	f6?

Black misses his chance: after 17...♗xa1! 18 ♕xa1 ♕xd6 19 ♕xh8+ ♚e7 20 ♕xh7 ♕e6 his passed a-pawn offers real counterplay.

18 ♘df7!

Fischer had no doubt planned his brilliant 21st move at this point.

18	...	♕xd1
19	♖axd1	♚e7
20	♘xh8	♖xh8 *(D)*

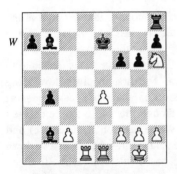

21 ♘f5+!

This is necessary as otherwise Black's a-pawn supported by his bishop pair could have proved dangerous.

21	...	gxf5

Black has to take the knight as 21...♚e6 22 ♖d6+ ♚e5 23 ♖d7 is even worse for him.

22	exf5+	♗e5
23	f4	♖c8
24	fxe5	

Timman gives 24 ♖d2 ♖c5 25 ♖de2 as an alternative.

24	...	♖xc2

25	e6	♗c6
26	♖c1!	♖xc1
27	♖xc1	♚d6

The ending is still quite compli-cated, but with such a monstrous e-pawn the result is never in doubt.

28	♖d1+	♚e5
29	e7	a5
30	♖c1	♗d7
31	♖c5+	♚d4
32	♖xa5	b3
33	♖a7	♗e8
34	♖b7	♚c3
35	♚f2	b2
36	♚e3	♗f7
37	g4	♚c2
38	♚d4	b1♕
39	♖xb1	♚xb1
40	♚c5	♚c2
41	♚d6	1-0

Game 28
Landa – Goldin
St. Petersburg 1993

1	e4	c5
2	♘f3	♘c6
3	♗b5	g6
4	♗xc6	dxc6 *(D)*

In my opinion this is the more natural recapture. Black will be able to develop freely and, if he plays acccurately, White will be unable to play d4 under favourable circum-stances.

5 h3

White tends to play this automat-ically, now or on the next move. If it

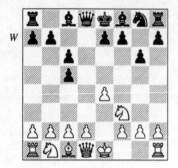

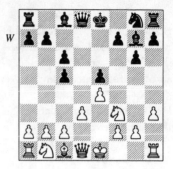

is omitted though, it's not clear whether Black should avail himself of the opportunity to play ...♗g4. One example where he did is Savon-Kiselev, Moscow 1992: 5 d3 ♗g7 6 a4 ♗g4 7 h3 ♗xf3 8 ♕xf3 ♘f6 9 ♘c3 0-0 10 0-0 ♘d7 11 ♕e2 when the players actually agreed to a draw. In my opinion, though, White has the better chances as Black will have difficulty in finding a constructive plan. Black is probably better off forgetting about ...♗g4 as sooner or later White will feel obliged to play h3. The annoyance value of something to g4 (especially ♗e3 ♘g4) will be too much to tolerate.

5 ...   e5!

After this it feels like colours have been reversed, but White is no doubt quite happy with this state of affairs as he is really playing an English Opening in reverse. 5...♗g7 6 d3 e5 leads to the same position.

6 d3

6 ♘xe5 ♕d4.

6 ...   ♗g7 (D)

7 ♕e2

This move is the first sign of the indecisiveness which plagues White throughout this game.

White has two plans available to him. The first involves developing with ♗e3 and ♘bd2, castling short (although this can often be delayed as White has such a solid centre), and then either throwing the a-pawn down the board (more attractive if Black has played ...b6) or playing for c3 and d4. The second plan is to play ♗e3, ♕d2 and ♗h6 to weaken the dark squares. White usually follows up by castling queenside and then continues his attack by either f4 or h4. Here are some examples:

a) 7 ♗e3. This might well be the best move as it is essential to both plans. Black now has to do something about his c-pawn:

a1) 7...b6?! 8 ♘bd2 ♘e7 9 a4! 0-0 10 a5 ♖b8 11 axb6 axb6 12 0-0 f6 13 ♕b1! ♗e6 14 b4 with some advantage for White; Nevednichy-Riegler, Bled 1992.

a2) 7...♕e7! (this doesn't create a target for the a-pawn to latch onto. If White now continues with 8 ♘c3 and 9 ♕d2 play transposes to the next note) 8 ♘bd2 f6 9 a4 ♘h6 10 0-0 ♗e6?! 11 c3 0-0 12 d4 cxd4 13 cxd4 ♘f7 14 dxe5 fxe5 15 ♕c2 and White stood slightly better in Zagrebelny-Ikonnikov, USSR team Ch 1991. However, I think that 10...♗e6 wasted precious time and gave White the opportunity to carry out d4 under favourable circumstances. Better would have been the immediate 10...♘f7 as after 11 c3 0-0 12 d4 cxd4 13 cxd4 exd4 14 ♘xd4 (14 ♗xd4 ♘e5 is OK for Black) 14...♘d6 Black should be able to free his game with ...f5 (even after 15 ♖e1).

b) 7 ♘c3 ♕e7 8 ♗e3 ♘f6 9 ♕d2 ♘d7 10 ♗h6 f6 (this move enables Black to cover the dark squares) 11 ♗xg7 ♕xg7 12 ♕e3 ♕e7 13 ♘d2 ♘f8 14 f4 ♘e6?! (Black's knight manoeuvre to e6 was the right idea, but he should have taken time out to capture on f4. After 14...exf4 15 ♕xf4 ♘e6, the game would have been about equal. The text saddles Black with a weak pawn on e5) 15 fxe5 fxe5 16 0-0-0 ♘f4 17 ♖hg1 ♗d7?! (Black's plan of going long is faulty. 17...0-0 would have minimized White's advantage. The rest of the game is very instructive and a perfect example of the sort of thing Black has to avoid) 18 ♘f3 0-0-0 (D)

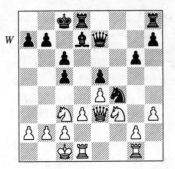

19 ♘b1! (Psakhis doesn't delay the transfer of the knight to its ideal square, c4) 19...g5 20 ♘bd2 h6 21 ♘c4 ♘g6 22 b4! g4 23 hxg4 cxb4 (what else?) 24 ♕xa7 ♗xg4 25 ♖df1 ♖de8? (Black should have removed the knight) 26 ♘fd2! (now it is heading for those juicy dark squares around Black's king) 26...♖hf8 27 ♘b3 ♗e6 28 ♘ba5 ♕c7 29 ♘b6+ ♔d8 30 ♘a8! 1-0 Psakhis-F.Röder, Vienna Open 1991. Some people might describe this game as a knightmare (I can hear you groaning but make sure that you don't end up on the receiving end of this kind of game).

7 ...　　　♕e7
8 ♗g5?

This move shows that White doesn't understand the position. As we saw from some of the above examples, Black is quite happy to play ...f6 (which bolsters the e-pawn and allows the knight to come to f7), even without White forcing him to do so. A very similar mistake has occurred quite often in a variation of the French Defence. After the moves 1 e4 e6 2 d4 d5 3 ♘c3 ♘f6 4 ♗g5 dxe4 ♘xe4 ♗e7 6 ♗xf6 gxf6 7 ♘f3 b6, even grandmasters have played 8 ♗b5+ in order to force ...c6. However, after 8 ♗d3 ♗b7 9 ♕e2 ♘d7 10 0-0-0 Black's only way to complete his development is to play 10...c6! followed by ...♕c7 and ...0-0-0. White's play cost a whole tempo, as does ♗g5 in this game.

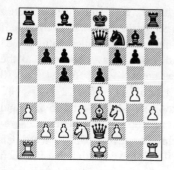

8	...	f6
9	♗e3	♘h6
10	♘bd2	♘f7
11	g4	

Another debatable decision. White prevents Black from playing ...f5 (for the moment) but one should remember that pawns don't move backwards.

| 11 | ... | b6 |

Now Black is not worried about a4-a5, as, if White follows that course, what is he going to do with his king? The same can be said for the plan he chooses in the game.

| 12 | a3?! *(D)* | |
| 12 | ... | ♘d8! |

This is the reason why Black is happy to develop his knight via h6. The knight heads for e6 from where it exerts a big influence on the centre and can hop in to either d4 or f4.

| 13 | b4 | |

The logical follow-up to his last move, but even without this dubious

queenside expansion Black would hold the advantage.

| 13 | ... | ♘e6 |
| 14 | 0-0 | |

The safest place for the king is in the centre, but then of course White will be unable to achieve any harmony amongst his forces.

14	...	♘d4
15	♕d1	h5!
16	♘h4	♕f7
17	♘g2	hxg4
18	hxg4	♗f8

Black prepares to double on the h-file, whilst the bishop is also removed from the g-file in anticipation of its opening after ...f5.

19	f3	f5
20	gxf5	gxf5
21	f4	

White, with good reason, decides he couldn't tolerate Black playing ...f4.

21	...	♕h7
22	fxe5	♕h2+
23	♔f2	♖g8
24	♖g1	f4

25	♗xd4	♕g3+
26	♔f1	♗g4
27	♕e1	

27 ♗f2 ♕h3 28 ♕b1 f3 and Black has a very strong attack.

| 27 | ... | cxd4 |
| 28 | ♕xg3 | fxg3 (D) |

The exchange of queens on g3 has certainly not eased White's defensive task. Now the f-file has been opened and Black's bishop has access to the powerful h6-c1 diagonal.

29	♘h4	♗h6
30	♘df3	♗h3+
31	♘g2	

31 ♔e1 ♗e3.

31	...	♖f8
32	♔e2	♗g4
33	♘gh4	♗f4
34	♘g6	♔d7!
35	♘xf4	

35 ♘xf8+ ♖xf8 36 ♖af1 ♗xe5 is completely hopeless for White.

35	...	♖xf4
36	♖xg3	♖xf3!
37	♖xf3	♖f8 (D)

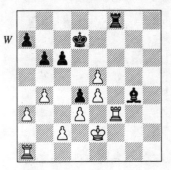

White finds himself in a final and terminal pin. The rest of the game must have been sheer bliss for Mr Goldin: **38 ♖f1 ♔e6 39 ♖f2 ♔xe5 40 ♖f1 ♖f6 41 ♖f2 ♖f7 42 ♖f1 a5 43 bxa5 bxa5 44 ♖f2 c5 45 ♖f1 c4 46 ♖f2 c3 47 ♖f1 ♔d6 48 ♖f2 ♔c5 49 ♖f1 ♖f4 50 ♖f2 ♔b5 51 ♖f1 ♔a4 52 ♖f2 ♔xa3 53 e5 ♔b2 54 e6 ♖f6 0-1**.

Game 29
Bronstein – Geller
Gothenburg 1955

1	e4	c5
2	♘f3	♘c6
3	♗b5	g6
4	c3 (D)	

This innocent-looking move is not all that it seems. With his tricky move order, White is hoping to lure Black into a dangerous gambit. As you will see, Geller fell for it hook, line and sinker. The usual 4 0-0 can be seen later in the Chapter.

| 4 | ... | ♗g7?! |

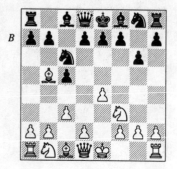

4...♘f6 is the safest reaction after which play should transpose into one of our subsequent games, e.g. 5 ♕e2 ♗g7 6 0-0 is considered in Game 30 (instead of castling Fischer once tried the greedy 6 e5 ♘d5 7 ♕c4 but after 7...♘c7 8 ♗xc6 dxc6 9 ♕xc5 ♕d3 10 ♕e3 ♗f5 11 ♕xd3 ♗xd3 he had to suffer considerably before obtaining a draw in Fischer-Matulović, Palma IZ 1970) and 5 e5 ♘d5 6 0-0 ♗g7 transposes to Game 31.

5   d4

5 0-0 transposes to subsequent games but if you're not going to play the text there's not much point employing this move order.

5   ...   ♕b6

5...cxd4 is worse as after 6 cxd4 ♕b6 White can defend his bishop with 7 ♘c3!. Suleimanov-Komozin, USSR 1972 is a game to be savoured: 7...♘xd4 (7...♗xd4 8 ♘xd4 ♕xd4 9 ♕e2 is very good for White) 8 ♘d5! ♘xf3+ 9 ♕xf3 ♕d6 10 ♗d2 e6 11 ♗b4 ♕b8 12 0-0! a6 13 ♖ac1 exd5 14 exd5 axb5 15 ♖fe1+ ♗e5 16

d6 ♔f8 17 ♖xe5 b6 18 ♖c7 ♖xa2 19 h3 ♕a8 20 ♕e3 ♗b7 (D)

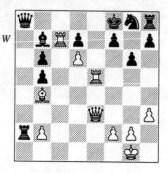

21 ♖xb7!! ♕xb7 22 ♖e8+ ♔g7 23 ♗c3+ f6 24 ♖xg8+! ♖xg8 25 ♗xf6+ ♔xf6 26 ♕e7+ ♔f5 27 g4+ 1-0. Breathtaking stuff.

6   a4

White has to give up a pawn to retain the initiative, but at least it will be a dangerous one.

6   ...   cxd4
7   0-0

7 cxd4 is an alternative course to follow. After 7...♘xd4 8 ♘c3 ♘xb5 9 axb5 ♗xc3+ 10 bxc3 ♕xb5 11 ♕d4 f6 12 c4 ♕b4+ 13 ♗d2 ♕d6 14 ♕e3 White undoubtedly has compensation, but who stands better is a very difficult question to answer (and probably not extremely relevant either).

7   ...   a6

7...d3 is safer. *ECO* considers the position to offer equal chances after 8 ♘a3 ♘f6 9 ♗xd3 although it's interesting to see that Grandmaster

Smirin is still playing this line and no doubt has some improvements on the published theory.

8 ♗xc6   ♛xc6

This is really asking for it. With 8...dxc6 9 cxd4 ♘f6 10 a5 ♛c7 11 ♘c3 Black could have kept his disadvantage to a minimum.

9 cxd4   ♛xe4
10 ♘c3   ♛f5
11 ♖e1   d5

The game Smirin-Dokhoian, Klaipeda 1988 continued 11...d6 12 ♘e4 ♛d5 (12...♗e6 13 ♘xd6+!) 13 ♗f4 ♗e6 14 ♘c3 ♛b3 15 d5 ♛xd1 16 ♖axd1 ♗d7 17 ♗xd6 ♗xc3 18 bxc3 ♗xa4 19 ♖d4 ♗d7 20 ♗a3 and White's initiative has hardly lessened with the exchange of pieces.

12 a5

White plans to transfer his knight to b6.

12 ...   ♗d7
13 ♛b3   ♘f6? *(D)*

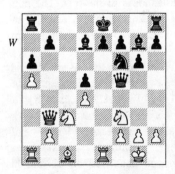

In his rush to get castled, Black overlooks a tactical coup. Necessary

was 13...♗c6 after which 14 ♛b4 still gives very good attacking chances for White.

14 ♖e5!   ♛d3
15 ♖xe7+!   ♔xe7

15...♔f8 16 ♖xf7+! doesn't help.

16 ♘xd5+   ♘xd5
17 ♛xd3

Black struggled on a few more moves: 17...f6 18 ♗d2 ♔f7 19 ♛b3 ♗c6 20 ♘e1 ♖he8 21 ♘d3 ♖e6 22 ♖c1 ♗f8 23 ♖xc6 1-0.

Game 30
Lutikov – Ermenkov
Albena 1976

1 e4   c5
2 ♘f3   ♘c6
3 ♗b5   g6
4 0-0   ♗g7 *(D)*

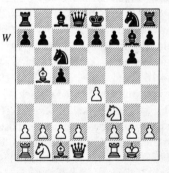

5 c3

5 ♖e1 is frequently seen and after 5...♘f6 6 c3 play has transposed to the next game. White does have a couple of alternatives to c3 though:

a) 6 e5 ♘d5 7 ♘c3 ♘c7 (7...♘xc3
8 dxc3 just speeds up White's development) 8 ♗xc6 dxc6 (the position
is virtually the same as note 'b', and
will often transpose) 9 ♘e4 ♘e6
(9...b6?! is inaccurate because of 10
♘f6+ ♔f8 11 ♘e4 when Black will
lose more time trying to castle by
hand than White has done with his
knight) 10 b4?! (White hopes to take
over control of the centre, but Black
will have resources. More prudent
was 10 d3 0-0 11 ♗e3 b6 12 ♕d2
♘d4 13 ♘xd4 cxd4 14 ♗h6 c5 with
about equal chances. Black should
always be able to defend his kingside
with a timely advance of the f-pawn)
10...cxb4 11 d4 0-0 12 a3 bxa3 13 c4
b5!. This is the star move, which enables Black to blockade the centre.
The immediate 14 d5 is premature,
as after 14...cxd5 15 cxd5 ♘c7 16 d6
exd6 17 ♘xd6 b4 Black's passed
pawns should decide the issue. The
game Hecht-Adorjan, London 1981
went instead 14 ♗xa3 bxc4 15 ♕a4
♘f4 16 ♕xc4 ♗g4 17 ♘fd2 ♖e8 18
♗c5 a5 with advantage to Black.

b) 6 ♘c3 0-0 7 e5 (7 ♗xc6 dxc6
leads to positions similar to those
considered in Game 28, but with
White having already committed his
king) 7...♘e8 8 ♗xc6 (otherwise
Black will play ...♘d4 with a good
game) 8...dxc6 (8...bxc6 allows White
to play 9 d4) 9 ♘e4 b6 10 h3 ♘c7 11
d3 ♘e6. The chances are about level
and a dour struggle lies ahead. For

the moment all the pawns are still
present, so the knights are more effective than the bishops, but of course
the game may well open up later.

5 ...   ♘f6
6 d4 (D)

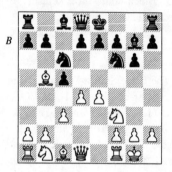

White gambits the e-pawn to gain
a lead in development. This is quite a
familiar idea when White plays ♗b5
against the Sicilian, e.g. 1 e4 c5 2
♘f3 d6 3 ♗b5+ ♗d7 4 ♗xd7+
♕xd7 5 0-0 ♘c6 6 c3 ♘f6 7 d4 with
similar ideas to the text. The main
line is 6 ♖e1, which is Games 32 and
33, whilst 6 e5 can be seen in Game
31.

From time to time White defends
the pawn with his queen, e.g. 6 ♕e2
0-0 7 d4 (7 ♖d1!?) 7...cxd4 8 cxd4
d5 9 e5 ♘e4 and now:

a) 10 ♘c3 ♘xc3 11 bxc3 ♘a5.
White's position is less good than if
his rook had been on e1 and his
queen on d1 (see Game 32, note to
Black's 7th move). There are less attacking chances here as his rook

won't be able to swing to the king-side with the same ease and in some lines he may regret the fact that the bishop's retreat to f1 is blocked. 12 h3 a6 (12...♗d7!?) 13 ♗d3 ♗d7= (*ECO*).

b) 10 h3 ♕b6 11 ♗e3 ♗d7 12 ♗d3 ♘b4 13 ♘e1 f5 with a good game for Black in Ledger-Ulybin, Hastings 1990.

6 ...   cxd4

Black could also take on e4 at once, but the text has the advantage of opening up the long diagonal for his bishop. 6...♕b6 is not to be rec-ommended. In the game Minasian-Gkountintas, London Lloyds Bank 1991, Black lost a piece in rather amusing fashion: 7 ♘a3 cxd4 8 e5 ♘e4 9 cxd4 0-0 10 ♗c4 d6 11 ♗d5! and 11...♗f5 can be met by 12 ♖e1.

7 cxd4   ♘xe4

There is little choice as 7...d5 8 e5 ♘e4 9 ♘e1! leaves Black's knight in trouble.

8 d5   ♘d6!

8...♘b8 is too passive. In the game Tseitlin-Suradiradja, Pernik 1977, Black found himself in diffi-culties after 9 ♖e1 ♘d6 10 a4 0-0 11 ♗g5 ♖e8 12 ♘c3 h6 13 ♗f4 ♘xb5 14 axb5 d6 15 ♕d2. The pawns on d5 and b5 severely restrict Black's position.

9 ♘a3 (D)

9 ...   ♘e5?!

Stronger is 9...a6! after which White has trouble proving that he

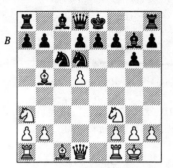

has sufficient compensation for the pawn, e.g. 10 ♕a4 ♘e5 11 ♘xe5 ♗xe5 12 ♖e1 ♗f6 13 ♗d3 0-0 14 ♗h6 ♖e8 15 h4 b5! (Black liberates his position) 16 ♘xb5 ♘xb5 17 ♗xb5 ♖b8 18 ♗d3 (obviously 18 ♗xa6 ♖a8) 18...d6 19 h5 ♖xb2 and White had nothing to show for his in-vestment in Barle-Matulović, Yugo-slavia 1976; or 10 ♗a4 b5 11 dxc6 (if the bishop had moved Black could have gained time hitting it with his knight, e.g. 11 ♗b3 ♘a5 or 11 ♗c2 ♘b4) 11...bxa4 12 ♗g5 dxc6 13 ♖e1 f6 14 ♕xa4 0-0 (not 14...fxg5 15 ♕xc6+ ♗d7 16 ♕xd6) 15 ♗d2 (Rogers-Zilberman, London Lloyds Bank 1991) and now I think that 15...♖b8 16 ♗c3 ♘b5 would have left Black with the better game.

10 ♘xe5   ♗xe5
11 ♖e1   ♘xb5?

A serious mistake. The resolute 11...f6 (Minev) was a better chance.

12 ♖xe5   f6

12...♘xa3 allows 13 ♗g5!.

13 ♘xb5!   fxe5

14	d6	0-0
15	♗g5	♕b6
16	dxe7	♕xb5
17	exf8♕+	♔xf8
18	♕d6+	♔g8
19	♗h6	1-0

19...♔f7 20 ♗f8! g5 21 ♕e7+ ♔g6 22 g4! leads to mate.

Game 31
Klovsky – Korsunsky
USSR 1978

1	e4	c5
2	♘f3	♘c6
3	♗b5	g6
4	0-0	♗g7
5	c3	♘f6
6	e5	♘d5
7	d4	cxd4
8	cxd4	0-0
9	♘c3 (D)	

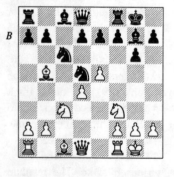

| 9 | ... | ♘c7 |

9...♘xc3 is also quite playable. After 10 bxc3 d6 11 exd6 exd6 (11...♕xd6 12 a4 is a little better for

White) 12 ♗f4 ♘e7 13 ♗c4 ♗g4 14 h3 ♖c8 15 ♗b3 ♗e6 the game was about equal in Matanović-Schweber, Sousse IZ 1967.

10 ♗f4

Not feeling too concerned about the bishop pair, White concentrates on his development and threatens to play d5. Retreating the bishop has not brought White any success either, e.g. 10 ♗a4 d6!. The reason why lines with an early e5 are not dangerous for Black is that he is able to break up the centre in this fashion. Now both 11 ♗f4 ♗g4 12 ♗xc6 bxc6 13 h3 ♘e6! Miagmasuren-Korchnoi, Sousse IZ 1967 and 11 h3 dxe5 12 dxe5 ♕xd1 13 ♖xd1 ♘xe5 14 ♘xe5 ♗xe5 15 ♗g5 ♗f6 16 ♗xf6 exf6 17 ♖ac1 Nezhmetdinov-Polugaevsky, USSR 1959 promise White no more than equality.

10	...	♘xb5
11	♘xb5	a6
12	♘c3	d6
13	exd6	♗g4!

13...exd6 should be about equal, but the text gives Black the chance to fight for the initiative.

14	dxe7	♕xe7
15	d5	♘d4
16	d6	♕d7 (D)
17	♘d5	

Bronstein once tried the incredible 17 ♕xd4 ♗xd4 18 ♘xd4 but after 18...g5!? 19 ♗g3 f5 20 ♗e5 ♖ae8 21 ♖fe1 ♖xe5 22 ♖xe5 ♕xd6 he was lucky to escape with a draw in

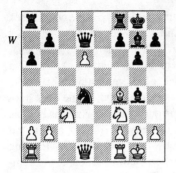

Bronstein-Schinzel, Sandamir 1976. Razuvaev has suggested 19 ♘d5 f5 20 ♗e5 as a possible improvement for White.

17	...	♗xf3
18	gxf3	♕h3
19	♗g3	h5!

Now White is faced with dangerous threats and feels forced into a dubious sacrifice. 20 ♘f4 ♕f5 doesn't help him.

20	♖e1	h4
21	♘e7+	♔h7
22	♖e4	hxg3
23	hxg3	

In view of what is about to happen on the h-file White might have considered 23 fxg3 but in that case 23...♘f5 would be very strong.

| 23 | ... | ♖ad8! |

23...♘f5 looks like a good alternative, although after 24 ♖g4! White has more chances than in the previous note.

24 ♖xd4

Taking the queen with 24 ♖h4+ ♕xh4 25 gxh4 ♖xd6 would leave

White with the difficult task of extricating his knight, e.g. 26 ♕d3 ♖e8 27 ♖e1 ♖d7 28 ♕a3 ♘c6 and Black wins.

24	...	♗xd4
25	♕xd4 (D)	

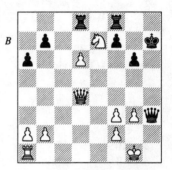

25 ... ♖h8!

Just when it looks like he should be thinking about defence, Black unleashes a nasty attack.

26 ♖e1?

The best chance was 26 ♕f6 although after 26...♕e6 27 ♕xe6 fxe6 28 ♖d1 ♖d7 29 ♖d4 ♖hd8 30 ♖h4+ ♔g7 31 ♖g4 ♖xd6 32 ♘xg6 ♖d2 Black's chances are to be preferred.

26 ... ♖xd6!

The point behind the previous move.

27 ♘d5

After 27 ♕xd6 ♔g7 the only way to avoid mate, 28 ♕d4+ f6 29 ♕h4 ♖xh4 30 gxh4, leaves White hopelessly lost.

27	...	♖hd8
28	♘f6+	♔h8

29 ♖e8+

This is certainly not the most accurate, but White would also lose after 29 ♕e5 ♕e6 30 ♕c3 ♕xe1+ or 29 ♕c3 ♖c6 30 ♕e5 ♕e6! when the queens are forced off.

29 ...   ♖xe8

0-1

Game 32
Vedder – Yakovich
Leeuwarden 1992

1	e4	c5
2	♘f3	♘c6
3	♗b5	g6
4	0-0	♗g7
5	c3	♘f6
6	♖e1	0-0
7	d4 *(D)*	

For 7 h3 see Game 33.

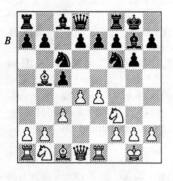

7 ...   d5!

Until recently Black has nearly always exchanged on d4 before playing this advance. After 7...cxd4 8 cxd4 d5 9 e5 ♘e4 10 ♘c3! (of course this isn't possible when Black hasn't captured on d4) 10...♘xc3 (10...♗f5 11 ♘h4!) 11 bxc3 a considerable amount of tournament practice has demonstrated that White has an edge. True, White does have some queenside weaknesses but this is compensated for by his central pawn wedge and kingside attacking chances. Here are a couple of examples:

a) 11...♕a5 12 a4 ♗g4 (and not 12...♕xc3? 13 ♗d2 ♕b2 14 ♖b1 ♕a2 15 ♕c1 ♗f5 16 ♖b2 ♕a3 17 ♖e3) 13 ♖e3 ♖fc8 14 h3 ♗xf3 15 ♖xf3 e6 16 h4! (the standard way to attack in these kind of positions) 16...a6 17 ♗f1 b5 18 h5 b4 19 cxb4 ♕xb4 20 ♗e3 ♘a5 21 ♖h3 ♘c4 22 hxg6 fxg6 (22...hxg6 23 ♗g5 with the intention of ♕g4-h4) 23 ♕g4 ♕e7 24 ♗g5 ♕f7 25 ♕h4 ♗h8 26 ♗d3 ♖a7 27 ♖b1 ♖ac7 28 ♖b3 ♘a5 29 ♖b6 ♖c6 30 ♖xa6 ♖xa6 31 ♗xa6 ♖a8 32 ♗b5 ♖f8 33 ♗h6 ♖c8 34 ♖f3 ♕c7 35 ♕g4 ♕e7 36 ♗g5 h5 37 ♕h3! ♕xg5 38 ♕xe6+ ♔h7 39 ♕xc8 ♕c1+ 40 ♕xc1 1-0 Torre-Van der Wiel, Thessaloniki OL 1988.

b) 11...♘a5 12 ♘g5!? h6 13 ♘f3 (at the cost of a tempo, White has bought something to get his teeth into on the kingside) 13...a6 14 ♗d3 ♗e6 15 ♘h4 ♖c8 16 f4 ♕d7 17 f5 ♗xf5 18 ♗xf5 gxf5 19 ♕h5 ♖c6 20 ♘xf5 ♔h7 21 ♗a3 ♖e6 22 ♖e3 ♘c6 23 ♘xg7 ♔xg7 24 ♕g4+ 1-0 Mainka-Reeh, Bundesliga 1992. I can't imagine a more direct attacking game than that one.

8 exd5

8 e5 ♘e4 9 ♘bd2 cxd4 10 cxd4 ♗f5 11 ♘b3!? (11 ♗xc6 bxc6 12 ♘b3 transposes to a line given in *ECO* which continues 12...a5 13 a4 f6 14 exf6 exf6 15 ♘fd2 ♖e8 ∓) 11...f6 12 exf6 (the attempt to win a piece with 12 ♘h4 is very dubious: after 12...fxe5! 13 f3 exd4 14 fxe4 dxe4 15 g4 e5! Black has excellent play) 12...exf6 13 ♘fd2 with a roughly level game.

8 ... ♕xd5

9 dxc5

After 9 c4 ♕d6 10 dxc5 ♕xd1 (10...♕xc5!?) 11 ♖xd1 ♘e4 12 ♗xc6 (or 12 h3 ♗e6 13 ♗xc6 bxc6 14 ♘d4 ♗xd4! 15 ♖xd4 ♖fd8 16 ♖xd8+ ♖xd8 with advantage to Black; Slobodjan-Ibragimov, Dortmund 1992) 12...bxc6 13 ♘a3 ♗g4 14 ♘c2 ♘xc5 Black has at least equality; Kotronias-Torre, Manila OL 1992.

9 ... ♕xc5 *(D)*

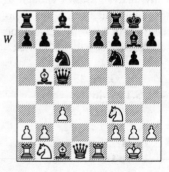

10 ♗xc6?!

It's not a good idea to grab the e-pawn, but even after a move like 10 a4 Black has a very comfortable game (an extra central pawn and White's queenside still undeveloped).

10 ... ♕xc6

11 ♖xe7 ♗e6

Of course the e-pawn wasn't free of charge.

12 ♘d4 ♕d6!

13 ♖xb7

White's play has been extremely optimistic and it's not surprising that Black is able to launch a vicious kingside assault.

13 ... ♘g4

14 g3

This horribly weakens the light squares, but there was no choice.

14 ... ♖fd8!

14...♗xd4 15 cxd4 ♕d5 16 ♖c7 ♘e5 looks crushing, but as Yakovich pointed out White can defend with 17 ♖c5 ♘f3+ 18 ♔h1 ♕b7 19 d5.

15 ♗g5

15 ♕e2? ♗xd4 16 cxd4 ♕c6 perfectly illustrates White's lack of co-ordination.

15 ... ♗xd4!

16 ♕xd4 *(D)*

After 16 cxd4 ♕d5! 17 ♗xd8 ♕xb7 lunch will be taken at b2 and d4.

16 ... ♕f8!

The weakness of the back rank now proves decisive. Unfortunately

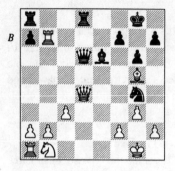

for White ♕a4 (with or without taking the rook) loses to 16...♕c5.

17	♗xd8	♖xd8
18	♕xa7	♕h6!

The threats are multiplying

19	♘d2	♕xh2+
20	♔f1	♖xd2
21	♔e1	♖d8
22	♖b8	♕h1+
23	♔e2	♗c4# (0-1)

Whilst 7...d5 is not completely uncharted territory, theory is still in its infancy. I find it rather surprising that this simple answer to White's system has not become more popular.

P.S. Some time after completing this chapter I was pleased to see the following encounter:

White: Channel 4 Commentary team in consultation (Carol Vorderman, Cathy Forbes and GM's Speelman, King and Keene)

Black: Kasparov and Short in consultation!!, Savoy Theatre 1993: 1 e4 c5 2 ♘f3 ♘c6 3 ♗b5 g6 4 0-0 ♗g7 5 c3 ♘f6 6 ♖e1 0-0 7 d4 d5! 8 exd5 ♕xd5 9 c4 ♕d6 10 d5 ♘d4 11 ♘xd4 cxd4 12 ♘d2 a6 13 ♗a4 b5 14 ♗b3 ♗b7 15 cxb5 axb5 16 ♘f3 ♘xd5 17 ♘xd4 ♖fd8 18 ♘f3 h6 19 ♕e2 e6 20 ♘e5 b4 21 ♗d2 ♗a6 22 ♕e4 ♘f6 23 ♕xb4 ♕xd2 24 ♕e7 ♖f8 25 ♘xf7 ♔h7 26 ♖ad1 ♕xb2 27 ♕xe6 ♗c8 28 ♕c4 ♘g4 29 ♖f1 ♗f5 30 h3 ♘e5 31 ♘xe5 ♕xe5 32 ♖fe1 ♕f6 33 ♕f4 ♖ad8 34 ♖xd8 ♕xd8 35 ♖d1 ♕b6 36 ♕d6 ♕a7 37 ♕d2 h5 38 ♕e2 ♗d4 39 ♖d2 ♗c8 40 ♗c2 ♔g7 41 ♕e4 ♗xf2+ 42 ♔h1 ♕b6 43 ♕e7+ ♖f7 44 ♕e8 ♗g3 45 ♖d1 ♗b7 46 ♗e4 ♕f2 47 ♗xb7 ♕f1+ 48 ♖xf1 ♖xf1# (0-1).

'In spite of choosing a well-known opening the White team was surprised by Black's 7...d5, which appears to be a theoretical novelty. 9 c4, although it drove back the queen, was an error and ultimately our side was reduced to fishing in muddy waters with a dubious piece sacrifice.' (Raymond Keene in *The Times* of November 3rd 1993).

If my analysis wasn't enough to convince you, then surely the combined efforts of the World Champion and his challenger will do the trick.

Game 33
M.S.Tseitlin – Neverov
Bucharest 1993

1	e4	c5
2	♘f3	♘c6

3	♗b5	g6
4	0-0	♗g7
5	♖e1	♘f6
6	c3	0-0
7	h3 *(D)*	

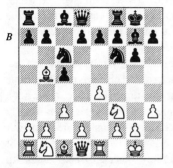

White doesn't wish to commit himself just yet and opts for a useful waiting move. He will now be able to plan his course of action depending on Black's next move. On the minus side a tempo has been spent.

7 ...   e5

Black has a large number of playable moves such as 7...♕b6, 7...♘e8 or even 7...a6. I like the text though, since if White plays quietly (d3), and statistical evidence seems to suggest that this is often the case, Black has a very comfortable position with many similarities to a favourable Ruy Lopez or Italian Game. I should just mention that 7...d5 would be a mistake, as after 8 e5 the e4 square is not available to the knight.

8 ♘a3

The attempt to win a pawn with 8 ♗xc6 dxc6 9 ♘xe5 runs into trouble: 9...♖e8 10 f4 (10 d4 is more natural, but after 10...cxd4 11 cxd4 c5! White is in difficulties) 10...♘xe4! 11 ♖xe4 f6 12 ♕b3+ ♗e6 13 ♘c4 ♗d5! and Black stood clearly better in Veingold-Kapengut, USSR 1975.

8 d4 is the sharpest move in the position after which Black has to take some care, e.g. 8...cxd4 9 cxd4 exd4 (9...♘xd4 10 ♘xd4 exd4 11 e5 ♘e8 12 ♕xd4 d6 13 ♘c3 ♗f5 14 ♗f4 dxe5 15 ♕xd8 ♖xd8 16 ♗xe5 gave Black equality in Kim-Kakarychev, USSR 1978. However, I think the simple 11 ♕xd4 should give White the advantage) 10 e5 *(D)* and now:

a) 10...♘d5 with another branch:
a1) 11 ♘a3 d6 12 ♗xc6 bxc6 13 ♘xd4 ♕c7 14 ♘db5 cxb5 15 ♕xd5 ♗e6 16 ♕d3 (16 ♕xd6 ♕xd6 17 exd6 a6 18 ♖e2 {the only way to try to stay material ahead} 18...b4 19 ♘c2 a5 with very good play for the pawn) 16...♗xe5 (16...dxe5!?) 17

♘xb5 ♕c4 18 ♕xc4 ♗xc4 19 f4 ♗g7 20 ♘xd6 ♗a6 21 ♗e3 ♗xb2 and a draw was agreed in Reyes-Wirthensohn, Novi Sad OL 1990.

a2) 11 ♘xd4 ♕b6 (11...♘xe5 12 ♘f5 gxf5 13 ♕xd5 d6 doesn't look out of the question) 12 ♘b3!? (White avoids the ugly capture on c6 with a little tactical resource) 12...♕xb5 13 ♘a3 ♕b4 14 ♘c2. Now 14...♕b5 is a draw, although Black would be quite justified in playing on with 14...♕e7 as in the game Miljanić-V.Spassov, Nikšić 1991. Play continued 15 ♕xd5 ♕e6 16 ♕d1 b6 17 ♘bd4 ♘xd4 18 ♘xd4 ♕d5 19 ♘f5 ♕xd1 20 ♘e7+ ♔h8 21 ♖xd1 ♗xe5 with advantage to Black.

a3) 11 ♗g5! ♕a5 12 ♘a3 a6 13 ♗c4 ♘b6 14 ♗b3 ♘xe5? (this loses by force but it was hard to meet the threat of ♖c1 and ♗d2) 15 ♘xe5 ♗xe5 16 ♗h6 d6 (moving the rook allows 17 ♕f3) *(D)*

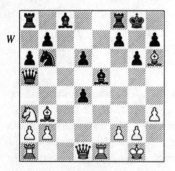

17 ♗d2! ♕c5 18 ♖c1 and the queen has been netted; Anand-Salov,

Paris Immopar rapid 1992. Black is obviously in need of an improvement on this *débâcle*. Salov based his whole strategy on taking the e-pawn, but this turned out to lose by force. 11...♕b6 or 11...♕c7!?, which is a more direct way of attacking the pawn on e5, are both worth investigation.

b) 10...♘e8!?. It seems to me that Black should give this retreat serious consideration. The d5 square is not a secure base and the knight is usually forced to move again quite soon after it has landed there. On e8 the knight is ideally placed to help break up White's centre with ...d6 or ...f6, whilst also retaining the option of ...♘c7-e6. 11 ♘xd4 can be met by 11...♘xd4 12 ♕xd4 d6 and 11 ♗g5 by 11...f6 (in Anand-Salov this would have been met by 12 ♕b3!) 12 exf6 ♗xf6 with a comfortable-looking game for Black.

8   ...   d6
9 ♘c2

9 ♗xc6 bxc6 10 ♘c4 (10 d3 leaves White with a rather passive position. Hübner-Adorjan, Bad Lauterburg Ct 1980 continued 10...a5! 11 ♗e3 a4 12 ♕c2 ♖e8 13 ♖ad1 ♗e6 14 ♕b1 ♕b8 15 d4 {White was in danger of suffocation} 15...exd4 16 cxd4 d5 17 e5 ♘d7 18 dxc5 ♗f5 19 ♕c1 ♘xe5 20 ♘xe5 ♖xe5 21 ♘c2 ♗xc2! 22 ♕xc2 ♕b4 and Black has the advantage) 10...♗e6 (10...♘xe4 looks tempting, but 11

♕a4! f5 12 d3 leaves White on top)
11 d3 ♘xe4!? (11...♕e7 is a solid
option) 12 ♖xe4 d5 13 ♖e1 dxc4 14
♘xe5 cxd3 15 ♘xd3 (Tseitlin-Sink-
ovics, Krumbach 1991). *New in
Chess* Yearbook 22 based a survey
of 7 h3 around this game, but after
15...c4 Black has at least equality.

9 ... ♖e8

Black indirectly attacks e4,
thereby preventing White from playing a sneaky d4.

10 d3 a6

Not strictly necessary but if Black
considers the exchange on c6 to be in
his favour then it's worth investing a
tempo.

11	♗xc6	bxc6
12	♗g5	h6
13	♗d2	♘h5 (D)

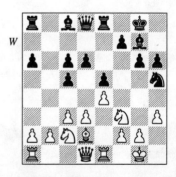

Black begins to think about a
kingside attack.

14 ♕c1 g5!?

14...♔h7 would have been less
committal, but maybe Black was
provoking White into taking action

in the centre so that the position
would be opened up for his bishops.

15	d4	exd4
16	cxd4	cxd4
17	♘cxd4	c5
18	♘f5	

18 ♘b3 ♗b7 is obviously not
what White had in mind when he
played 15 d4, but after the text Black
gets an extra central pawn at little
cost.

18	...	♗xf5
19	exf5	♖xe1+
20	♘xe1	♖b8
21	♘d3	

21 ♗c3 ♗xc3 22 ♕xc3 ♕f6!
forces the exchange of queens.

21	...	♕f6
22	♕c4	♕d4!
23	♕xd4	

23 ♕xa6? c4.

23	...	♗xd4 (D)

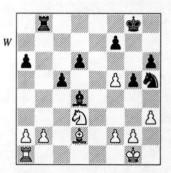

Black is in effect a pawn ahead,
which, combined with his play on
the b-file, gives him a winning ending.

24	g4	c4!
25	gxh5	cxd3
26	♗c3	♗xc3
27	bxc3	♖c8
28	f6	

White has to stop the king getting out via g7 and f6, but with a pawn structure like his, it's all pretty academic anyway. The game finished:

28	...	♖xc3
29	♖d1	♔f8

30	h4	gxh4
31	f4	♔e8
32	♔f2	♔d7
33	♖e1	d2
34	♖e7+	♔c6
35	♔e2	h3
36	♔xd2	h2
37	♖e1	♖h3
38	♖h1	♔d5
39	♔e2	♔e6
40	♔f2	♔xf6

0-1

7 1 e4 c5 2 ♘f3 d6 3 ♗b5+

B

For many years I lived in dread of 3 ♗b5+. How could anyone play so boringly? For me, it was the ultimate Anti-Sicilian. I didn't like the positions after 3...♘d7 or 3...♘c6 so I was reduced to playing 3...♗d7 and struggled to beat many a weaker player after a sequence of moves such as 4 ♗xd7+ ♕xd7 5 0-0 ♘c6 6 c3 ♘f6 7 ♖e1 e6 8 d4 cxd4 9 cxd4 d5 10 e5 ♘e4 11 ♘bd2 ♘xd2 12 ♗xd2. It's true that White could play more excitingly (7 d4!?), but they never did. Occasionally they aimed for a Maroczy set-up (6 c4) and I didn't even like this and usually played 6...e5 with games at least as dull as the above. Finally I decided that I was going to have to play 3...♘d7,

like it or not. To my surprise I began to enjoy the positions that arose, although the first dozen or so moves were usually pretty nerve-racking, as I often found myself lagging behind in development. To compensate for this Black often has long term advantages: the bishop pair and, most importantly, a rock-like centre which usually enables him to get his pieces out without suffering a catastrophe. To summarise, if Black can avoid being 'murdered in his bed' (D.King) he can look forward to a bright future.

Game 34
Bologan – Istratescu
Mamaia junior Wch 1991

1	e4	c5
2	♘f3	d6
3	♗b5+	♘d7
4	0-0	

For 4 d4 see Games 35 and 36.

| 4 | ... | ♘f6 |
| 5 | ♖e1 | |

5 d4 is a major alternative after which we have a position which is just as likely to have arisen from

the alternative move order 4 d4 ♘f6
5 0-0 *(D)*.

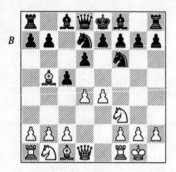

Black now has three possibilities:
a) 5...♘xe4. I am amazed at how
few examples of Black accepting the
sacrifice I have been able to dig up. I,
for one, am willing to suffer considerably for a central pawn. Its bad
reputation can be traced back to the
game Bonchev-Ničevski, Sofia 1976
which continued 6 ♕e2 ♘ef6 7 dxc5
(this is usually accompanied by an
exclamation mark. The alternative 7
♗g5 led to an unclear position in
the game Peters-Mestel, Hastings
1978 after the moves 7...cxd4 8
♗xf6 gxf6 9 ♘xd4 a6 10 ♗xd7+
♗xd7 {10...♕xd7!?} 11 ♘c3 ♕a5
12 ♕f3 0-0-0 13 ♘d5 e6 14 ♘xf6
♗g7) 7...dxc5 8 ♗g5 a6 9 ♗xd7+
♗xd7 10 ♖d1 ♕c7 11 ♘e5 ♗c6 12
♘c3 e6 13 ♗f4 ♕c8? 14 ♘c4 b5 15
♘b6 ♕b7 16 ♘xa8 ♕xa8 17 f3 with
advantage to White. The position after 13 ♗f4 *(D)* demanded some con-
crete calculation.

Black would obviously like to
play 13...♗d6, but White has a couple of dangerous-looking replies in
14 ♘xf7 and 14 ♖xd6. On closer in-
spection though, Black has nothing
to worry about:
a1) 14 ♘xc6 ♗xf4.
a2) 14 ♘xf7 ♗xf4 15 ♘xh8 (15
♕xe6+ ♕e7) 15...♗xh2+ 16 ♔h1
♔e7 17 ♖e1 and even if there's nothing better than 17...♖xh8 18 ♕xe6+
♔f8 Black has a good game as his
minor pieces cover all the important
central squares. After 19 ♖ad1,
19...h5! both activates the rook and
offers dangerous counterplay to
Black.
a3) 14 ♖xd6 ♕xd6 15 ♘g6 (15
♘xf7 ♕xf4 16 ♕xe6+ ♔f8 17 ♘xh8
♘g4 and suddenly the boot is on the
other foot; 15 ♖d1 ♕e7 16 ♘xc6
bxc6 17 ♗d6 ♕b7 should be favourable for Black) 15...♕d4 16 ♗e3 (16
♗e5 ♕g4 wins) and now Black has a
safe line in 16...♕g4 17 ♕xg4 ♘xg4
18 ♘xh8 ♘xe3 19 fxe3 ♔e7 20
♘xf7 ♔xf7 with a likely draw, or he

can play what appears to be an irresistible queen sacrifice: 16...hxg6!
17 ♗xd4 cxd4 18 ♘d1 0-0-0 *(D)*

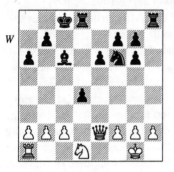

Black's central control, combined
with White's lack of activity should
more than compensate for the queen.
To sum up, 5...♘xe4 certainly deserves more attention than it's cur-
rently receiving, but if ever it were
to come under the microscope, improvements would no doubt be
found for White as well.
   b) 5...a6 6 ♗xd7+ and now:
   b1) 6...♘xd7 7 ♘c3 transposes
to the next game, but White has the
additional possibility of playing 7 c4
or even 7 d5.
   b2) 6...♕xd7!? 7 ♘c3 cxd4 8
♕xd4 e5 9 ♕d3 h6! (it's extremely
important to stop ♗g5 in this type of
position) 10 a4 ♗e7 11 ♘d2 ♕c7 12
♘c4 ♗e6 13 ♘e3 ♖c8 14 ♗d2 ♗c4
and Black had a good Najdorf in
Shabanov-Obukhov, USSR 1991. I
wouldn't hesitate to recommend
6...♕xd7 to you, if it weren't for

Obukhov's suggested improvement
for White, 8 ♘d5!. After the forced
8...♘xd5 9 exd5 Black is going to
have a lot of trouble completing his
development. White has achieved
the type of position normally associ-
ated with a pawn sacrifice (in the
♗b5+ lines) but for no cost as the
black pawn on d4 is obviously about
to drop off.
   c) 5...cxd4 6 ♕xd4 a6 (6...e5 7
♕d3 h6 is possible, but again White
has the possibility of 8 c4. This pawn
structure is also known from the
Kalashnikov variation {1 e4 c5 2
♘f3 ♘c6 3 d4 cxd4 4 ♘xd4 e5 5
♘b5 d6 6 c4}. It's curious to note
that this is quite a fashionable line
offering Black excellent chances of
equality, whereas the position after 8
c4 is usually dismissed as better for
White) 7 ♗xd7+ ♗xd7 8 ♗g5 h6?!
(8...e6 looks better) 9 ♗xf6 gxf6 10
c4! (again we can see this cramping
– or clamping – move) 10...e6 11
♘c3 ♖c8 12 ♔h1 h5 13 a4 h4 14 h3
♗e7 15 b4 a5 16 b5 ♕c7 17 ♘d2
♕c5 18 ♕d3 ♖g8 19 ♖ae1 ♕g5 20
♖g1 *(D)*
   We have been following the famous game Ivanchuk-Kasparov, Linares 1991. After 20...b6, Black's
position would not be too bad, but at
this moment the World Champion
made a serious error with 20...♕f4
which turned out to give White the
tempo he needed to launch an attack.
The ease with which Ivanchuk now

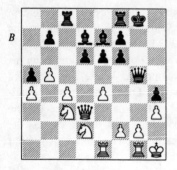

B

dispatched Kasparov sent tremors through the chess world: 21 ♖ef1 b6 22 ♘e2! ♛h6 23 c5!? (White considers the c4 square to be worth at least a pawn. 23 f4 was safer) 23...♖xc5 (according to Ivanchuk, Black's best chance was to curl up with 23...dxc5 24 ♘c4 ♖b8 25 f4 ♗c8 26 f5 ♔f8 but it's understandable that a player of Kasparov's nature would not like this. The problem with the text is that ultimately the c-file is sure to fall into White's hands) 24 ♘c4 ♔f8 25 ♘xb6 ♗e8 26 f4 f5 27 exf5 ♖xf5 28 ♖c1! ♔g7 29 g4 ♖c5 30 ♖xc5 dxc5 31 ♘c8 ♗f8? 32 ♛d8 ♛g6 33 f5 ♛h6 34 g5 ♛h5 35 ♖g4 exf5 36 ♘f4 ♛h8 37 ♛f6+ ♔h7 38 ♖xh4+ 1-0. In several reports I've seen 3 ♗b5+ praised as a brilliant psychological choice. Whilst this might be true, it was more by accident than design. Ivanchuk's flight arrived at four in the morning the day before the game and he simply didn't feel up to facing the Najdorf.

Before continuing with our main game, 5 e5 deserves a brief mention. The game Mantovani-Gallagher, Swiss League 1991 went on 5...dxe5 6 ♘xe5 a6 (6...e6 looks perfectly OK as well) 7 ♗xd7+ ♘xd7 8 d4 and instead of the risky 8...cxd4 9 ♛xd4 f6 which I chose, Black should play 8...♘xe5 9 dxe5 ♛xd1 10 ♖xd1 ♗f5 with a pleasant endgame. I simply couldn't bring myself to exchange queens after such an insipid opening by White, but a few moves later I was desperate to swap them off in order to dampen my opponent's increasing initiative.

5 ...   a6
6 ♗f1

The retreat of this bishop seems to be automatic when it can be tucked away on f1, but 6 ♗xd7+ is equally playable. For instance, after 6...♘xd7 7 d4, play is likely to transpose to Game 35 or 36, whilst 7 c3 also comes into consideration.

6 ...   b6 (D)

This very natural continuation is directed against White's standard plan of c3 and d4. If White wishes to carry this out he will first have to waste a tempo defending his e-pawn.

However 6...♘e5 also deserves consideration. The one known example is Marantz-Grünfeld, Israel 1988, which continued 7 ♘xe5 dxe5 8 a4 ♗g4 9 ♗e2 ♗e6 10 d3 g6 11 a5 ♗g7 12 ♘d2 0-0 13 b3 ♛c7 with an unclear game.

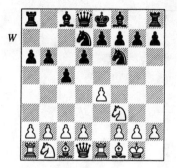

7 d4!?

The majority of people who play ⌞b5+ are looking for a quiet time, possibly even a quick draw, but consider yourself forewarned if ever you find yourself opposite Mr Bologan, whose style will become apparent as this game unfolds. The alternative is 7 c3. The game Wahls-Renet, Dortmund 1989 continued 7...⌞b7 8 d3 e5 (8...g6 is an equally valid approach. *ECO* gives 9 c3 e5 10 d4 ♛c7 11 dxe5 dxe5 with equality) 9 ⌞bd2 ⌞e7 10 d4 0-0 11 dxe5 dxe5 12 a4 ♛c7 13 ♛c2 ⌞c6 14 ⌞d3 b5 with a very comfortable game for Black.

7	...	cxd4
8	⌞xd4	⌞b7
9	⌞c3	e6
10	g4!?	

This looks crazy, but in my view shows good understanding of the position. White has appreciated that with quiet play he may well drift into a bad position, as so often happens in the Open Sicilian, of which this is

not a particularly good version for White. In fact some people have claimed, only half tongue in cheek, that 3 d4 is a decisive positional error. I certainly don't belong to that group, but it does demand great energy to play the Open Sicilian successfully which is probably why we so often find ourselves facing the variations in this book.

10	...	h6
11	⌞g2	♛c7

I'm not convinced by Black's plan of castling long. I would be very tempted to play 11...g5!? here, in order to highlight the drawbacks of White's play. Black could follow up with ...⌞e5 and decide later, when he has a clearer picture of the situation, what to do with his king, if anything.

12	f4	0-0-0
13	a4	♚b8
14	a5	b5
15	⌞e3	b4 *(D)*

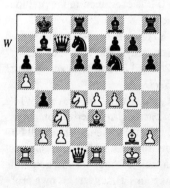

| 16 | ⌞cb5! | axb5 |

17	♘xb5	♛c6
18	♘a7	♛c7
19	a6	♗xe4
20	♘b5	♛c6
21	♘d4	♛c7
22	♘b5	♛c6
23	♘d4	½-½

Black could consider playing on with 23...♛d5, but I have a feeling that White was trying to lure his opponent into continuing the battle (instead of 19 a6 he could simply have repeated). After 24 c4 bxc3 25 ♗xe4 ♘xe4 26 bxc3 ♘dc5 27 c4 Black has an extremely exposed queenside.

Game 35
S.Clarke – Gallagher
Hastings 1993

1	e4	c5
2	♘f3	d6
3	♗b5+	♘d7
4	d4	♘f6
5	♘c3	

5 0-0 is examined in the previous game.

5 e5 gives rise to a virtually forced sequence: 5...♛a5+ 6 ♘c3 ♘e4 7 ♗d2 ♘xc3 8 ♗xd7+ ♗xd7 9 ♗xc3 ♛a6! *(D)*

It is essential to prevent White from castling in order to contain his lead in development. White will find it very difficult to launch a successful attack without the participation of his rooks. Black has his own problems in getting his kingside out and

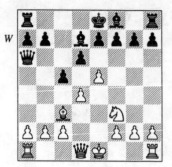

although he possesses the bishop pair this can hardly be counted as an asset in the middlegame. He will not be without counterplay, however, while White's king remains in the middle of the board. White now has:

a) 10 d5 with the following examples:

a1) 10...♗f5 11 ♘h4 ♗d7 12 e6 fxe6 13 ♛h5+ ♔d8 14 0-0-0? ♛xa2 15 b3 c4 16 b4 ♗a4 17 ♛e2 g6 with a clear advantage for Black in Dobosz-Georgiev, Varna 1979. 14 0-0-0 looks like madness; 14 dxe6 would offer White some play for his pawn.

a2) 10...♗g4 11 h3 ♗h5 12 exd6 exd6 13 g4 (the ending after 13 ♛e2+ ♛xe2+ 14 ♔xe2 f6 is fine for Black, whose bishop pair may eventually begin to tell) 13...♗g6 14 ♘h4 ♔d7 (Ftačnik probably didn't want to give White the chance of reaching an ending after 14...0-0-0 15 ♘xg6 hxg6 16 ♛e2 ♛xe2+ 17 ♔xe2, although I believe he can maintain the balance with 17...♖h7!;

Nunn's suggestion 16...♕a4!? also deserves attention). Dobosz now chose the strange 15 ♘f5 and Black gained the upper hand after 15...♗xf5 16 gxf5 ♖e8+ 17 ♔d2 ♕c4 18 ♕f3 ♖e4. Polugaevsky in *ECO* suggests that 15 ♘xg6 hxg6 16 ♕f3 gives White a clear advantage, but Razuvaev has shown this assessment to be incorrect. Black can obtain very good attacking chances with 16...♖e8+ 17 ♔d2 ♗e7! as 18 ♗xg7 loses to 18...♗g5+ 19 ♔d1 ♖xh3!.

b) 10 ♕d2 (White completes his development rather than trying to blast his way through the middle) 10...0-0-0 11 a3 ♗c6 12 ♕e3 dxe5 (12...cxd4!?) 13 dxe5 and now in O'Donnell-Tukmakov, Toronto 1990 Black headed straight for the endgame with 13...♕c4 14 ♖d1 ♕e4. More ambitious would have been 13...e6 when there is no need to fear 14 ♘g5, because of 14...♖d7 15 ♖d1 ♖xd1 16 ♔xd1 ♗xg2 17 ♖g1 ♕c6.

5 ... a6

Black has a solid alternative in 5...cxd4 6 ♕xd4 e5 (other moves allow White to free a hand in the centre) 7 ♕d3 h6 but White should be able to gain a slight advantage with 8 ♗e3!. The game Chandler-Mestel, Brighton 1984 now continued 8...♗e7 9 ♗c4 0-0 10 0-0 ♘b6 11 ♗b3 ♗e6 12 ♘h4 ♖c8 (12...♕d7 13 ♗xe6 fxe6 14 ♘g6 was also slightly better for White in Kupreichik-

Polugaevsky, USSR 1976) 13 ♘g6! ♖e8 14 ♖fd1 ♘c4 15 ♗xc4 ♖xc4 16 ♘xe7+ ♖xe7 17 ♕xd6 ♕xd6 18 ♖xd6 ♘xe4 19 ♘xe4 ♖xe4 20 b3 a6 21 c4 and Black's rook finds itself in an embarrassing position.

6 ♗xd7+ ♘xd7

6...♗xd7 7 dxc5 favours White.

7 ♗e3

7 0-0 is the next game.

7 ♗g5 has been tried a few times, e.g. 7...h6 8 ♗h4 (this only encourages Black to develop his kingside. 8 ♗e3!? is safer although I don't know what White has gained by forcing ...h6. The game A.Ivanov-Spraggett, Roses 1992 continued 8...e6 9 dxc5 dxc5 10 a4 ♗e7 11 a5 b5 12 axb6 ♕xb6 13 ♘a4 ♕c7 14 0-0 0-0 15 ♘d2 and a draw was agreed in a position where Black is certainly not worse. His strong bishop pair fully compensates for his inferior pawn structure) 8...g5 9 ♗g3 ♗g7 10 0-0 g4 11 ♘h4 cxd4 12 ♘f5 dxc3! 13 ♘xg7+ ♔f8 14 ♘f5 cxb2 15 ♖b1 ♘f6 with advantage to Black; Dvoretsky-Ljubojević, Wijk aan Zee 1976.

7 ... cxd4

This capture is quite risky but I can't see a way for White to exploit his lead in development. During the game I felt that it would be bad to allow dxc5, but having now seen the game Ivanov-Spraggett (previous note) I'm no longer so sure.

8 ♕xd4 e6 (D)

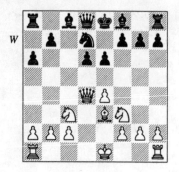

At first glance this position looks terrible for Black who is miles behind in development, but the fact is that it will be almost impossible for White to pierce Black's position without the assistance of pawns. If White could get in a quick f4-f5 or e4-e5 Black would indeed be in trouble, but White is in no position to carry out either of these breaks before Black is ready to meet them. To complete his development, Black first has to play ...♕c7 in order to bolster e5 so that he can follow up with ...♘e5, which in turn enables Black to develop his king's bishop. White often captures on e5 but Black then gains control of a large number of central squares.

9 0-0

At the board I was anxious about 9 0-0-0 ♕c7 10 ♗f4 as I couldn't work out the consequences of 10...e5 11 ♘d5 ♕c6 12 ♗xe5 dxe5 13 ♘xe5, but I calmed down when I realized that 9...♕a5 also allows Black to carry out his planned ...♘e5.

9 ...   ♕c7

I believe Black has equal chances in this position.

    10 ♖fd1   ♘e5
    11 ♘xe5   dxe5 (D)

Despite the fact that he has doubled pawns and White has a three *vs* two queenside majority, Black's pawn structure is favourable (at least while there are pieces on the board). His control of the centre severely restricts White's pieces and with a later ...f5 he may well be able to create a passed pawn in the centre.

12 ♕b6?!

The game Antonio-Gallagher, Biel 1991 also reached this position, but through a different move order (7 0-0 cxd4 8 ♕xd4 e6 9 ♗e3 etc). Play continued 12 ♕a4+ ♗d7 13 ♕b3 ♗e7 14 ♖d2 (or 14 ♘a4 ♗xa4 15 ♕xa4 b5 with equality) 14...0-0 15 ♖ad1 ♗e8 (15...♗c6 looks more natural but I wanted to keep this square free for my queen) 16 ♘a4 b5 17 ♘b6 ♖d8 18 ♖xd8 ♗xd8 19 c4

♗c6 20 f3 ♗e7 with an unclear game.

12	...	♛xb6
13	♗xb6	♗d7
14	♖d3	♗c6
15	♖ad1	

White's position still gives the illusion of being active but in reality there is little for him to do.

15	...	♗e7
16	♗c7	f6
17	♗d6	♖d8!
18	♗xe7	♖xd3
19	♖xd3	♚xe7

White has deprived Black of the bishop pair but has also allowed the exchange of one rook, which favours Black. In the ensuing ending White has no choice but to remain passive, whilst Black can advance on either side of the board, probing for weaknesses. With accurate defence White should be able to hold the draw, but there lies an unpleasant period ahead for him.

20	f3	g5!
21	♚f2	h5
22	♘d1	

I believe my opponent was trying to lure me into playing ...f5, but he overlooked something simple.

| 22 | ... | f5 (D) |
| 23 | exf5? | |

This is a horrible move. White had to return the knight to c3 after which nothing would have been lost (after all, he's only marking time). In that case Black would probably have

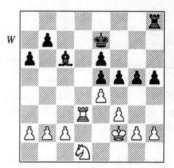

continued with 23...g4, not fearing 24 exf5 exf5 25 ♘d5+ ♚f7. However kingside play on its own will not be enough, so Black would have to try to stretch White's defences by opening some lines on the queenside at some point.

23	...	exf5
24	♘e3	♚e6
25	♖d2	

The explanation for the last few moves is that White intended 25 ♘c4 here, missing 25...♗b5.

| 25 | ... | b5 |

As ♘c4 was now threatened, Black takes a time out before continuing his kingside offensive.

| 26 | c3 | g4 |

26...f4 was also possible.

| 27 | ♘c2 | a5 |
| 28 | f4!? | |

White ensures that his knight will have at least one secure square on the board, but the cost of opening up the long diagonal is very high.

| 28 | ... | ♗e4 |
| 29 | fxe5 | ♚xe5 |

30	♘a3	♖b8
31	♘c2	h4
32	♘e1	f4
33	♘d3+	♔f5
34	♘c5	g3+

Now White will have the additional worry of getting mated on the back rank. He will also have to make sure that his knight doesn't stray too far from the kingside as Black will then be able to win by sacrificing his bishop on g2.

35	hxg3	hxg3+
36	♔g1	♗c6
37	♘b3	♔g4! *(D)*

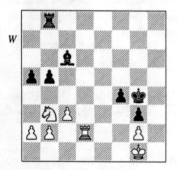

38   ♘d4

Here is a fine example of the previous note: 38 ♘xa5 ♖e8 39 ♔f1 ♗xg2+!? 40 ♖xg2 (40 ♔xg2 ♖e2+!! 41 ♖xe2 f3+ 42 ♔f1 fxe2+ 43 ♔xe2 ♔h3 and the pawn queens) 40...f3 41 ♖d2 g2+ (41...♔h3 42 ♖d7 ♖h8 43 ♔g1) 42 ♖xg2+ fxg2+ 43 ♔xg2 ♖e2+ 44 ♔f1 ♖xb2 and Black wins.

38	...	♗d5
39	a3	

39 b3 a4!.

39	...	♗c4!
40	b3	♖e8

The point of Black's last move is revealed; White is unable to oppose on the e-file and is forced back even further.

41	♖d1	♗d5
42	♖c1	a4!
43	bxa4	bxa4

Black's queenside play has borne fruit. A weak pawn on a3 has appeared and with the b-file open it will be impossible for White to prevent Black from penetrating.

44   ♘c2?

This rather accelerates matters.

44	...	♖e2
45	♘e1	♗xg2!
46	♘xg2	f3
47	♘e1	♖xe1+!
48	♖xe1	f2+
49	♔f1	♔f3! *(D)*

0-1

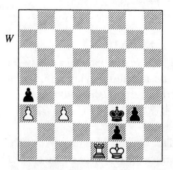

I must admit that I didn't think much of this game until afterwards in the bar where grandmasters Mestel and Speelman expressed their admiration. It is true that it's quite rare these days to play an endgame which flows so nicely from start to finish.

Game 36
Ljubojević – Kasparov
Amsterdam 1991

1	e4	c5
2	♘f3	d6
3	♗b5+	♘d7
4	d4	♘gf6
5	0-0	a6
6	♗xd7+	♘xd7
7	♘c3 (D)	

7 ...   e6

I have experimented with 7...cxd4 on a number of occasions as I prefer my knight to stay on course for e5 rather than being diverted to c5 in the event of White exchanging pawns. One example was the game against Antonio, given in the notes

to the previous game. Another was Belkhodja-Gallagher, Antony 1992 which continued 8 ♕xd4 e6 9 ♗g5 ♕c7 10 ♖ad1 (10 ♖e1 transposes to the main game) 10...f6 (obviously not 10...♘e5?? 11 ♘xe5 dxe5 12 ♕d8+. 10...f6 looks ugly but it supports the e5 square and gives the king the useful option of moving to f7) 11 ♗c1 ♗e7 (11...♘e5 at once looks better) 12 ♕e3 ♘e5 13 ♘d4 ♘c6 14 ♕g3 0-0 15 ♗f4 ♖d8 16 ♗e3 b5 17 a3 ♖b8 18 f4 ♘xd4 19 ♗xd4 a5 with a good game for Black.

8 ♗g5

8 dxc5 ♘xc5 is what I was trying to avoid in the previous note but this is really just a matter of taste, as the positions which arise are quite playable for Black:

a) 9 ♗g5 ♕c7 (9...♕b6 10 ♖b1 ♗d7 11 b4 ♘a4 12 ♘xa4 {12 ♘d5!? has been suggested} 12...♗xa4 13 ♕d3 h6 14 ♗e3 ♕c7 15 c4 ♗e7 was unclear in Keres-Ljubojević, Petropolis 1973. Ljubojević was the main champion of this line for Black in the seventies, so it's interesting to see him playing White against Kasparov in the nineties) 10 ♖e1 f6 (Black needs a bolt-hole for his king in the event of ♘d5) 11 ♗h4!? (11 ♗d2 had occurred before, after which Black should play 11...♗e7) 11...b5 (11...♗e7 is more solid) 12 ♘d4 b4 13 ♘d5! exd5 14 ♕h5+ ♕f7 15 exd5+ ♗e7 16 ♕e2 0-0!? (it would have been too nerve-racking to try to hold on to the piece) 17 ♕xe7 ♕xd5 18 ♖ad1 ♗b7 19 ❹f3 ♕xa2 with a very unclear position in Ricardi-Gallagher, Benidorm 1991. To add to the chaos both players had hardly any time till move 40. The game continued 20 ♗g3! ♖f7 21 ♕xd6 ♖c8 22 ♖e7 ♕xb2 (D) (greedy)

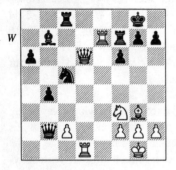

23 ❹e5! ❹e4 (White's evil idea was 23...fxe5? 24 ♗xe5 ♕xc2 25 ♕d8+! ♖xd8 26 ♖xd8+ ♖f8 27 ♖xg7+. As the move chosen also loses I should have tried 23...♖xe7 24 ♕xe7 ♗d5) 24 ♕e6? (24 ♕d7! wins as 24...♖xe7 loses to 25 ♕xc8+!) 24...❹g5! 25 ♕xc8+ ♗xc8 26 ❹xf7 ❹e6 27 ❹d6 ♕xc2 28 ♖e1 h6 (no more explanations until the time control has passed) 29 ♖e8+ ♔h7 30 ♖xc8 ♕d2 31 ♖cc1 b3 32 ♖cd1 ♕c2 33 ♖c1 ♕d2 34 ❹c4 ♕d5 35 h4 a5 36 ♖ed1 ❹d4 37 ♔h2 a4 38 ♗f4 ♕e4 39 ♗g3 ❹c2 40 ❹d6 ♕b4 41 ❹f5 ♔g6 42 ♖d5 b2 43 h5+ ♔h7 44 ♖xc2 b1♕ 45 ♖c7 ♕f8 (it was

only here that we stopped blitzing, neither player having a clue how many moves had been played) 46 ♗d6! ♕xf5 47 ♖xg7+! ♕xg7 48 ♖xf5 ♕g4 49 ♖f3 ♕xh5+ 50 ♔g1 and White has an unbreakable fortress, although I continued in vain for another couple of hours (there were one or two tricks). It was after this hair-raising experience that I began to contemplate 7...cxd4.

b) 9 ♗f4 (it's quite logical to pressurize d6 now that the knight is far from e5, but Black still has sufficient resources) 9...♕c7 10 ♕d2 b5! 11 b4!? ❹d7 12 ♖fd1 ♗b7 13 ♗xd6 ♗xd6 14 ♕xd6 ♖c8! 15 ♕d4 ❹f6 16 ♖d3 0-0 and White's extra pawn counted for little in Rechlis-Mestel, Beersheba 1988.

8	...	♕c7
9	♖e1	

9 dxc5 ❹xc5 transposes to Ricardi-Gallagher from the previous note.

9	...	cxd4
10	♕xd4	❹e5! (D)

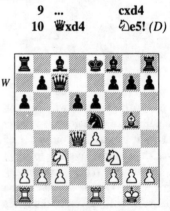

Once the knight arrives here Black can usually breathe a sigh of relief as nothing terrible is likely to happen to him any more.

11 ♖ad1   ♗d7

11...♘xf3+ looks tempting, but after 12 gxf3 f6 13 ♗f4 e5 14 ♘d5 ♕c6 15 ♕b6 ♕xb6 16 ♘xb6 ♖b8 17 ♗e3 White has a slightly better ending.

12 ♘xe5

Did Ljubojević wait with baited breath for 17 years to play this novelty? I doubt it. The game Gufeld-Ljubojević, Belgrade 1974 went instead 12 ♗f4 f6 13 ♘d2 ♗e7 14 ♗g3 g5 15 f3 b5 16 ♔h1 ♕a7 17 ♘e2 ♕xd4 18 ♘xd4 ♔f7 with a slight advantage for Black.

12 ...   dxe5
13 ♕d2   b5!?

Whilst this move is not a mistake, I would certainly be looking at ways to develop my kingside. 13...f6, 13...♗c5 and 13...♗b4 all come into consideration whilst Kasparov proposes 13...♖c8. The problem with the inclusion of ...b5 and a3, which one would normally expect to favour Black, is that in some lines White has the chance to activate his miserable knight via the a2 square.

14 a3   ♖c8?!

In *Informator* Kasparov criticized this move, giving instead 14...f6 15 ♗e3 ♗e7 16 ♗b6 ♕xb6 17 ♕xd7+ ♔f7 with equality. (I prefer Black but he's the World Champion).

15 ♖e3?!

Here Ljubojević misses his first chance. After 15 ♘a2! f6 16 ♗e3 ♗e7 17 ♘b4 ♖a8 18 f3 Kasparov considers White to be slightly better.

15 ...   f6
16 ♖d3   ♗c6
17 ♗e3   ♔f7?!

According to Kasparov, another inaccuracy. Black should have started his queenside play at once with 17...a5!.

18 f3   a5
19 ♕f2?!

The difference is now that the e-pawn is defended, White has another chance to play 19 ♘a2!. This holds up Black's queenside play and after a continuation like 19...♗e7 20 ♕f2 Black might begin to regret having advanced his pawns.

19 ...   b4
20 axb4   axb4 (D)

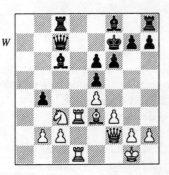

21 ♘a2?

Finally Ljubojević plays his knight to a2, but this time it's a mistake.

Very interesting play would have arisen from 21 ♗b6! ♕b7 22 ♖a1 bxc3! 23 ♖a7 ♕xa7 24 ♗xa7 cxb2 25 ♖b3 ♗a3! (Kasparov).

21 ...   ♗b5
22 ♖3d2   ♖a8
23 ♘c1   ♗e7
24 ♗b6

Black already stands very well, but this is a pretty pointless move.

24 ...   ♕c6
25 ♘b3   ♖hc8
26 ♗e3

Of course 26 ♘a5 loses to 26...♖xa5.

26 ...   g5?

Kasparov makes life difficult for himself. It would have been better to play 26...♔g8 followed by ...f5.

27 g4!

White's best chance lies in sealing up the kingside and trying to prevent Black from entering on the queen-side.

27 ...   h5
28 h3   ♔g6
29 ♔g2   h4!

This ensures that if the position ever opens up the white king will be in for a torrid time.

30 ♕g1   ♖a2
31 ♖b1   ♗c4
32 ♘c1   ♖aa8
33 ♘b3   ♖d8
34 ♖bd1   ♖xd2+
35 ♖xd2   ♖a2
36 ♕b1   ♕a4 (D)
37 ♗c5?

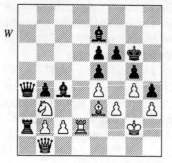

A time trouble blunder. White had to remain passive. Kasparov gives 37 ♕c1 ♔f7 38 ♗f2 ♕c6 39 ♕b1 ♖a8 with just a slight advantage to Black. It's very hard to break into White's fortress. ...f5 will probably have to be played at some moment although this may entail some risk.

37 ...   ♗xc5
38 ♘xc5   ♕a7!
39 b3

39 ♘b3 ♗xb3 40 cxb3 ♖a1 41 ♖d7 ♕a6! (stronger than Kasparov's 41...♖xb1) 42 ♕d3 ♕b6 doesn't save White and neither does 39 ♕g1 ♖a1 40 ♕e3 ♕a2 when Black gets in round the back.

39 ...   ♖a1
40 bxc4

Was this Ljubojević's way of re-signing? 40 ♕xa1 ♕xa1 41 bxc4 would have prolonged the game but after 41...♕c3 42 ♖f2 ♕xc4 43 ♘b3 f5! White is soon going to find out how weak g3 really is.

40 ...   ♖xb1

0-1

8 1 e4 c5 2 ♘f3 d6 3 c3

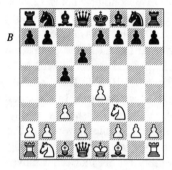

B

The main difference between this version of the c3 Sicilian and the lines studied in Chapter 3 is that in answer to ...♘f6 White doesn't have the possibility of playing e5. Play is therefore of quite a different nature. White has two main ways of playing after 3...♘f6: 4 ♗e2 is featured in Games 37 and 38, whilst in Game 39 White plays the manoeuvre ♗d3-c2, with or without h3.

Game 37
Hodgson – Suba
Blackpool Z 1990

1	e4	c5
2	♘f3	d6
3	c3	♘f6!

This makes it difficult for White to carry out his planned d4. If he is reduced to playing d3 his position could become quite passive.

4 ♗e2

As the e-pawn is not really *en prise* (4...♘xe4 5 ♕a4+ and Black will have to take himself off for an early bath) this looks more natural than ♗d3, which along with other 4th move alternatives can be seen in Game 39.

4 ... ♘c6 (D)

W

Suba is a principled man and he no doubt wanted to encourage White to part company with a central pawn. Of course it's very unlikely that Mr Hodgson would need any

encouragement to sacrifice a pawn
or two. He is not noted for his timid-
ity in this area of the game. I imagine
most of you will prefer the more
solid approach of Game 38.

5 d4   cxd4

The e-pawn cannot be taken at
once: 5...♘xe4 6 d5 and there is no
saving check at a5.

6 cxd4   ♘xe4
7 d5   ♕a5+
8 ♘c3   ♘xc3

ECO gives 8...♘e5 9 ♘xe5 dxe5
10 0-0 (Palatnik-Ljubojević, Belgrade 1974) 10...♘xc3 11 bxc3 e6 12
♗f3 exd5 13 ♗xd5 ♗c5 14 ♖e1 0-0
15 ♖xe5 ♗e6 as equal (Palatnik).
However instead of 10 0-0, White
can play 10 ♗b5+ ♔d8 11 ♕b3.

9 bxc3   ♘d8

9...♘e5 led to a famous victory
for White in the game Basman-
Stean, Hastings 1973/74: 10 ♘xe5
♕xc3+ 11 ♗d2 ♕xe5 12 0-0 *(D)*

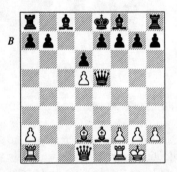

12...♕xd5 13 ♖b1 e6 14 ♗b5+
♗d7 15 ♗xd7+ ♔xd7 16 ♕a4+

♔d8 17 ♖b5 ♕c6 18 ♖c1 ♕a6 19
♖a5 ♕d3 20 ♗e3 d5 21 ♖xa7 ♖xa7
22 ♕xa7 ♗a3 23 ♕b8+ ♔e7 24
♗g5+ f6 25 ♕xb7+ ♔d6 26 ♕c7#
(1-0).

Recently several attempts have
been made to improve upon Black's
play, the most notable being 12...a6,
as in Nikolenko-Obukhov, Smol-
ensk 1991 which was agreed drawn
after 13 ♖b1 g6 14 ♖c1 ♗g7 15 ♗c3
♕xc3 16 ♖xc3 ♗xc3 17 ♕c2 ♗f6
18 ♗xa6 0-0 19 ♗d3 ♖a3 ½-½, although I prefer Black in the final
position. White's bishop is a truly
awful piece. White, however, either
missed or rejected a very interesting
possibility on his fourteenth move,
namely 14 ♖xb7. Now 14...♗xb7 allows mate in three: 15 ♕a4+, 16
♗a5+ and 17 ♕e8#. So Black's only
move is 14...♗g7 after which White
has to prevent castling with 15 ♕a4+
♔f8 16 ♖c7!. Now 16...♕xe2 loses
to 17 ♕c6 ♗b7 18 ♕xb7 ♖e8 19
♖c8 ♕b5 20 ♖xe8+ ♕xe8 21 ♖c1 so
Black has to play 16...♗f5 where-
upon 17 ♕c6 ♖d8 18 ♗xa6, with the
threat of ♖e1, looks good for White,
but the game is clearly more of a
fight than Basman-Stean.

10 0-0   e5

Of course the c-pawn can't be
touched on account of ♗b5+.

11 dxe6   ♘xe6
12 ♘d4   ♗e7

Hodgson gives the following variation in *Informator*: 12...♘xd4 13

♕xd4 ♕e5 14 ♖e1! ♕xd4 15 ♗b5+
♔d8 16 ♖e8+ ♔c7 17 cxd4 ±.

13 ♗b5+

The black king just fails to make
it to safety.

13	...	♔f8
14	♖b1	a6
15	♗c4	♕c7
16	♗xe6	fxe6
17	♖e1	e5
18	♕f3+	♗f6 (D)

Better was 18...♔e8 but after 19
♘f5 ♗xf5 20 ♕xf5 White still has a
dangerous attack.

19 ♗a3!!

White wastes no time in high-
lighting the drawback of Black's last
move – the weakening of d6 – and
finds a quite brilliant combination.

19 ... exd4

Black accepts the offer as he understandably wasn't attracted to the
position after 19...♔g8 20 ♘c2
when the knight is within hopping
distance of the killer square d5 and
Black is also struggling to complete

(or should I say begin) his development.

20	♕d5	♗e7
21	♖xe7!	♔xe7
22	♖e1+	♔f6

22...♔d7 23 ♖e6 and 22...♔d8 23
♗xd6 are not better.

23	♗xd6	♕d7
24	♖e5!	

The net is closing.

24	...	♖e8

Hodgson planned to meet 24...h6
with 25 h4.

25	♕f3+	♔g6
26	♕h5+	♔f6
27	♕f3+	♔g6
28	♕h5+	♔f6
29	♖xe8!	♕xd6
30	cxd4! (D)	

Black is virtually in zugzwang.
The queen has to stay defending both
e5 and f8 whilst ...♗g4 fails to
♕e5+.

30	...	h6
31	h4	a5
32	♕f3+	♔g6

33	h5+	♚g5

33...♚h7 34 ♕f7.

34	♖e5+	♕xe5
35	dxe5	♗e6
36	♕xb7	♖g8
37	♕e7+	♚f5
38	g4+	♚xe5
39	f4+	♚xf4
40	♕xe6	♖d8
41	♕f7+	1-0

Game 38
Torre – Ftačnik
Biel 1988

1	e4	c5
2	♘f3	d6
3	c3	♘f6
4	♗e2	♘bd7!? *(D)*

The text has certain advantages over the normal 4...g6. Firstly White is forced to defend his e-pawn at once, secondly the line with 6 ♗b5+, which can often be very drawish, is avoided. Another point is that as the move is still quite unusual, your opponent might have to think for himself at an earlier stage than he's used to.

However 4...g6 is also a good move, so we shall also examine it in some detail. After 5 0-0 ♗g7 White has:

a) 6 ♗b5+!? *(D)*

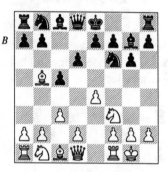

This original move is a speciality of the Filipino grandmaster Torre. Basically White wants to play d4, but if he continues in normal fashion with 6 ♖e1 this will be almost impossible to carry out (see 'b' below). The check on b5 helps him to implement this advance as each of Black's replies lessens the pressure on d4: 6...♘c6 allows 7 d4 due to the threat of d5; 6...♗d7 allows an exchange of bishops, thereby denying Black the possibility of ...♗g4, and 6...♘bd7 doesn't hinder d4 at all. Nevertheless, even if White manages to play d4 Black should still be able to equalize quite easily. After all, to play ♗e2 and then ♗b5 is an incredible luxury to take in the opening. I believe that I became the first victim of this line in the game Torre-Gallagher, St John 1988. I was so taken aback by this check that I conducted the rest of the game in a very miserable manner. Firstly, I chose 6...♘c6, the weakest of the three plausible ways to escape the check. Play then continued 7 d4 cxd4 8 cxd4 0-0 9 ♘c3 ♗g4 10 ♗e3 ♘d7 11 ♗e2 e5 12 d5 ♗xf3 13 dxc6! ♗xe2 14 ♘xe2 ♘f6 15 cxb7 ♖b8 16 ♘c3 with a clear advantage to White. I soon blundered the exchange and then left a piece *en prise* in time trouble, but you've seen enough. Black's other two moves should offer about equal chances, e.g. 6...♗d7 7 ♗xd7+ ♘bxd7 8 ♖e1 0-0 9 d4 cxd4 (9...e5) 10 cxd4 e5 11 ♘c3 h6 12 h3 ♖e8 13 ♗e3?! d5! 14 exd5 e4 15 ♘d2 ♘b6 with good play for Black in Preismann-Gallagher, Geneva 1989. The problem, if you're playing for a win, is that White could have exchanged on e5 on several occasions, leaving a very dull position; 6...♘bd7 7 ♖e1 a6 8 ♗f1 0-0 9 d4 e5 10 dxe5 ♘xe5 11 ♗g5 ♕b6 12 ♘xe5 dxe5 13 ♕c2 ♗e6 14 ♘d2 h6 15 ♗h4 (Kengis-Lukin, Groningen 1991) and now 15...♕c6 is about level.

b) 6 ♖e1 0-0 7 ♗f1 ♘c6. White will find it very difficult to achieve d4 under favourable circumstances (8 d4?! cxd4 9 cxd4 ♗g4). He has several options in this position, the following two are the most common:

b1) 8 a3 e5 9 d3 d5 10 ♘bd2 d4 (why release the tension? 10...♖e8 looks perfectly OK) 11 cxd4 cxd4 12 b4 ♘e8 13 ♘b3 ♘d6 and a draw was agreed in Torre-Wang Zili, Shenzen 1992.

b2) 8 h3 e5 9 d3 a6 (9...h6!?, to prevent ♗g5, is quite a good move. My experience is that White's queen's bishop and queen's knight are often reduced to waging a private battle for the e3 square) 10 ♘a3 ♖e8 11 ♗g5 h6 12 ♗h4 ♗e6 13 ♘c4 b5 14 ♘e3. This type of position is quite typical of this line. Black stands very comfortably as he has an advantage in space. 14...♕d7 15 ♘d2 ♘e7 16 a4 ♘h5 17 ♕f3 ♘f4 18 ♗xe7 ♕xe7 19 ♔h2 ♕b7 20 g3 ♘h5 21 ♗g2 ♘f6 22 ♖eb1 h5 23 b4 ♕c7 24 c4 cxb4 25 ♖xb4 ½-½ Yudasin-Khalifman, Leningrad 1989.

5   d3

5 ♕c2 is not better than the text, as after 5...♕c7 White will be unable to play d4 because of the pin on the c-file.

5   ...   b6

Black's position is not under any pressure so he has the time to post his bishops as actively as possible; this means on the long diagonals.

5...c4 is a disruptive move which also deserves attention. After 6 d4 ♘xe4 7 ♗xc4 e6 8 0-0 ♗e7 the game is about equal.

6	0-0	♗b7
7	♘bd2	g6
8	♖e1	♗g7
9	♗f1 *(D)*	

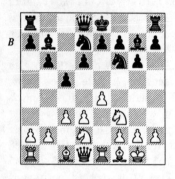

9 ...   ♘e5!

Ftačnik grasped the subtleties of this position at the second attempt. In a previous game he had played 9...0-0 but after 10 d4 White obtained a slight advantage. The secret is to exchange off a pair of knights as Black's position feels considerably more comfortable with fewer minor pieces.

10 d4

10 ♘xe5 dxe5 gives Black a firm grip in the centre.

10	...	♘xf3+
11	♕xf3	0-0
12	♗d3	♘d7!

Black starts to enjoy the benefits of his accurate ninth move. He is able to clear the diagonal for his bishop without having to put this knight on an inferior square.

13 ♘b3 *(D)*

Not a good place for the knight, but the only way to hold the centre.

13 ...   d5!

Excellent play. Now 14 exd5 cxd4 15 cxd4 (15 ♘xd4 ♘e5) 15...♘f6 is good for Black, so the threat of ...c4 forces White into:

14 dxc5   bxc5

14...♘e5 15 ♕e2 ♘xd3 16 ♕xd3 dxe4 is less clear.

15	exd5	♘e5
16	♕e2	♕xd5
17	♗e4	♕xe4
18	♕xe4	♗xe4
19	♖xe4	f5
20	♖e2	♘d3

Although Black's pawn structure is less than perfect, his active pieces guarantee him a good game. If White now plays 21 ♖xe7 there follows 21...♖fe8 22 ♖xe8+ ♖xe8 23 ♗e3 c4! with advantage to Black.

21	♘a5	e5
22	f3	e4

Black employs a little tactical trick to obtain a passed e-pawn.

22...♖ab8 23 ♘c4 would not be too
bad for White.

23	fxe4	♖ae8
24	♘c4	♖xe4
25	♖xe4	fxe4
26	♗e3 *(D)*	

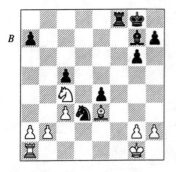

26 ...   ♘xb2!?

Black wins a pawn, but has no
winning chances due to the weakness of his own pawns. 26...♖b8!?,
threatening 27...♘xb2 28 ♖b1 ♗xc3
29 ♗c1 (29 ♗xc5 ♖c8) 29...♖b4! 30
♘xb2 ♗d4+ 31 ♔f1 c4 winning,
would have forced White to find the
active defence 27 ♖d1!, after which I
can't see how Black can improve his
position; 27...♘xb2 28 ♘xb2 ♖xb2
29 ♖d8+ ♔f7 30 ♖d7+ ♔g8 is a
draw and 27...♔f7 allows ♘d6+,
whilst 27...♔f8 28 ♘d2! shows that
Black's king cannot make his jour-
ney to the centre via the dark
squares. There's not much point in
considering 27...h5 as a prelude to
...♘xb2, as the white rook will always be too active in these lines.

27	♘xb2	♗xc3
28	♖c1	

28 ♖b1 ♖b8 29 ♗c1 ♗d4+ 30
♔f1 c4 wins.

28	...	♗xb2
29	♖xc5	♖d8

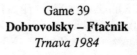

30 ♖c4 wins back the pawn.

Although Black was unable to
convert his initiative into victory, it's
most enjoyable to be pressing right
from the word go with the black
pieces.

Game 39
Dobrovolsky – Ftačnik
Trnava 1984

1	e4	c5
2	♘f3	d6
3	c3	♘f6
4	h3 *(D)*	

What's this? Is one really allowed
to play such moves so early in the
game? It's all part and parcel of

White's super-sophisticated strategy. The plan is to bring his bishop to c2 via d3 in order to bolster the defences of e4, thereby enabling White to carry out d4 with greater ease than in the 4 ♗e2 line. Experience has proved that if White tries to do without the precautionary h3, Black can achieve a comfortable game with ...♗g4. Nevertheless 4 ♗d3 is still seen just as often as the text, so let's take a look at some examples: 4 ♗d3 ♗g4 (4...♘c6 5 h3 transposes to the main game) and now White has two main approaches:

a) 5 h3 ♗xf3 6 ♕xf3 (Black has sacrificed the bishop pair for a noble cause – control of d4 {White's knight was a more important player in this battle than Black's bishop}. An added bonus is that White's queen is now misplaced on f3) 6...♘c6 7 ♗c2 g6 8 0-0 ♗g7 9 ♕e2 0-0 10 d3 (10 a4 a6 11 ♘a3 ♖b8 and White won't be able to hold up Black's queenside advance for long) 10...b5! (it's time to soften up the long diagonal for the lurking bishop) 11 ♗e3 ♘d7 12 ♖d1 b4 13 ♗a4 ♖c8 14 d4 (it's too late for this to trouble Black) 14...bxc3 15 bxc3 ♕a5 16 ♗b3 (inconsistent, but after 16 ♗xc6 ♖xc6 Black can prepare an invasion on the b-file) 16...cxd4 17 cxd4 ♕b4 18 ♕b2 (ugly, but 18 ♕d2 ♕xd2 19 ♖xd2 ♘c5 20 f3 ♘a5! is extremely unpleasant) 18...♖b8 19 ♘a3 ♘c5! 20 ♘c2 ♕b7 21 ♖ab1 ♘a5 22 ♕a3

♘cxb3 23 axb3 ♕xe4! 24 ♘b4 ♖b5 25 ♘a2 ♘c4! 26 ♕c1 ♘xe3 27 ♘c3 (White finds the path of least resistance, as Tal once commented on a similar finish) 27...♕xg2# (0-1) Jokšić–Har-Zvi, Biel 1992. A model game.

b) 5 ♗c2 *(D)*.

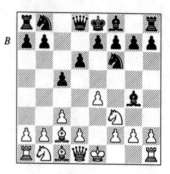

This time the plan is to play d3 and ♘bd2 before putting the question to the bishop. If White can answer ♘xf3 to ...♗xf3, his position would be very satisfactory. Of course Black could take unprovoked on f3, but a plan involving ...e6 and ...d5 has proved quite successful against White's set-up, e.g. 5...♘c6 6 d3 e6 7 ♘bd2 d5 (White has already relinquished all the advantage of moving first) 8 ♕e2 (or 8 ♗a4 ♕c7 9 ♕e2 ♗e7 10 h3 ♗h5 11 ♘f1 0-0 12 ♘g3 ♗g6 13 ♗xc6 bxc6 14 ♘h4 ♗d6 15 ♘xg6 fxg6 16 0-0 ♗xg3 17 fxg3 dxe4 18 dxe4 ♘h5! with a clear advantage for Black in Ničevski-Magerramov, Cheliabinsk 1992;

8 0-0!?) 8...♗e7 9 h3 ♗h5 10 ♘f1 c4!? (10...♕a5 is a sounder alternative, e.g. 11 g4 ♗g6 12 ♘3d2 ♕c7 13 ♘g3 h5 14 g5 ♘d7 15 h4 0-0-0 with a good game for Black; Bisguier-Panno, Gothenburg 1955) 11 ♘g3? (11 dxc4 is a more critical test of Black's play. A possible continuation is 11...dxe4 12 ♗xe4 ♘xe4 13 ♕xe4 ♗g6 {13...♗xf3!?} 14 ♕e3 ♗d3 with compensation for the pawn) 11...♗xf3 12 gxf3 cxd3 13 ♗xd3 ♕c7 14 f4 dxe4 15 ♘xe4 ♘d5 with a clear advantage to Black in Martinović-Brenninkmeijer, Groningen 1989.

4 ♕c2 deserves a brief mention, although it's hardly ever played these days. Smyslov-Fischer, Zagreb 1959 continued 4...♘c6 (4...♕c7 is a good alternative) 5 d4 cxd4 6 cxd4 (White has quickly achieved the desired d4, but his queen is rather exposed on c2) 6...d5 7 e5 ♘e4 8 ♘c3 ♗f5 9 ♕b3 ♘xc3 10 bxc3 ♕d7 11 ♗a3 ♖c8 12 ♘h4 ♗g4 (12...♗e4) 13 h3 ♗h5 14 g4 ♗g6 15 ♘xg6 hxg6 16 ♗g2 ♘a5 17 ♕xd5 ♕xd5 18 ♗xd5 e6 19 ♗xf8 ♖xf8 20 ♗g2 ♖xc3 with a slight advantage for Black.

4 ... ♘c6
5 ♗d3

The sacrifice 5 d4 is dubious here. Of course the position is the same as Hodgson-Suba (Game 37) apart from one crucial difference – pawn on h3 replacing the bishop on e2.

The game Barlov-Velimirović, Yugoslav Ch 1983 continued 5...cxd4 6 cxd4 ♘xe4 7 d5 ♕a5+ 8 ♘c3 ♘xc3 9 bxc3 ♘d8 10 a4 ♗d7 11 ♕b3 g6 and White had nothing for the pawn.

5 ... g6

5...d5!? *(D)* is worth considering for the more adventurous among you.

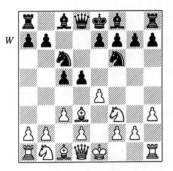

White has:

a) 6 exd5?! ♕xd5 7 ♕e2 ♗f5 8 ♗xf5 (8 ♗c4 ♕d7 9 d4 cxd4 10 cxd4 e6 11 ♘c3 ♗b4 is fine for Black) 8...♕xf5 9 d4 cxd4 10 ♘xd4 ♘xd4 11 cxd4 e6 12 ♘c3 (Kosanski-Ničevski, Yugoslav Ch 1991) 12...♗d6 with a good game for Black.

b) 6 e5 ♘d7 7 e6 fxe6 (perhaps 7...♘de5!?) 8 ♘g5 ♘f6 9 ♗xh7 ♘xh7 10 ♕h5+ and now in the game Mokry-Watson, Gausdal 1988 Black played 10...g6?, after which White could have got the advantage by 11 ♕xg6+ ♔d7 12 ♘f7! ♕c7 13 d4! cxd4 14 f4 (Watson). According to

Mokry, Black should have played 10...♔d7 11 ♘xh7 e5 12 ♘f6+ exf6 13 ♕xh8 b6 with a position to play rather than try to evaluate.

6 0-0

6 ♗c2 ♗g7 7 d4 cxd4 8 cxd4 ♘b4 looks OK for Black.

6 ...   ♗g7

7 ♗c2 (D)

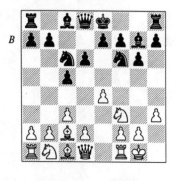

7 ...   0-0

7...e5 is a major alternative. Now 8 ♖e1 0-0 transposes to the main game, but White has two other possibilities:

a) 8 d3 0-0 9 ♗e3 b6 (9...♖e8 should be considered in order to slow down d4) 10 d4 exd4 11 cxd4 ♘b4 12 ♘c3 ♘xc2 13 ♕xc2 ♖e8 14 ♖fe1 (if 14 dxc5 then it's important to recapture with the b-pawn to avoid getting blown away in the centre) 14...♗b7 15 ♗g5 (15 d5 b5) 15...h6 16 ♗h4 cxd4 17 ♘xd4 ♖c8 with an unclear position in the game Chiburdanidze-Polugaevsky, Haninge 1988.

b) 8 d4 and now:

b1) 8...cxd4 9 cxd4 0-0 (9...exd4 10 ♘xd4 ♘xd4 11 ♕xd4 0-0 12 ♖d1 ♗e6 13 ♕xd6 ♕xd6 14 ♖xd6 ♖ac8 15 ♘c3 b5 16 ♗b3 is good for White) 10 ♗e3?! d5! 11 exd5 exd4 12 ♘xd4 ♘xd5 13 ♘xc6 ♘xe3 14 ♕xd8 ♖xd8 15 fxe3 bxc6 with a good game for Black in Abravanel-Gallagher, Dijon 1987. Better was 10 d5 ♘e7 with a King's Indian position. Black can follow up with ...♘e8, ...h6 and ...f5.

b2) 8...exd4 9 cxd4 0-0 10 d5 (10 dxc5 dxc5 11 ♘c3 ♗e6 is equal according to *ECO*) 10...♘b4 11 ♘c3 ♘xc2 12 ♕xc2 with a typical Benoni position, which should not be unfavourable for Black.

As our opponents are 1 e4 players they might not be familiar with the whole crop of Benonis and King's Indians that seem to arise from this variation (of course I'm assuming that my readers are fountains of knowledge).

8 ♖e1

8 d4 is more critical. After 8...cxd4 9 cxd4 ♘b4 (9...d5!?) 10 ♗b3 d5 (10...♘xe4?? 11 ♕e1) 11 e5 ♘e4 12 ♖e1 ♗f5 13 g4 ♗c8 (13...♗e6 14 ♘h2 and the knight on e4 is embarrassed) 14 ♘h2 h6! 15 f3 (15 h4? e6! 16 f3 ♘g3 17 ♗f4 ♕xh4 18 ♔g2 ♘h5) 15...♘g5 the game is unclear (Mokry).

8 ...   e5 (D)

8...♘d7 is very interesting. In the

game Davies-Rashkhovsky, Vrnjačka Banja 1988, White made the mistake of playing 9 d4 and after 9...cxd4 10 cxd4 ♕b6 11 d5 ♘d4 12 ♘c3 ♘xf3+ 13 ♕xf3 ♘e5 14 ♕e2 ♗d7 it was clear that he had lost the opening battle.

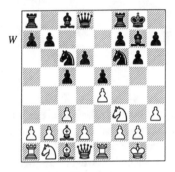

9 d4?!

If White wanted to play d4 he should have played it on the previous move. Now Black has the chance to liquidate the centre and be left with the more active pieces. Better was 9 d3 with a balanced game. Here are a couple of examples:

a) 9...h6 10 ♗e3 b6 11 d4 exd4 12 cxd4 ♘b4 13 ♘c3 ♗b7 (13...♘xc2 14 ♕xc2 ♖e8 15 dxc5 bxc5) 14 ♗b1 ♖e8 15 d5 ♘a6 with another Benoni; Smagin-Yrjölä, Voronezh 1987.

b) 9...b5!? 10 a4 b4 11 ♗e3 ♖b8 12 ♘bd2 ♘a5 13 d4 exd4 14 cxd4 c4 with chances for both sides in Conquest-Gallagher, Bern 1987.

9 ...	**exd4**
10 cxd4	**cxd4**

11 ♘xd4	**♘xd4**
12 ♕xd4	**♗e6**
13 ♕b4 *(D)*	

13 ♗b3 ♖e8 and 13 ♘c3 ♘d5 are both good for Black.

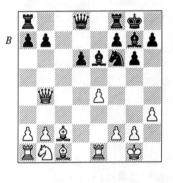

13 ...	**d5!**
14 ♘c3	

White shouldn't even contemplate grabbing the pawn on b7, e.g. 14 exd5 ♘xd5 15 ♕xb7 ♕d6 16 ♕b5 ♘b4 17 ♗e4 ♖ab8 with a clear advantage for Black; 14 e5 ♘d7 15 f4 b6 with ...f6 to follow is also better for Black.

14 ...   ♘xe4

Ftačnik also gives 14...dxe4 15 ♘xe4 ♕b6 16 ♕xb6 axb6 with a slightly better ending for Black. The main difference in the respective positions is the activity of the bishops.

15 ♘xe4	**dxe4**
16 ♗xe4	**♕h4!?**
17 ♗d2	

White's queen is in need of protection in order to break the pin along the rank. Again taking the b-pawn is too dangerous, e.g. 17 ♕xb7 ♗d4! 18 ♗e3 ♖ab8 19 ♕c6 ♖fc8 20 g3 ♕xh3 with advantage to Black.

17 ...   ♖ad8
18 ♗xb7

White finally succumbs to the temptation. More prudent would have been 18 ♗c3 ♗xc3 19 ♕xc3 b6 when Black has a slight initiative, but of course White's position is defendable.

18 ...   ♖d4
19 ♕a5   ♖a4!
20 ♕b5   ♖b8
21 ♖ac1

21 b3 ♗xa1 (21...♖d4 – Ftačnik) 22 bxa4 (22 ♖xa1 ♕d4) 22...♗d4 23 ♗e3 ♗xe3 24 ♖xe3 ♕e7.

21 ...   ♖xa2
22 ♗c3?!

White misses a chance to complicate the game with 22 ♖c8+!. Ftačnik gives the following complex variation: 22...♖xc8 (22...♗xc8? 23 ♖e8+ ♗f8 24 ♕c5) 23 ♗xc8 ♗d4! 24 ♕e8+! ♚g7 25 ♗e6 ♕xf2+ 26 ♚h2 ♖xb2 27 ♖e2! ♗e5+ 28 ♖xe5 ♖xd2 29 ♕xf7+ ♕xf7 30 ♗xf7 ♚xf7 31 ♖a5 with excellent drawing chances for White.

22 ...   ♗xc3
23 ♖xc3   ♕d4
24 ♖ec1

The passive 24 ♖c2 was preferable, although Black is clearly better after 24...♗f5.

24 ...   a6!

25 ♕c6 (D)

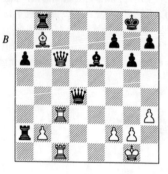

25 ...   ♖xb2

In his notes to the game Ftačnik awards this move a question mark and recommends 25...♕a7 as winning a piece. However, he overlooked an incredible resource, 26 ♗c8!, with the ideas 26...♖xc8 27 ♕xe6!! and 26...♗xc8? 27 ♕e8+ ♚g7 28 ♖c7. Nevertheless, I think that Black can retain some advantage with 26...♖bxb2!, e.g. 27 ♗xe6 ♕xf2+ 28 ♚h1 fxe6 29 ♕xe6+ ♚g7 30 ♕e5+ ♚h6 31 ♖g3 although it's far from clear if he can win.

26 ♗a8?

The last chance was 26 ♗xa6. After 26...♕xf2+ 27 ♚h1 ♖d8 Black is a pawn up with an active position, but the reduced amount of material offers White some hope.

26 ...   ♕xf2+
27 ♚h1   ♕a7

This time there's no miracle.

0-1

9 Others

This chapter deals with several systems which have been unable to find another home in this book and don't quite merit a chapter of their own.

They are:

Game 40: 1 e4 c5 2 ♘f3 e6 3 d3 (3 c4)

Game 41: 1 e4 c5 2 g3 (2 d3; 2 c4 and 2 ♗c4)

Game 42: 1 e4 c5 2 ♘c3 ♘c6 3 ♗b5

Game 40
Bologan – Lautier
Chalkidiki 1992

1	**e4**	**c5**
2	**♘f3**	**e6**
3	**d3** *(D)*	

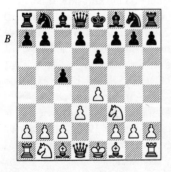

This usually signifies White's intention to transpose into a King's Indian Attack, a favourite variation of the young Fischer. Whilst this is quite a major topic in itself, I don't wish to devote twenty pages or so of this book to a variation that takes up about 2% of the anti-Sicilian systems. However, I think that by studying this game you will acquire sufficient knowledge to deal confidently with this line whenever it arises.

3 c4 is rare but still deserving of a mention. If it suits his style, there is nothing wrong with Black playing moves like 3...a6 and 4...♕c7 with a very likely transposition to some sort of Hedgehog after White plays d4. An alternative approach was seen in the game Bologan-Rublevsky, Jurmala 1991 which continued 3...♘c6 4 ♘c3 ♘f6 5 ♗e2 d5 6 exd5 exd5 7 d4 ♗e7 8 ♗e3 cxd4 9 ♘xd4 ♘xd4 10 ♗xd4 dxc4 11 0-0 0-0 12 ♗xc4 b6 13 ♖e1 ♗b7 14 ♕a4 a6 15 ♖ad1 b5 16 ♕b3 ♕c7 17 ♗d5 ♗xd5 18 ♘xd5 ♘xd5 19 ♕xd5 ♖fd8 20 ♕b3 ♗f8 with a drawish position.

3	**...**	**♘c6**

Obviously Black can also play in this fashion after 1 e4 c5 2 ♘f3 ♘c6 3 d3, but there he has the very sound alternative 3...g6.

4 g3   d5

Black has to be careful with his move order. For example, the immediate 4...g6 is met by 5 d4! when according to *ECO* White holds some advantage (although 5...d5 is not so clear). 4...♘ge7 is, however, an alternative move order.

5 ♘bd2

5 ♕e2 is also seen from time to time when White wishes to avoid the congestion which can be caused by ♘bd2. However it's far from clear if the queen is any better placed on e2 than on its original square. The game Psakhis-Khenkin, Chalkidiki 1992 continued 5...♘ge7 6 ♗g2 g6 7 0-0 ♗g7 8 e5 h6!? 9 h4 ♕c7 10 ♖e1 ♘d4 11 ♘xd4 cxd4 12 c4 dxc4 13 dxc4 ♗d7 with a double-edged position.

5 ...   g6

The fianchetto is a good idea as it makes it extremely difficult for White to organize a successful kingside attack (just as in the King's Indian, this is White's most dangerous plan in the KIA).

6 ♗g2   ♘ge7
7 0-0   ♗g7 *(D)*

As already mentioned, White can play the King's Indian Attack against several different openings, but the diagram position can be regarded as

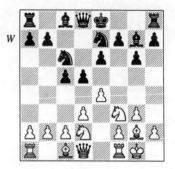

particularly important for the variation as it is the meeting point of the two most popular move orders – the first, via the Sicilian or French (this game actually started 1 e4 e6 2 d3 c5) and the second via a Réti move order such as the following: 1 ♘f3 d5 2 g3 c5 3 ♗g2 ♘c6 4 d3 e6 5 0-0 g6 6 ♘bd2 ♗g7 7 e4 ♘ge7.

8 ♖e1   0-0

8...b6 is a popular alternative.

9 h4

White declares his hand. The text is the necessary preparation for blocking the centre with e5, which in turn is a necessary measure before attacking on the kingside. If he plays e5 at once, Black has 9...♕c7 10 ♕e2 g5! after which White will have nothing better than to exchange his e-pawn for Black's g-pawn, e.g. 11 h3 (11 ♘xg5 ♕xe5 12 ♕xe5 ♘xe5 13 ♘f1 ♘f5 was agreed drawn at this point in Damljanović-Georgadze, Belgrade 1992) 11...♘g6 12 ♘b3 h6 13 ♘xc5 ♘cxe5 with good play for Black.

9 c3 is an alternative, usually quieter, approach, although not when Grandmaster Ljubojević has control of the white pieces. His game with Hulak, Zagreb 1975 was pure coffee-house from start to finish: 9...♕c7 10 exd5 ♘xd5 11 ♘c4 b6 12 ♘g5 ♗b7 13 ♕g4!? ♖ad8 *(D)*

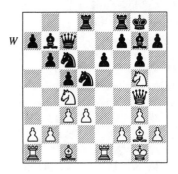

14 ♖xe6 (at any rate consistent) 14...h6! (Ljubojević was probably tempted by the variation 14...fxe6 15 ♕xe6+ ♔h8 16 ♗xd5 ♘d4 17 ♕h3! – not so good is 17 ♘f7+ ♖xf7 18 ♕xf7 ♕xf7 19 ♗xf7 ♘f3+ 20 ♔f1 ♖d7! with advantage to Black) 15 ♘xf7 ♕xf7 16 ♕e2 ♘xc3! 17 bxc3 ♗xc3 18 ♗xc6 ♗xc6 19 ♗b2 ♖de8 20 ♗xc3 ♖xe6 21 ♘e5 ♗f3 22 ♕f1 ♕f5 23 ♖e1 ♖fe8 24 d4 cxd4 25 ♕c4 dxc3 26 ♘xf3 ♕c5 27 ♕b3 ♔f7 28 ♖d1 ♔f8 29 ♖d5 ♕c7 30 ♘d4 ♖e4 31 ♘b5 ♕c4 32 ♘xc3 ♖e1+ 33 ♔g2 ♕f1+ 34 ♔f3 ♖1e3+ 35 ♔g4 ♕xf2 36 ♕c4 ♕f3+ 37 ♔h3 ♖xc3 38 ♕h4 ♕f1+ 39 ♔g4 ♖c4+ 0-1.

Black could also consider 9...d4 in reply to 9 c3, with the idea of 10 cxd4 ♘xd4 11 ♘xd4 ♗xd4 with an unclear game.

9 ... h6

A very important move ensuring that Black can meet h5 with ...g5.

10 e5 f5!
11 exf6 ♖xf6

Black has allowed his kingside to be seriously weakened but in compensation he has a potentially massive centre.

12 ♘h2

Against 12 ♘f1 Lautier intended 12...♕d6! followed by 13...e5. If White tries to prevent this with 13 ♗f4 then Black need not think twice about sacrificing the exchange: 13...♖xf4! 14 gxf4 ♗xb2 15 ♖b1 ♗c3 gives Black an excellent game.

12 ... ♖f7
13 ♘g4 ♕d6
14 ♘f3? *(D)*

This is a serious mistake. Better was 14 ♘f1. After 14...♔h7 15 c4 the game is unclear.

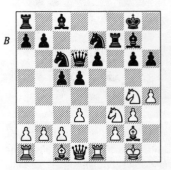

14 ...   e5!
15 ♘e3

White must have assumed that he could play 15 ♘xh6+ here, but after 15...♗xh6 16 ♗xh6 ♗g4 he is caught in a deadly pin.

15 ...   ♗e6
16 c4   ♖af8
17 ♘d2

Faced with the threat of 17...d4 followed by ...♗g4, White has no choice but to seek complications.

17 ...   ♖xf2!
18 cxd5   ♖xg2+

18...♘xd5 19 ♘e4 ♖xg2+ leads to the same position.

19 ♔xg2   ♘xd5
20 ♘e4   ♕e7
21 ♗d2? *(D)*

21 ♘xd5 ♗xd5 would have made a fight of it although Black remains with more than enough for the exchange.

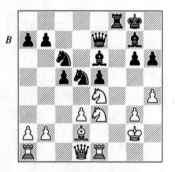

21 ...   ♘f4+!

Lautier has conducted the game in a very energetic manner and he

doesn't miss his chance to strip the white king of his remaining cover.

22 gxf4   exf4
23 ♘f1   ♕xh4

Black now threatens 24...♕h3+ followed by ...♗d4+ in addition to 24...f3+.

24 ♘h2

24 ♕f3 loses to 24...♘d4 25 ♕f2 ♕h3+ 26 ♔g1 ♘f3+.

24 ...   f3+
25 ♕xf3

25 ♘xf3 ♕h3+ 26 ♔f2 ♕h2+ leads to mate but the text only manages to delay things for a few moves.

25 ...   ♖xf3
26 ♘xf3   ♕h3+
27 ♔f2   ♘d4
28 ♘xd4   ♗xd4+
29 ♗e3   ♗g4!
30 ♗xd4   ♕f3+
31 ♔g1   ♗h3

0-1

Game 41
Nadyrkhanov – Serper
Tashkent 1993

1 e4   c5
2 g3 *(D)*

White has the devious idea of playing a Closed Sicilian without ♘c3, giving him the useful option of playing c3. A study of Chapter 1 will reveal that White usually works very hard to get this little pawn move in. The drawback with the text is that White is not particularly well placed

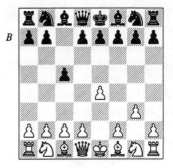

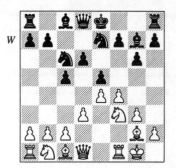

to meet an immediate counter in the centre (see main game).

2 d3 is an alternative way for White to implement his idea as now 2...♘c6 3 g3 d5 can be met by 4 ♘d2 with a King's Indian Attack where White still has the option of playing f4. Instead of 3...d5 play can continue 3...g6 4 ♗g2 (4 ♗e3 d6 5 ♗g2 ♗g7 6 c3?! {better 6 ♘c3} 6...♕b6! 7 ♕b3 {7 ♕c2 is met by 7...♘e5!, with threats of ...♕xb2 and ...♕a6} 7...♗e6 8 ♕xb6 axb6 and Black has the advantage; Boog-Gallagher, Biel 1991) ♗g7 5 f4 d6 6 ♘f3 e5 (6...e6 is less good, a recent example being Nadyrkhanov-Zagrebelny, Tashkent 1992 which continued 7 0-0 ♘ge7 8 c3 0-0 9 ♗e3 b6 10 ♘a3 ♗a6 11 ♗f2 ♕d7 12 ♖e1 ♖ac8 13 ♕d2 f5 {13...e5!?} 14 exf5 gxf5 15 d4 c4 16 ♘g5 ♘d8 17 ♖e2 d5 18 ♖ae1 with a clear advantage to White) 7 0-0 ♘ge7 *(D)* with the alternatives:

a) 8 ♘c3 transposes to the 6 f4 e5 line of the Closed Sicilian, but with White's knight already committed to f3. After the moves 1 e4 c5 2 ♘c3 ♘c6 3 g3 g6 4 ♗g2 ♗g7 5 d3 d6 6 f4 e5 7 ♘h3! Black cannot normally avoid exchanging on f4 for long (he has to steer clear of lines like 7...♘ge7 8 0-0 0-0? 9 f5!). White then recaptures with the knight which will be very well placed on f4. In view of this 8 ♘c3 is quite rare. One example is Larsen-Portisch, Rotterdam 1977: 8...0-0 9 ♗e3 ♘d4 10 ♕d2 exf4 11 ♗xf4 (11 gxf4 looks very loose) 11...♘xf3+ 12 ♖xf3 ♕b6 13 ♖b1 ♗e6 with a pleasant game for Black.

b) 8 f5 is a speculative pawn sacrifice by which White hopes to gain a bind on the light squares. Davies-Horvath, Budapest 1987 continued 8...gxf5 9 ♘h4 fxe4 10 dxe4 0-0 11 ♘a3 ♗e6 12 ♘f5 ♗xf5 13 exf5 f6 14 ♗e3 ♕d7!? 15 ♗xc5 ♖ad8 16 ♗e3 ♘xf5 17 ♗h3 ♘xe3 18 ♗xd7 ♘xd1 19 ♗e6+ ♔h8 20 ♖axd1 ♘e7 and White didn't have enough for the pawn even though he finally won the ending.

c) 8 c3 0-0 *(D)* with the further division:

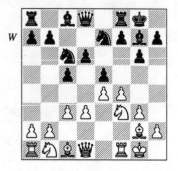

c1) 9 ♗e3 b6!. Not only does this provide the bishop with an extra diagonal, but it also protects the c-pawn, enabling Black to think about pushing ...d5. We shall now follow the game Todorčević-Mirallès, Marseille 1990: 10 ♘bd2 (10 ♕d2 can be met by 10...exf4 followed by 11...d5) 10...♗a6 11 ♘e1 exf4 12 gxf4 f5 13 ♕a4 (13 ♖f2 would be more prudent) 13...♘a5! (Black is not forced to retreat his bishop and thereby maintains the pressure on the a6-f1 diagonal) 14 ♘df3?! (probably the exchange had to be taken: 14 exf5 ♘xf5 15 ♗xa8 ♕xa8 16 ♗f2 with a double-edged, but uncomfortable game for White) 14...fxe4 15 ♕xe4 ♘f5 (White is already positionally lost, but he had clearly pinned his hopes on the coming attack) 16 ♕e6+ ♔h8 17 ♘g5 ♖c8! 18 ♖f3 ♖c7 19 ♖h3 ♗f6!. Black's pieces have defended beautifully and

White's attack has now run its course leaving him with no good defence to 20...♖e7, as 20 ♗d2 ♖e7 21 ♕d5 ♗b7 nets the queen. The game finished 20 b4 cxb4 21 ♘c2 ♖e7 22 ♕d5 ♗b7 23 ♕b5 ♗xg2 24 ♔xg2 ♗xg5 25 fxg5 ♖xe3! 0-1.

c2) 9 ♘a3 exf4!? (9...♖b8 is a good alternative. The game Todorčević-Kir.Georgiev, Yugoslavia 1991 was a wild affair: 10 ♘c2 exf4 11 gxf4 b5 12 a3 a5 13 ♘e3 b4 14 axb4 axb4 15 c4 f5 16 exf5 ♘xf5 17 ♘g5 ♗d4! 18 ♗xc6 ♘xe3 19 ♗xe3 ♗xe3+ 20 ♔h1 ♗xf4 21 ♗d5+ ♔h8 22 ♘f7+ ♖xf7 23 ♗xf7 ♗xh2! 24 ♕d2 ♗e5 25 ♕h6 ♗g7 26 ♕h2 ♗b7+ 27 ♗d5 ♗xd5+ 28 cxd5 ♕g5 with a winning position for Black) 10 ♗xf4 d5 11 ♘b5 ♗g4 12 h3 ♗xf3 13 ♕xf3 d4! (the motive behind Black's last few moves is to ensure that the e5 square is firmly under his control) 14 c4 ♘e5 15 ♕e2 ♘7c6 16 ♘a3 h5 17 b3 a6 18 ♘c2 b5 19 ♘e1 bxc4 20 bxc4 ♖b8 21 ♘f3 ♘xf3+ 22 ♕xf3 ♘e5 with advantage to Black; Morović-Larsen, Buenos Aires 1992.

Before returning to the main game I should like to examine briefly, for the sake of completeness, a couple of extremely rare alternatives: 2 c4 and 2 ♗c4.

2 c4 ♘c6 3 ♘c3 e5 obviously gives Black simple equality. *ECO* now quotes Keres: 4 g3 h5! 5 h4 d6 6 ♗g2 ♗g4 7 f3 ♗e6 8 d3 ♗e7 =. The

pawn structure is very similar to a line in the English where Black's bishop is on the inferior g7 square, but even that is considered equal. I have been able to trace one recent grandmaster game with 2 c4, but the only explanation I can think of to explain White's poor performance is that he must have been totally inebriated. Judge for yourselves: 2 c4 d6 3 ♘f3 ♗g4 4 d4 cxd4 5 ♕xd4 ♗xf3 6 gxf3 ♘c6 7 ♕d1 g6 8 ♘c3 ♗g7 9 ♗e3 ♗xc3+ 10 bxc3 ♕a5 11 ♕b3 ♘f6 12 0-0-0 0-0 13 h4 ♘d7 14 ♖d5 ♘c5 15 ♗xc5 dxc5 16 f4 e6 17 ♖g5 ♕c7 18 e5 ♖ad8 19 h5 ♘e7 20 hxg6 fxg6 21 ♗h3 ♕c6 22 ♗g2 ♕d7 23 f5 0-1 I.Ivanov-Dzindzichashvili, USA Ch 1989.

2 ♗c4 is clearly premature. After 2...e6 Black already has the initiative. There are no worthwhile examples from modern practice, but *ECO* gives 3 ♕e2 ♘c6 4 c3 ♗e7 5 d3 d5 6 ♗b3 ♘f6 =.

2 ...   d5

2...♘c6 3 ♗g2 g6 4 d3 transposes to 2 d3 (see above).

3 exd5

3 ♗g2 dxe4 4 ♗xe4 ♘f6 and 3 ♘c3 d4 4 ♘ce2 e5 are not especially attractive for White.

3 ...   ♕xd5
4 ♘f3   ♗g4
5 ♗g2

5 ♗e2 would be extremely passive and White would still have a problem with his king after 5...♗h3.

5 ...   ♕e6+
6 ♔f1 (D)

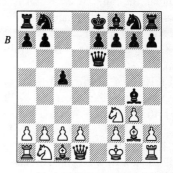

White has lost the right to castle, but in return his bishop is master of the long diagonal and Black will have to move his queen again before long in order to develop his kingside. 6 ♕e2 ♕xe2+ 7 ♔xe2 ♘c6 is not an alternative.

6 ...   ♘c6

6...♗h3 is less good as an exchange on g2 would only relieve White's kingside congestion. 7 b4!? would be a dangerous reply.

7 h3   ♗h5
8 ♘c3

This looks the most natural, but White has an alternative plan based on ♘a3-c4. This is usually preceded by 8 d3 ♕d7 (it's too early to contemplate castling long) 9 ♘a3 e6 and now:

a) 10 g4 ♗g6 11 ♘c4 f6! 12 a4 ♘ge7 13 h4 e5 14 ♘fd2 ♗f7 15 ♘e3 (White can't afford to allow ...♗d5) 15...0-0-0 16 a5 (Balashov-

Filipenko, Katowice 1992) 16...♘g6! (White often has to play g4 in order to break the pin, but the result is a weakening of the f4 square) 17 a6 b6 18 ♕f3 ♔c7 19 ♖h2 ♘f4 20 ♗h1 ♖b8! with advantage to Black (Filipenko).

b) 10 ♘c4 ♗d6!? (10...♘f6 or 10...f6 are possible alternatives) 11 ♕e1 f6 12 ♘xd6+ ♕xd6 13 ♗e3 ♘ge7 14 g4 ♗f7 15 ♕c3 b6 16 d4 cxd4 17 ♘xd4 ♖c8 18 ♘b5 ♕d7 19 ♕d2 and a draw was agreed in Jansa-Emends, Münster 1992. I think we can safely assume that Grandmaster Jansa offered a draw to his lower rated opponent as he wasn't overly keen on his position. 19...♘d5 looks best.

8 ... ♕d7 (D)

Black can also play 8...♘f6, although this rules out the possibility of ...f7-f6 (it can sometimes be useful to have e5 under control). Nadyrkhanov-Stefansson, Lucerne team Wch 1993 continued 9 d3 ♕d7 10 g4 ♗g6 11 ♗f4 e6 12 g5 ♘h5 (this looks like an improvement on the previously played 12...♘g8) 13 ♘e5 ♘xe5 14 ♗xe5 ♗d6! 15 ♗xd6 ♕xd6 16 h4 (16 ♗xb7 ♖b8 17 ♗f3 ♘f4 with compensation for the pawn) 16...♕c7 17 ♗f3 ♘f4 18 ♕d2 ♖d8 19 ♘b5 ♕b8 20 h5 ♗xd3+!? (the simple 20...♗f5 deserves attention) 21 cxd3 ♖xd3 22 ♕c2 ♖xf3 23 ♕e4! ♖h3 (23...♖d3 24 ♖h3) 25 ♖xh3 ♘xh3 25 ♕e3 ♕h2 26 ♕xc5

♕g1+ (26...♕h1+ 27 ♔e2 ♘f4+ 28 ♔e3 ♘d5+ 29 ♔d2 ♕xa1 30 ♕c8+ leads to a draw by perpetual) 27 ♔e2 ♕g4+ (27...♕xa1?? 28 ♕c8+ ♔e7 29 ♕c7+ mates) 28 ♔f1 ♕g1+ 29 ♔e2 ♕xg5?? (the Icelandic team captain was probably in need of medical assistance after this move) 30 ♘c7+ ♔d7 31 ♖d1+ ♔c8 32 ♘d5+! ♔b8 33 ♕d6+ 1-0

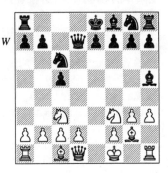

9 ♘e5!?

The sort of move which makes you jump out of your chair. Previous practice has seen: 9 d3 e6 10 a4 (10 g4 ♗g6 11 ♘h4 ♗e7 12 ♘xg6 hxg6 13 ♗e3 ♘f6 14 ♘e4 b6 with equality; Suetin-Sveshnikov, Dubna 1979) 10...♘f6 11 a5 ♖d8 (the plan of pushing the a-pawn in order to soften up the long diagonal had brought Short a previous success in his game with Hjartarson, European club Ch 1990. That game had continued 11...♖c8 {less active than 11...♖d8} 12 g4 ♗g6 13 ♘h4 ♗e7 14 ♘xg6 hxg6 15 h4 0-0 16 h5 gxh5? 17 g5!

♘g4 18 ♖xh5 and White soon won)
12 g4 ♗g6 13 ♘h4 ♗e7 14 ♘xg6
hxg6 15 h4 (this looks premature, although Short got away with it in the
above game. Sveshnikov recommends 15 ♗d2) 15...a6! (rather than
castling into an attack, Black fixes
the pawn on a5 which is now seriously weak) 16 ♗e3 ♕c7 17 g5 ♘h5
18 ♗xc6+ (this must be a candidate
for anti-positional move of the year,
but what was White to do about his
a-pawn? Sveshnikov's own suggestion of 18 ♘a4 ♘xa5 19 b4 fails to
19...♘c4! with the idea of 20 ♗xc5
♗xc5 21 ♘xc5 ♘g3+!) 18...♕xc6
19 ♖h3 (Short-Sveshnikov, European club Ch 1992) and now 19...f5!
would have left Black with a clear
advantage.

9 ...   ♗xd1

9...♕f5 10 ♘g4 was White's idea.

10 ♘xd7   ♗xc2
11 ♘xc5   0-0-0
12 b4

The two players, analysing in *Informator*, consider that after this
White has a slight advantage. Whilst
I agree that 12 b4 is the only move
(White's only trump in this position
is the long diagonal – he has to try to
exploit this at once) their assessment
appears to be based on an oversight
(see later).

12 ...   e6

12...a6 13 a4 only helps White.

13 ♘xb7

13 b5 ♘a5.

13 ...   ♔xb7
14 b5   ♘ge7
15 ♗a3

15 bxc6+ ♘xc6 and White is unable to exploit the pin.

15 ...   ♘d5!
16 bxc6+   ♔xc6
17 ♘xd5 (D)

Better would have been 17 ♗xf8
with a probable transposition to the
game.

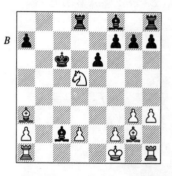

17 ...   exd5?

It seems that neither player no-
ticed 17...♗d3+! 18 ♔g1 ♗xa3!.
Now the bishop is defended, so there
is no devastating discovered check.
After 19 ♘f4+ (or 19 ♘c3+ ♔d6)
19...♔c7 20 ♔h2 (20 ♘xd3 ♖xd3 21
♔h2 ♖xd2 22 ♖ab1 ♗b2) 20...♗a6
Black is better.

18 ♗xf8?!

And now White also misses a
chance. Stronger was 18 ♗b2! ♗d3+
19 ♔g1 f6 20 ♖c1+ ♔d6 21 ♔h2 after which Black's pieces are somewhat awkwardly placed.

18 ...   &d3+

The bishop has to be removed from the same file as the king.

19 &g1   Hhxf8
20 Hc1+   &d6
21 Hc3   &e4
22 &xe4   dxe4
23 d3   ½-½

Game 42
Rausis – Benjamin
Lucerne team Wch 1993

1 e4   c5
2 &c3   &c6
3 &b5 *(D)*

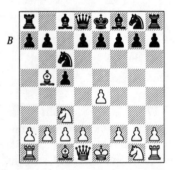

The big difference between this move here and in Chapter 6, is that Black has one important alternative not really available to him with the knights on b1 and f3, namely:

3 ...   &d4!

White is now unable to remove the intruder with c3, so will probably be forced to play &xd4 at some point. If you've already studied the

section with 3 f4 (Chapter 2) you will understand that this type of position should not pose Black any opening problems.

4 &c4

4 a4 is the alternative, favoured by German master Keitlinghaus who is one of the rare few to play this line with any regularity. 4...g6 5 &ge2 (if White plays 5 f4 and 6 &f3, we'll have transposed into Game 13) 5...&g7 6 0-0 b6!? (there's nothing wrong with 6...e6, e.g. 7 &xd4 cxd4 8 &e2 &e7 9 c3 a6 10 &d3 &c6 11 f4 0-0 12 &h1 d6 with a good game for Black in Thesing-Bönsch, Bundesliga 1990/91) 7 &xd4 cxd4 8 &e2 &b7 9 d3 Hc8 10 a5 a6 11 &c4 b5 12 &b3 d5 13 f3 e6 14 We1 &e7 15 &g5 h6 16 &h4 (16 &xe7 is best met by 16...&xe7!) 16...0-0 and Black has a good game; Keitlinghaus-Blatny, Münster 1992.

4 ...   e6
5 &f3

About a week after this game with Benjamin, Rausis found himself facing this strange variation. His opponent varied here with 5 &ce2. The game continued 5...&f6 6 &xd4 cxd4 7 We2 d5 8 &b5+ &d7 9 &xd7+ Wxd7 10 e5 &g8 11 &f3 &c5 12 Wd3? (an extremely ill-considered move. It is obvious that White won't be able to take the d-pawn without losing his e-pawn and after the text his queenside development will be laborious at best)

12...♕c7 13 0-0 ♘e7 14 ♘xd4 (14 ♖e1 ♘g6 with ideas of ...♘f4 and ...f6) 14...♗xd4 15 ♕xd4 ♕xc2 with a clear advantage to Black; Kamber-Rausis, Chiasso 1993. Rausis later managed to lose a totally winning position, completing a rather miserable time with this variation.

5 ... ♘f6!?

The text looks more active than the choice of the World Champion, 5...♘e7. Spassky-Kasparov, Reykjavik 1988 continued 6 0-0 ♘ec6 7 d3 g6 8 ♘xd4 cxd4 9 ♘e2 ♗g7 10 ♗d2 0-0 11 b4 b6 12 b5 ♘e7 13 ♗b4 d6 14 a4 a5 15 ♗a3 ♗b7 16 f3 d5 17 ♗b3 ♕c7 18 ♕e1 ♖ad8 19 ♕h4 and a draw was agreed.

6 0-0

Black intended to meet 6 e5 with 6...d5!.

6 ... a6
7 d3

White's position reminds me of my primary school days where my opponents invariably met the Sicilian with a set-up rather like this one, only to be driven back soon by ...d5 or ...b5.

7 ... d5
8 ♗b3

White could also take on d5 at once as after 8 exd5 exd5 9 ♗b3 ♗g4 he has 10 ♕e1+ with an unclear game. Black could of course play 9...♘xb3.

8 ... ♗e7
9 exd5 ♘xb3

Black avails himself off the opportunity to retain the d5 square for his pieces.

10 axb3 ♘xd5
11 ♘xd5 ♕xd5
12 ♖e1 0-0

There can be no doubt that Black's opening has been a success. If he wished to avoid the game continuation he could have played 12...♗f6 as after 13 ♘d2 b6 14 ♘e4 ♗b7 15 ♘xf6+ is obviously risky. 12...f6 is also not out of the question.

13 ♖e5 ♕c6
14 ♖h5 f6!

Black prepares to defend his kingside along the second rank as well as covering the e5 square.

15 ♖a4!? ♖f7
16 ♖g4 (D)

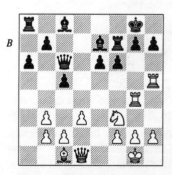

With some imaginative play White has managed to swing his rooks into the vicinity of the black monarch. Nevertheless, with care Black should be able to repulse the attack; and let's not forget that White has totally ignored the centre.

16	...	e5
17	♖g3	♗e6
18	♘h4	g5!?

Obviously Black would prefer to do without this move, but as well as 19 ♘f5 he has to worry about 19 ♖xh7. The text has the advantage of gaining time and Black judges that his rook will be able to defend along the second rank. Another point is that White's rook is very unlikely to emerge unscathed from h5, although Black has to take care that it can't sacrifice itself under favourable circumstances.

19	♘f3	♖g7
20	♕e2	♖d8
21	h4	

Of course White has to try to prise open the kingside.

21	...	g4
22	♘h2	♕d7
23	f3	♗f7
24	♖h6	gxf3
25	♕xf3?	

It's strange that White did not prefer 25 ♖xg7+ ♔xg7 26 ♕xf3 which would have given him more chances, e.g. 26...♔h8 27 ♖xf6 e4 (threat ...♕d4+) 28 ♕f2 ♗g6 looks unclear.

25	...	♖xg3
26	♕xg3+	♔h8
27	♕g4	♕d4+!

Black is quite happy to exchange queens, but on his own terms.

28	♔f1	♖g8
29	♕f5	♖g7
30	♖xf6!?	

The best practical chance.

30	...	♗xf6
31	♕xf6	e4!
32	♕xd4	cxd4
33	dxe4	♗g6
34	♗f4	♖f7
35	g3	♗xe4
36	c3	d3?

Black should have played 36...dxc3 37 bxc3 a5! after which the outcome would not be in doubt.

37	♔e1	♖e7
38	♔d2	♗f5
39	♗e3	♗e4
40	♘g4 (D)	

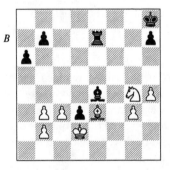

0-1

Somewhat fortunately for Black, White overstepped the time limit. The position should now be a draw as White can win the d-pawn by force.

10 Move Order Tricks

1 e4 c5 2 ♘c3 ♘c6 3 ♘ge2/♘f3

This chapter is for those of you who wish to follow the repertoire recommended in this book but are embarrassed by the above move order (for example, Najdorf players). However, there is no great cause for concern and there are a number of ways to deal with the situation. The first and in some ways most simple is to play 3...e5. This has quite a bad reputation (especially against 3 ♘ge2) but I feel this is not totally justified. It was games such as the following which were instrumental in creating this reputation:

Game 43
Fischer – Naranja
Manila 1967

1	e4	c5
2	♘c3	♘c6
3	♘ge2	e5
4	♘d5	♘f6
5	♘ec3	♗e7
6	♗c4	0-0
7	d3	h6
8	f4	d6

9	f5	b6
10	h4	♗b7
11	a3	♖c8
12	♘xf6+	♗xf6
13	♕h5	♘e7 *(D)*

14	♗g5!	d5
15	♗xf6	dxc4
16	♕g4	g6
17	dxc4	♕d6
18	♗xe7	♕xe7
19	fxg6	fxg6
20	♕xg6+	♕g7
21	♕xg7+	♔xg7
22	♖d1	♖cd8
23	♖xd8	♖xd8
24	♘d5	b5
25	cxb5	♗xd5
26	exd5	c4

27	a4	Rxd5
28	♔e2	Rd4
29	Rd1	Re4+
30	♔f3	Rf4+
31	♔e3	c3
32	b3	1-0

A crushing victory for White, but Black's opening play was of a very low standard and I would say that he was simply lost by move 9. The rest of the games in this chapter are devoted to 3...e5 against 3 ♘f3 or 3 ♘ge2 so if you take some time to study them you should at least fare better than Mr Naranja. I believe that with careful and solid play Black should be able to reduce White's slight initiative until it completely disappears. However, herein lies the main problem. Playing 3...e5 drastically reduces Black's chances of winning the game and the rather dry positions that arise may not be to the taste of the counter-attacking Sicilian player. The ideal solution is to have a second Sicilian in your repertoire, and one which includes ...♘c6. Of course not everyone has the time or the inclination to learn a second variation, but if you do, and you don't have a variation already, I can highly recommend the Dragon (i.e. 1 e4 c5 2 ♘c3 ♘c6 3 ♘ge2/♘f3 g6!). The point is that after White has played 2 ♘c3 he is unable to play the positionally unpleasant Maroczy Bind, nor with this move order is he

able to get a good version of the dangerous Yugoslav Attack. You will appreciate, however, that a further discussion of the Dragon is beyond the scope of this book.

There is another, slightly riskier, approach to the move order problem. Play the man! Very often you will know your opponent and can make your decisions accordingly. For example, in a recent tournament I had to play Black against American grandmaster Nick De Firmian. I knew that he always played into Open Sicilians so when he played 2 ♘c3 I treated it like the little joke it was and played 2...d6 and sure enough he followed up with 3 ♘ge2 and 4 d4. On the other hand, if I'm up against Mark Hebden, former world expert on the Grand Prix attack but recently converted to the Open Sicilian (when he's not playing 1 d4), and he plays 2 ♘c3 it has to be taken seriously. You can be pretty sure that if you play 2...d6, still hoping for a Najdorf, the answer will be 3 f4 and we will find ourselves in the most dangerous system of the Grand Prix Attack. Therefore against Mark I play 2...♘c6 and then he plays 3 ♘f3 or 3 ♘ge2 with a cheeky grin on his face (he's avoided the Najdorf), and I have to find another Sicilian or play 3...e5. Obviously you'll have to work out for yourselves how to respond to each of your likely opponents but at club level things are usually more straightforward than at international level. In my experience most people who play 2 ♘c3 are not bluffing but really intend to play the Closed Sicilian or possibly 3 f4. Of course there are always a few spoilers around.

Before moving on to the games I would just like to mention a couple of other move order problems which might affect some of you. The first occurs after the moves 1 e4 c5 2 ♘c3 ♘c6 3 ♘ge2 e6 4 g3 *(D)*

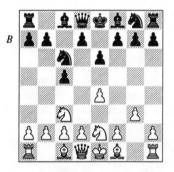

Black will now not be able to reach our proposed repertoire against the Closed Sicilian as 4...g6 can be met by 5 d4. 4...a6 is a possibility, but recent practice suggests that Black can equalize with 4...d5. For example, the 17th game of the Fischer-Spassky match, Belgrade 1992, continued 5 exd5 exd5 6 ♗g2 d4 7 ♘d5 ♘f6 8 ♘ef4 ♘xd5 9 ♘xd5 ♗d6 10 0-0 0-0 11 d3 ♗e6 12 ♘f4 ♗f5 13 h3 ♖b8 14 ♗d2 ♖e8 15 ♖e1

♖xe1+ 16 ♕xe1 and according to Matanović in *Informator* 16...♕e7 (instead of 16...♕d7) leads to equality. The 23rd game of the match saw something slightly different as Fischer played 6 d3, but after 6...♘f6 7 ♗g2 ♗e7 8 ♗g5 d4 9 ♗xf6 ♗xf6 10 ♘e4 ♗e7 11 ♘f4 0-0 12 0-0 ♖e8 13 ♕h5 g6 14 ♕d5 ♗f5 Black had equalized.

The second is a warning for those of you who play the Kan Sicilian. After the moves 1 e4 c5 2 ♘f3 e6 3 ♘c3 a6 4 g3, the natural 4...b5 looks risky on account of 5 d4!. Shabalov-Benjamin, Philadelphia 1993 continued 5...cxd4 6 ♘xd4 ♗b7 7 ♗g2 d6 8 0-0 ♘d7 9 ♖e1 ♕c7 10 ♗g5 ♘gf6 11 a4 b4 *(D)* (Shabalov himself once played 11...bxa4 here, but 12 ♘d5! would still be strong)

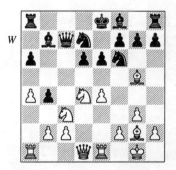

12 ♘d5! exd5 13 exd5+ ♘e5 14 f4 ♘xd5 15 ♘f5! ('once the key to White's attack is found, namely to hold the f8 bishop on its starting square, the next series of flashing

moves becomes clear' – Shabalov)
15...♕c5+ 16 ♔h1 f6 17 fxe5 fxg5
(17...dxe5 18 ♗xf6!) 18 exd6+ ♔d7
19 ♘d4! ♕xd6 20 ♖e6! ♕c5 21
♖e5 (this is the point at which Shabalov concluded his home analysis!)
21...♘e3 22 ♖xe3 ♗xg2+ 23 ♔xg2
♕d5+ 24 ♘f3! with a winning position for White.

Black should probably content
himself with the modest 4...d6, with
a likely transposition to a g3
Scheveningen.

Game 44
Rublevsky – Ernst
Helsinki Open 1992

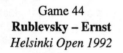

1	e4	c5
2	♘c3	♘c6
3	♘ge2	e5 *(D)*

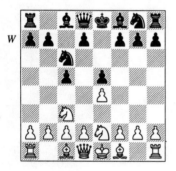

4 ♘d5

4 g3 d6 5 ♗g2 g6 6 d3 ♗g7 7 0-0
♘ge7 8 f4 0-0 9 ♗e3 ♘d4 10 ♕d2
♗e6 11 ♖ae1 ♕d7 was approxi-
mately equal in Korchnoi-Hübner,

Barcelona 1989. This position is
much more likely to have arisen
from the Closed Sicilian, e.g. 1 e4 c5
2 ♘c3 ♘c6 3 g3 g6 4 ♗g2 ♗g7 5 d3
d6 6 ♘ge2 e5 etc.

4 ...   d6

4...♘ce7 is less convincing, e.g. 5
♘e3 (5 ♘ec3 also offers White the
chance of an edge, e.g. 5...♘xd5 6
♘xd5 ♘f6 7 ♘xf6+ ♕xf6 8 ♗c4
♗e7 {8...♕g6 9 0-0 ♕xe4 10 d4!
with an attack} 9 0-0 0-0 10 ♗d5
{10 d3, 10 b4!?} d6 11 b4!? ♗e6 12
♖b1 ♖ab8 13 ♕e2 ♕g6 14 d3 with a
slight plus for White, Gallagher-
Scherbakov, Metz 1994) 5...♘f6 6
♘c3 a6 7 a4 d5 8 exd5 ♘exd5 9
♘cxd5 ♘xd5 10 ♕h5 ♗e6 11 ♕xe5
♗e7 12 ♕xg7 ♗f6 13 ♕g3 ♕e7 14
♗e2 0-0-0 and Black had reasonable
compensation for his investments in
Nikolenko-Sveshnikov, Moscow Tal
mem 1992. Safer, for White, would
have been 10 ♘c4 with a small advantage.

5 ♘ec3   ♘ge7
6 ♗c4

6 g3 ♘xd5 7 ♘xd5 ♗e7 transposes into Fischer-Spassky, Belgrade (19) 1992. After 8 ♗g2 h5!? 9
h4 ♗e6 10 d3 ♗xd5 11 exd5 ♘b8 12
f4 ♘d7 13 0-0 g6 White could have
obtained a good game with 14 f5
since against 14...g5 there is the dangerous sacrifice 15 f6!. Matanović
considers 9...♗g4 10 f3 ♗e6 to be a
possible improvement whilst I believe that Black might be able to

improve upon 7...♗e7 with 7...♘e7 or 7...g6.

6	...	♘xd5
7	♘xd5	

7 ♗xd5 occurred in the game Tischbierek-*Deep Thought*, Hannover 1991. If I remember correctly, this was a tournament between seven of Germany's top players and the new improved version of the monster. This game caused great embarrassment to the Deep Thought team and you will understand why if you play through the moves: 7...♗e7 8 d3 ♘d4?! 9 0-0 *(D)*

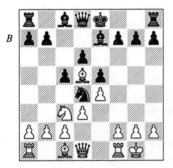

9...♗h4? (how on earth did the machine arrive at this choice?) 10 f4 0-0 11 f5 ♖b8 12 a4 ♗d7 13 g3 ♗g5 14 ♖f2 ♗xc1 15 ♕xc1 ♗c6?? 16 f6 gxf6 17 ♕h6 ♕b6 18 ♕xf6 ♗e8 19 ♖af1 ♕xb2 20 ♕g5+ ♔h8 21 ♘d1 ♕b4 (apparently 21...♕a3 would have lost even more quickly, but no human would ever play 21...♕b4) 22 c3 1-0. If Black wants to avoid the possibility of 7 ♗xd5 he can play

4...♘ge7 and 5...♘xd5 before playing ...d6.

7	...	♗e7
8	d3	

The game Vogt-Lücke, Bundesliga 1992 continued slightly differently with 8 0-0 0-0 9 f4 exf4 10 ♘xf4!? (10 d3 ♘e5 11 ♗xf4 ♘xc4 12 dxc4 ♗g5 13 ♗g3 f5 14 ♕d3 g6 15 e5 dxe5 16 ♗xe5 ♖f7 17 ♖ae1 and White has the initiative; Rublevsky-Krasenkov, USSR 1991. Black probably would have done better not to capture on c4) 10...♗g5 11 d3 ♖b8 12 c3 b5 13 ♗d5 ♘e5 14 h3 ♗b7? *(D)*

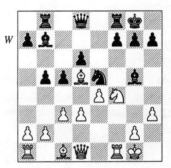

15 ♘e6! fxe6 16 ♗xe6+ ♔h8 (the main point of the combination is 16...♘f7 17 ♖xf7! ♖xf7 18 ♗xf7+ ♔xf7 19 ♕h5+ winning) 17 ♖xf8+ ♕xf8 18 ♗xg5 with a clear advantage for White.

8	...	0-0
9	0-0	♗e6

In the game Adams-Ubilava, Manila OL 1992, Black delayed ...♗e6, preferring instead 9...♗g5. After 10 f4 exf4 11 ♗xf4 ♘e5 12 ♗b3 ♗xf4 13 ♖xf4 ♘g6 14 ♖f2 ♗e6 15 ♕h5 ♕d7 16 ♖af1 White held a slight initiative.

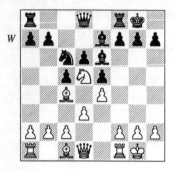

10 f4

After this, play becomes very similar to many lines in the King's Gambit Declined with Black having the doubtful ...c7-c5 thrown in. The alternative is to play in the centre and queenside with 10 c3. The game Berg-Vologyin, Copenhagen 1991 now continued 10...♗g5 11 ♕e2 ♗xc1 12 ♖axc1 ♕d7 13 a3 ♘e7 14 ♘e3 b5 15 ♗xe6 ♕xe6 16 ♖fd1 d5? (16...f5 is much more to the point. The text is a horrible blunder) 17 exd5 ♘xd5 18 ♘xd5 ♕xd5 19 c4! bxc4 20 dxc4 ♕e6 21 ♖d5 and White won a pawn followed by the game.

10	...	exf4
11	♗xf4	♘e5
12	♔h1	♗g5
13	♗xe5	

Now the draw becomes the odds-on favourite. 13 ♗g3 would keep a bit more life in the position.

13	...	dxe5
14	♕f3	♔h8

Black prepares to play ...f6, after which White will have no weak points to attack.

15	♕g3	f6
16	♗b3	♖c8
17	♖ad1	♕e8
18	♘c3	♗d7! *(D)*

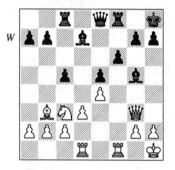

Black should avoid the exchange of the light-squared bishops, not only because his is theoretically the good bishop, but also because White's minor pieces don't coordinate very well. With the knight on d5 the bishop's scope has been severely restricted, whilst with the bishop on d5 the knight needs to find a new home.

19	♗d5	b6
20	♕f3	♕g6
21	♘e2	♕h6
22	♘g1	♗f4

23	g3	♗g5
24	♖de1	♛g6
25	♕e2	♗h6
26	♘f3	♛h5
27	♘h4	♗g4
28	♕g2	♗g5
29	h3	♗d7
30	♘f5	♗xf5
31	♖xf5	♛e8
32	♖ef1	♛e7
33	h4	♗h6
34	♖5f3	½-½

There is nothing for either side to do.

Game 45
Gallagher – Muse
Biel 1989

1	e4	c5
2	♘c3	♘c6
3	♘f3	e5 *(D)*

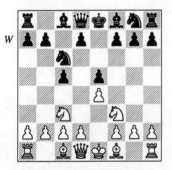

Blocking the centre with ...e5 has a much better reputation after 3 ♘f3 than 3 ♘ge2, probably because White's knight is a lot further from

d5 when it's on f3 than when it's on e2. However, as we have seen, control of d5 is not so important, as whenever White puts a piece there Black can just hack it off. From White's point of view, the main advantage in playing 3 ♘f3 as opposed to 3 ♘ge2 is that Black's options are reduced. For example, I knew that Muse played the Sveshnikov Variation and I was trying to coax him into some other line with which he might be less familiar. If I had played 3 ♘ge2 he could simply have answered 3...♘f6, but after the text this would be quite risky as White has two interesting systems in 4 e5 or 4 ♗b5 (my opponent wasn't to know that I knew nothing about either of them and would have simply replied 4 d4).

4	♗c4	d6
5	d3	♗e7

Of course Black has to get his move order right, and not play 5...♘f6 on account of 6 ♘g5. 5...h6 is an alternative which rules out all the lines with ♘g5, but as we shall see there is no need to spend a tempo to prevent them.

6 0-0

This is the most common, but by no means only move at White's disposal. The alternatives are:

a) 6 ♘g5?! is an extremely dubious sacrifice. 6...♗xg5 7 ♕h5 ♗e7! (7...g6? 8 ♕xg5 was the inexplicable continuation of Tseshkovsky-

Dvoirys, USSR 1983) 8 ♕xf7+ ♔d7 9 ♕xg7 (9 ♗e6+ ♔c7 10 ♘d5+ ♔b8 doesn't help) 9...♘f6 and Black has quite a safe position; Adams-Coleman, British Ch 1989. Everybody was amazed that Adams would risk playing such a line but the explanation was quite simple – he'd overlooked 7...♗e7.

b) 6 ♘d2!? is an interesting idea of Tony Kosten's. White immediately sends his knight off on a long voyage to the e3 square, from where it can keep an eye on the strategically important d5 and f5 squares. White probably assumes that because of the blocked nature of the position, the three tempi spent on getting the knight there are of little consequence. This might be true, but it's also not clear how much is gained by this lengthy manoeuvre. The game Kosten-Sadler, Hastings 1991 continued 6...♘f6 7 ♘f1 ♗g4 8 f3 ♗e6 9 ♘e3 ♘d4 (in view of the fact that this knight soon gets kicked away by c3, one could question this move) 10 0-0 0-0 11 a4 ♘d7 (11...♔h8!?) 12 ♘cd5 ♗g5 13 c3 ♘c6 14 g3 ♗xe3+!? 15 ♗xe3 ♔h8 16 ♕d2 ♘b6 17 ♗g5 ♘xc4 18 dxc4 f6 19 ♗e3 and now 19...♘e7 (instead of the over-ambitious 19...♗h3) gives equality.

c) 6 ♘d5. White plans to follow up with c3 and possibly d4, but Black is able to free his position by exchanges on d5. For example the game Gdanski-J.Polgar, Budapest

1993 continued 6...♘f6 7 c3 0-0 8 0-0 ♗e6 9 ♖e1 ♗xd5 10 ♗xd5 (10 exd5 ♘a5) 10...♘xd5 11 exd5 ♘b8 12 d4 (otherwise ...f5 will give Black the better game) 12...exd4 13 cxd4 ♘d7 14 dxc5 ♘xc5 15 ♗e3 ♗f6 with equality. White could also have tried 8 h3, as in the game Hebden-Gallagher, Hastings Masters 1990, which continued 8...♘xd5 (8...♗e6) 9 ♗xd5 ♗f6 (I wanted to provoke White's next) 10 g4?! ♕e8! (vacating d8 for the bishop) 11 ♗e3 ♗e6 12 ♘d2 ♗d8 13 ♘c4 ♗c7 14 ♗g5 ♗xd5 15 exd5 ♘e7 16 ♘e3 f6 17 ♗h4 ♕g6 18 ♕d2 ♕h6! 19 ♗g3 f5 with a clear advantage to Black.

| 6 | ... | ♘f6 |
| 7 | ♘g5 | |

White's only active idea (apart from 7 ♘d5 which leads to play very similar to note 'c' just above) is to play f4.

7	...	0-0
8	f4	exf4
9	♗xf4	h6
10	♘f3	♗e6 *(D)*

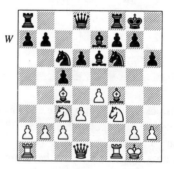

11 ♕d2

I played this quickly and confidently as it was all part of my faulty pre-game preparation, which had consisted of five minutes memorizing a game in *Informator*. White has a couple of other tries:

a) 11 ♕e1. *ECO* now gives the game Kovalev-Andrianov, USSR 1983, considering the position as equal after 11...♕d7 12 a3 d5 13 exd5 ♘xd5 14 ♘xd5 ♗xd5 15 ♕g3 ♔h8 16 ♗e5 f6 17 ♗xd5 ♕xd5 although it's worth knowing that Kovalev is still playing this line with White. Black could also play 11...d5 at once, for example 12 exd5 ♘xd5 13 ♘xd5 ♗xd5 14 ♕g3 ♔h8 15 ♕h3 ♖e8 16 ♗xh6?! (this looks irresistible but it's probably not very good) 16...gxh6 17 ♕xh6+ ♔g8. If you compare this position with the note to Black's 15th move in the main game you will see that the only difference is that White has a bishop on c4 rather than a knight on c3 (this makes the defence simpler). Here the queen has taken the scenic route to h6 via e1-g3-h3 whilst in Gallagher-Muse the direct route via d2 was used. Black, meanwhile, has balanced the tempi by oscillating with his king from h8 to g8. Play now continued 18 ♖ae1 ♗xc4 19 ♖e4 (there is no time for 19 dxc4 ♕d6 after which the attack is beginning to fizzle out) 19...♗e6 20 ♖xe6 ♗f8! 21 ♖xe8 (21 ♖g6+ fxg6 22 ♕xg6+

♗g7 23 ♘g5 fails to 23...♕d4+ and 24...♕h4) ♕xe8 22 ♕g5+ ♗g7 and Black stood clearly better in Grosar-Kragelj, Bled 1992.

b) 11 ♘d5 is an idea of Mitkov who is probably the leading expert on this line. His game with Roman, World Junior Ch 1991 continued 11...♗xd5 12 exd5 ♘a5 13 b3!? b5 14 ♗xb5 ♘xd5 15 ♗d2 ♗f6 16 ♕e1 and now Black should have played 16...♕b8! with a good game, e.g. 17 ♗xa5 ♕xb5 18 c4 ♕a6! with ...♖ae8 to follow.

11 ...   d5!
12 exd5   ♘xd5
13 ♗xd5

13 ♖ae1 ♘xf4 ½-½ was the inglorious outcome of the game Mitkov-Gallagher, Lyon 1993. I won't try to find any excuses for such cowardly behaviour, except to say that the position is equal after the continuation 14 ♕xf4 ♘d4 15 ♗xe6 fxe6! 16 ♕d2 ♘xf3+ 17 ♖xf3 ♖xf3 18 gxf3.

13 ...   ♗xd5 *(D)*

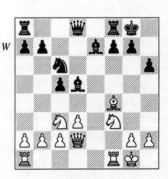

14 &xh6?

By now I had smelt a rat as my opponent had kept pace with my extremely rapid play. But I was also curious to see what he had in mind so there could be no question of bottling out now.

14 ... gxh6
15 &xh6 &e6!

And here it is! Up until now we had been following the game Kupreichik-Sveshnikov, Kuibyshev 1986 which had continued 15...&d4? 16 &xd4 &g5 17 &h5 cxd4 18 &xd5 &xd5 19 &f4! &ae8 20 h4 &e5 21 hxg5 &xg5 22 &g4 f6 23 &f1 &g7 24 &xf6 &xf6 25 &h6+ &e7 26 &xg5 1-0. In fact it seems that 15...&e6 is not the only good move in this position. 15...&e8! also appears to do the trick, e.g. 16 &ae1 &xf3! 17 &xf3 &d4+ 18 &ee3 &e5 19 &h3 &g6 20 &d5 &h4! 21 &h5 &e5 0-1 Yurtaev-Meshkov, USSR 1990; 16 &h1 is a better try, which cuts out a multitude of defences starting with ...&d4+. However, Black has a very strong riposte: 16...&e5!!. If 17 &xe5, then 17...&g5 regains the piece, so the game Landa-Gagarin, Bratislava 1990, continued 17 &h5 &f6 18 &ae1 &xf3! 19 gxf3 &g6 after which it was clear that Black held the advantage.

16 &e4

I must have spent an hour on the clock here but was unable to escape the conclusion that I was just lost.

It's incredibly infuriating to lose in this fashion, so you are warned yet again to check all analysis for yourselves.

16 ... &f5

Black's strong fifteenth move has enabled him to rush this bishop to the aid of his king, whilst also clearing the way for the queen to check on d4, from where it also defends key kingside squares.

17 &ae1

17 &g3 is insufficient: 17...&g6 18 &h5 &f6 19 &g5 &d4+ 20 &h1 &g7 repels the attack.

17 ... &g6!
18 &g3 &d4
19 &e5

The only chance.

19 ... &g5
20 &h3 &xc2
21 &e4! &xe4
22 &xe4 (D)

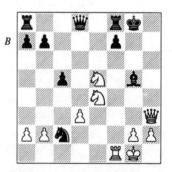

Here I began to have a glimmer of hope again but my opponent's reply destroyed my unfounded optimism.

22 ...   f5!

Of course Black avoids transparent traps like 22...♕d4+ 23 ♔h1 ♕xe5 24 ♖f5.

23 ♖xf5

I saw what was coming but there was no choice.

23 ...   ♕d4+

24 ♘f2

The cruel point (from my side of the board) is that 24 ♔h1 ♕xe5! 25 ♖xg5+ ♕xg5! wins for Black by exploiting the weak back rank.

24 ...   ♕e3!

25 ♖xg5+

25 ♖xf8+ is also hopeless after 25...♖xf8 26 ♕e6+ ♔h8 27 ♘g6+ ♔g7.

25 ...   ♕xg5

26 ♕e6+   ♔g7

27 ♕d7+   ♔h8

28 ♕h3+   ♔g8

29 ♕e6+   ♔h7

30 ♕d7+   ♔h8??

This is incredibly careless and allows a draw by threefold repetition. 30...♕g7 31 ♕h3+ ♕h6 32 ♕d7+ ♔h8 wins.

31 g3??

My flag was absolutely hanging. I should have kept checking as after 31 ♕h3+ ♔g7 (31...♔g8 32 ♕e6+ ♔h7 33 ♕d7+ ♔g7 34 ♕h3+ ♕h6 35 ♕d7+ ♔h8 would win easily for Black if it weren't for the fact that after 32 ♕e6+ White can claim a draw) 32 ♕d7+ and Black cannot make progress without playing ...♔g8 after which White can always claim a draw with ♕e6+.

31 ...   ♕c1+

32 ♔g2   ♘e1+

33 ♔h3   ♕h6+

0-1

Index of Variations